The Spot the War Forgot

───────────

The Spot the War Forgot

World War I Berrima German POW Camp

Written by

Wendy Hamilton

ZealAus Publishing

The Spot the War Forgot
World War I Berrima German POW Camp

Copyright © 2023 by Wendy Hamilton

www.zealauspublishing.com

All rights reserved. No part of this book may be reproduced or transmitted in any form or by any means without written permission of the author. Attitudes expressed in this book are not necessarily the attitudes of Wendy Hamilton or ZealAus Publishing.

The historical spelling 'gaol' has been updated to the modern spelling 'jail.'

Modified Cover Images were sourced from Berrima Historical Society.
This is the Second Edition of "The Spot the War Forgot"

ISBN: 978-1-925888-99-7 (sc)
ISBN: 978-1-922734-01-3 (hc)
ISBN: 978-1-922734-04-4 (e)

Contents

Captured 1
Berrima 7
Castle Foreboding 11
The First Day 24
Clean Ship Day 33
The Village 40
Snakes, the Unlikely Peacemakers 51
Moonshine and a Fugitive 62
A Boat a Bridge and a Mystery 73
Locked Up 80
A Gala for the Hansa Bridge 86
The Mystery Man tells his Story 92
The Hurtzigs arrive from Enoggera 97
I Get a Cell mate 111
Two Lovely Visitors 119
How Hugo Bahl was Captured 124
Secrets 133
Troubles and Disappointments 143
Christmas Preparations 150
Harmless Waves in the Sea of Romance 157
Moving Day 163
The Day Before Christmas 169
The Battle of Pooh 180
The Fight 188
Blackberries and a Good Idea 191
Bush Fires 199
Frienemies and a Carnival 219
Troubles and Another Carnival 228

Focus on Music	237
A New Theatre	250
Booze Smugglers	259
The Machotka Family Arrive	268
The Beautiful Woman	276
Machotka Begins a Garden	283
The Orchestra	290
Rats and Food Cuts	298
Disappointments and Surprises	307
An Escape	316
The Kaiser's Birthday is Overshadowed	323
A Picnic and a Plan	333
A School	342
A New Baby	350
Christmas and Swimming Lessons	356
The Boating Carnival	365
The Kaiser's Birthday	372
Henry Allen Strikes Out	378
Reshuffles and Upheavals	386
Armistice	395
Packing	402
Goodbye Berrima	413
A Century Later	417
References	432
Glossary	433

Acknowledgements

Many thanks to John Schweers for his encouragement. This book would not have been possible without documents from the Berrima District Historical and Family History Society, or the extensive research compiled by the late John Simons in his book Prisoners in Arcady. Also, thanks to Colin Gelling for his valuable help with the cover and permission to use the River Walk Map. Cover images were sourced from the Berrima District Historical and Family History Society. Additional images of the internees can be viewed at https://www.berrimadistricthistoricalsociety.org.au and visit the award wining Berrima District Historical & Family History Society Museum at the corner of Market Place and Bryan St, Berrima NSW 2577.

Foreword

A great deal of research has been undertaken by the author to produce a fascinating novel based on three-hundred internees who spent the duration of World War One interned in the jail in Berrima. This is not a dull history book but a look at what life was like for the German internees in the four-and-a-half years they were housed in the jail. The reader will discover and learn about the lifestyle of both the internees and the residents of Berrima and the Southern Highlands in this period of World War 1. The internees were resourceful and inventive. This novel is a wonderful way of exploring this small slice of history.

John Schweers - Manager / Volunteer
Berrima District Museum and Story Centre
Berrima District Historical & Family History Society Inc.

The World War 1 German internment camp at Berrima is an illuminating beacon in our district's history. Despite our plethora of archival material, the routines of the maritime internees were virtually unknown. This finely crafted historical fiction changes all that. Meticulous research clearly defines the lifestyle of the POWs, their hardships and triumphs. The congeniality apparent between the community and the internees is a feature, along with the creative and imaginative ingenuity of the German people

Phil Leighton - Volunteer
Berrima District Museum and Story Center

Introduction

Candlelight is not impressive at noon on a sunny day, its glory is only revealed in darkness. If the story of Berrima had taken place in a time of peace it would have been little more than a summer camp where men holidayed in a village by a river. The story's power lies in the blackness of its place in history. Nation fought against nation and hatred spread like cancer until it got to the derelict village of Berrima. In that humble spot, the war stopped. Within a two-mile radius, German prisoners, military men, and Australian citizens, all dwelt together in peace and harmony.

The character, Wolfgang Schmitt, and the conversations in the book are imaginary, but the people and the events portrayed are real. They are based on the diaries, photographs, and documents, left by over three-hundred men, six women, and six little girls. One woman was married to the Bohemian, Paul Machotka, perhaps the most influential man in the camp. Edna was the only American woman to live in a German Prisoner-of-War camp in Australia. She finishes her diary with these poignant words:

The old jail is soon to be torn down to make room for the progress which has come to the once-forgotten village, and soon there will be nothing left to remind the stranger of the prisoners who spent four years behind its walls.

Thankfully she was wrong. The kindly prison still stands like a foreboding ogre, and Berrima enjoys the reputation of the best-preserved Georgian village in Australia. Despite Edna's fears, the people of Berrima did not forget the Germans, instead, they built a museum to keep their memory alive. And rightly so, for the conduct of the villagers, the prisoners, and the guards, during World War One was outstanding, and a badge of honour on Australia's sleeve.

Isaiah 2:4

And he shall judge among the nations, and shall rebuke many people: and they shall beat their swords into plowshares, and their spears into pruninghooks: nation shall not lift up sword against nation, neither shall they learn war any more.

King James Version (KJV)

W.E. Hamilton

August 1914
Britain declares war on Germany.

Captured

They called World War One the Great War, but it was not a good war. I was on the ship that drew Australia's first shot on August the 5th 1914. Capture within the first three hours of war is not glorious. But what can you do? That is life. It happened this way…

I, Wolfgang Schmitt, was an ordinary seaman of the cargo steamer the Pfalz, of the North German Lloyd Line. At that time, the war was uppermost in everyone's mind. As Germans, we were particularly jittery, for we were foreigners in a land teetering on hostility. On August the 3rd 1914 we were docked in Port Phillip Bay, Melbourne when our captain received news that war was imminent.

"Men, I have had word that Germany intends to ignore Britain's request to respect the neutrality of Belgium," said Captain Kühlken as we stood assembled before him, "therefore prepare to leave."

The Spot The War Forgot

"But Captain," broke in the First Officer, "it is late, and we won't have enough coal to get us back to Germany, for many of the ports where we stop for fuel are under the control of the British."

The captain rubbed his chin and gazed with unseeing eyes at the night sky. We waited silently, staring at the top knuckle of his hand which repeatedly appeared and disappeared under his luxurious handlebar moustache. At last, he spoke.

"A small delay will probably not matter. Everyone, regardless of rank or shift, is to haul coal into the bunker, we will leave as soon as it is filled to capacity."

"Jawohl" we said, saluting.

Then we all pitched in, from the captain to the laziest man aboard, and by morning the bunker was filled. When there was no room for another lump of coal, Captain Kühlken gave the order:

"Prepare to sail."

Although we had worked all night and our uniforms were begrimed with black dust, we readied the ship with urgency powered by anxiety. We stowed things away and toiled to build up a head of steam, while the cook laid in provisions and the captain hustled about getting the paperwork in order. Despite our best efforts it was mid-morning when (with trembling hands) we loosened the ropes that held us to the docks and steamed slowly towards the Heads.

"So far so good, Billy," I said to my friend Wilhelm Köster. "We just need to get past the Royal Navy examination vessel at Portsea."

"I hope we will make it," said Billy, "the captain should have gone last night while we had the chance. Better to be stuck at sea without coal, than captured and imprisoned."

"I agree, they could have sent a message to Germany and a collier would have come to refuel us."

"It doesn't matter how right we are nobody will listen to a couple of nineteen-year-olds."

I nodded. "I think the captain is trying to make up for lost time," I said, noticing our steady increase in speed. "This is rather fast."

"It is risky," said Billy. "Phillip Bay Heads is dangerous. All the captains fear the boiling bubbly water between Portsea and Point Lonsdale."

I looked at my watch as we neared Queens cliff. "12:45, not much longer before we reach the ocean."

"And here comes the sea pilot," said Billy, pointing at a boat labouring against the swift incoming tide.

"It is a pity we need an Australian pilot to ferry us through the gap," I said, as a man leapt from the moving boat to a ladder dangling down the side of the Pfalz. "For if war is declared, it will be very difficult if he's still on board."

"It'd be worse trying to get to open water without the expertise of a local sailor," said Billy, as the pilot clambered on board and headed up to the bridge. "I expect the pace will drop to a safe speed once Captain Robinson takes the wheel from Captain Kühlken."

The words were barely out of his mouth before the ship slowed, and shortly after, the Royal Navy examination vessel the, Alvina, pulled alongside us. It was less than ten minutes from the time the inspector came on board until we got clearance and he left, but it felt like hours. I blew a sigh of relief as we picked up speed again. But when we approached Fort Nepean

The Spot The War Forgot

on our port side, Billy's faced tensed as we moved into the path of the Fort's guns and our apprehension turned to fear when we saw the Fort hoist the 'HALT' signal.

"I don't like the look of this," said Billy. "I suspect war has been declared for they are trying to see our flag."

Unfortunately, Billy's guess was correct. Germany and Britain had been at war for almost three hours but Fort Queenscliff had only just heard the news.

"So close and yet so far," I said, as the ship slowed,"all we needed was ten more minutes to be free."

Suddenly we heard a commotion and looking towards the bridge, we saw Captain Kühlken push the pilot aside before grabbing the wheel.

"The captain is going to make a run for it," I shouted over the noise of the accelerating engines.

"He'll never make it without Pilot Robinson!" cried Billy, gripping the side rail with unusual strength. "He doesn't know the waterway."

Montgomery Robinson thought so too, for as soon as he was on his feet, he lunged at Captain Kühlken with the fury of a man being kidnapped or about to die.

Then everything happened at once.

The pilot leapt on the captain and knocked him to the ground.

They struggled.

The wheel spun.

The ship drifted off course.

And the Alvina hoisted the H flag.

When Fort Nepean saw the H for, 'hostile,' a warning shot flew across the bows of our ship. As it hit the water, a wave burst up and over the bridge.

"YOU FOOL," shouted the pilot. "They are not bluffing. If you don't stop, the next shot will hit the ship and we will all be killed."

"I WILL NOT STOP," shouted our heroic Captain.

But he did, for the Australian was younger and stronger. He punched our captain on the nose, knocking him out. This was the first arm to arm conflict between Australia and Germany. I should have been disappointed Germany was defeated, but I am glad the enemy won, for our chances of surviving that bubbling cauldron if the ship had gone down, were very slim. The First Officer, seeing the captain was overcome, shouted:

"STRIKE THE FLAG."

Then the man closest to the mast quickly lowered it so the second shot was never fired, and consequently, nobody was hurt or killed. Billy and I slumped against the rail, now there was no hope of escape we suddenly felt very tired. I dimly remember the pilot heaving to and the ship slowing to a halt. Then the Pfalz was escorted by an armed guard back to Portsea, before, exhausted, we fell into a deep sleep.

We awoke to endless waiting.

"If I had known I would be imprisoned on my ship, I would have signed on for a luxury cruise liner, not a freighter," I grumbled to Billy. "I am tired of sitting on crates and playing cards."

"It is not so bad," said Billy.

"It is not bad for you because you enjoy playing your viola."

"I could teach you to play, Wolfie."

"If I had an instrument, I might take you up on that. I used to play the violin when I was a kid. As it is, there is no point for

The Spot The War Forgot

I could only borrow yours. It's not worth losing your friendship over a viola."

Billy laughed and slapped me on the shoulder. "You know me better than I know myself. I like you, Wolfgang, but not enough to let you saw away on my viola. I would not trust a beginner to touch it. You would need your own instrument."

Because the ship was guarded it was impossible to buy a violin, so I continued fishing and playing cards with my shipmates while Billy played music hour after hour. Meaningless day followed meaningless day, and we hung in a state of limbo until the beginning of October. Then suddenly without warning, we were hustled off to Sydney.

———————

W.E. Hamilton

January 1915
German Zeppelins Bomb Great Britain.

Berrima

In Sydney, we were placed in accommodation and allowed to move about freely, provided we reported to the Victoria Barracks once a week. To make doubly sure we appeared, they paid us an allowance when we turned up. Life settled into a new routine. We found ways to keep ourselves occupied, and made new seafaring friends during our visits to the Barracks.

"Germany will win and the war will be over by Christmas," we said to one another.

But Christmas came and went and the war continued. One day in March 1915, Billy and I were commanded to report to the Barracks with our gear packed, ready to move out. When we got there, we were grouped with eighty-six other German mariners, among them, Captain Kühlken, and our shipmates from the Pfalz. Then we were marched under armed guard to Sydney Central Station where we boarded the Southern Highlands train destined for Moss Vale. We were barely settled

The Spot The War Forgot

when the train pulled out.

"Did you hear where they are taking us?" I asked Billy, as we chugged out of the city and into flat brown hills, spotted with sheep and the occasional herd of kangaroos.

Billy lifted his viola case onto the overhead rack and sat down beside me. "The Captain said someplace called Berrima, but that is all I know. It must be a hole in the corner because nobody has heard of it."

On overhearing this, the young man in the seat opposite frowned. "Oh no, I hope they are not sending us to work on a farm, I turned myself in to escape from farm work, and my sister Maria is very angry that I did. She said I should stay hidden in Victoria. I tried to (for her sake) but the work was hard and the locals so naïve and uninformed in politics it was a terrible bore. I didn't have one intelligent conversation the whole time I was there. My name's Michael Becker by the way," he ended, sticking out his hand.

"I'm Wolfgang Schmitt," I said shaking it. "And this is my good friend Wilhelm Köster.

"My friends call me Billy," said Wilhelm, shaking Michael's hand. "We are from the steamer Pfalz. What ship did you sail on?"

"The Prinz Sigismund under the command of Captain Hurtzig."

My eyebrows shot up and Billy whistled. "The Kaiser's private yacht?"

"*Ja*, but the NGL own it now." His face darkened. "Or they did until it was seized as a war trophy."

"Now that is the sort of ship to be confined to. I've heard it is handsomely fitted out and beautifully furnished."

Michael nodded. "It is a fine ship, which makes the loss worse."

I pulled a face. "We were stuck on a freighter for weeks, how long were you kept onboard?"

"I wasn't, because when we docked at Brisbane I got word that my sister had sailed to Sydney with friends of ours, William de Haas and his family, who had accepted a post at the German Consulate. I hadn't seen her for a year and thought it would be fun to go down and surprise her. So, I got leave and set off. But when I got to Sydney the surprise was on me because she had gone to a small place near Victoria's border called Burrumbuttock."

Billy and I burst out laughing.

"Burrumbuttock! Can you believe the names of this country?" I said. "What did she go down there for?"

"To stay with some friends called the Schilgs," said Michael. "When I heard this, I was not sure what to do because Britain had just declared war on Germany. But de Hass said my best chances of avoiding arrest and internment was to work on a farm. I took his advice and caught the first train to Burrumbuttock, where I stayed with my sister at the Schilgs until I got a job at a nearby farm called Rose View. I thought if I could avoid arrest until Christmas the war would be over and then I could go back to sea."

Billy nodded calmly, but I burst out:

"*Ja*, we all thought that. I even wrote to my parents and told them I was coming home for Christmas and I was bringing a boomerang for Papa and a wombat fur for Mama."

"This war is a sad business," said Michael. He looked out the window and our eyes followed his gaze. By now the brown

The Spot The War Forgot

hills had given way to acres and acres of scraggly eucalyptus trees. "If it is a farm we are going to, it will not be so bad this time," he said. "For at least there is intelligent conversation."

"And we will not be there for long," I added. "We will win, and the war will be over soon."

"This is also true," said Michael, smiling.

We continued talking as the train clattered over a bridge spanning a deep ravine, unaware of our steady climb as we moved south, for the land rose gently. The conversation had reached a small lull when we heard singing.

Michael hummed a few bars of the tune. "That's a military song. I bet it is the Emden men. I overheard the commandant say seven of the Emden crew are with us."

Billy's eyes lit up. "I would like to hear about their raiding adventures. Wouldn't you, Wolfgang?"

"*Ja* and *nein*, I want to hear their stories but I don't want to admit how easily I was captured, especially to battle-scarred soldiers."

"At least we weren't on the Ernst that sailed through Port Jackson Heads ninety-nine days after war was declared."

"Don't speak of it. As Germans, we all share the shame of it."

At that, the topic switched to sea stories and tales of terrific storms. With such companionable conversation the time flew, and after two hours the train pulled up at the Moss vale station.

W.E. Hamilton

February 1915
Germany Attacks Merchant Ships and Submarines of Neutral Countries.

Castle Foreboding

"EVERYONE OUT, LINE UP BEHIND YOUR CAPTAINS."

We stood and Billy lifted his viola off the overhead shelf, while I hung my heavy overcoat over my arm before shuffling down the aisle of the train and onto the platform.

"What am I to do," said Michael, following? "Captain Hurtzig is not here, I am by myself."

"Stick with us," I said.

The train disappeared into the distance as we lined up behind Captain Kühlken, and waited aimlessly in the heat, watched by a small band of Australian soldiers with bayoneted rifles over their left shoulders.

Michael nudged me, "most of the guard look unfit for service."

"Shh, they might hear you."

The Spot The War Forgot

"I could do with a cup of tea and something to eat," said Billy, "breakfast seems a long time ago."

"It's lunchtime, we'll get something soon, I expect," I said. "I suppose we are waiting for transport to arrive."

But sadly, neither lunch nor transport came. Instead, the commandant shouted:

"FORWARD MARCH"

Cockatoos with yellow crests screeched and flew overhead as we trudged down the road through brown fields where rabbits outnumbered cattle. As we were seafaring men who had done time on windjammers, we were accustomed to singing while we wound the windlass or hoisted the sails, so naturally, it was not long before someone started singing a rousing marching tune. Our spirits lifted at the sound and we strode along in time with the beat as we sang. At least we did for the first few miles. Our pounding feet pummeled the dirt road into a fine dust that the hot wind swirled around our heads in the most tiresome manner. It was bad enough for us younger ones, but our captains (who were podgy with comfortable living) found it exceptionally hard. Two older captains collapsed and a soldier stayed with them until a cart came by to give them a lift. By the seventh mile, there was no singing and our marching dwindled to methodically putting one foot in front of the other. Moreover, a rumour circulated that the end of our destiny was prison.

"At first I thought going to jail was terrible," I said to Billy, as we plodded along, "but the longer we go, and the hungrier I get, the less awful the idea seems."

"I know what you mean, even prison is preferable to endlessly marching under a hot sun."

W.E. Hamilton

We kept moving, moving, moving, and by the time we finally straggled into Berrima, we viewed the jail as a temple of salvation.

Berrima was a small poverty-stricken village. Many ruined cottages suggested the village once enjoyed prosperity. If so, it was long departed. Through a haze of exhaustion, I vaguely noticed two stone churches, a hotel, several shops, and many slab huts with earthen floors. Along the main street were better cottages of brick or timber; each with a corrugated iron roof that sloped down to a veranda. Barefooted children dressed in sacks stood in the dusty front yards, watching us with open curiosity, while their parents spied through the curtains.

Amid this destitution rose the jail, like the fortress of a castle. Its tall outer wall was built to last from huge slabs of yellow sandstone. The front corners were flanked by two houses; a handsome stone house on the left, and a smaller brick villa on the right. Across the road was an imposing courthouse. Oddly, a white picket fence separated the prison's front yard from the road, and tall trees lined the wide path to the gatehouse in the centre of the prison-wall. Behind the picket fence was a sign that said:

Berrima Detention Barracks
Public Notice!
NO ADMITTANCE
By Order of R.S. Sands, Major Commandant.
German Concentration Camps.

"We are finally here," said Michael, sighing with relief. "The first thing I am going to do when I get inside is have a drink of water, I'm parched."

"I hope dinner is beef stew, I'm starving," I said. "If I'd

The Spot The War Forgot

known they were not going to feed us I would have packed a cut lunch and a bottle of rum."

"And worn boots," said Billy. "These civilian shoes are alright for walking the streets of Sydney, but no good for tramping cross-country."

I nodded. "At least we didn't have to carry our luggage on our backs."

We passed into the yard, and with aching feet, half stumbled, half trotted down the path, eager to get inside. But to our dismay, the jail was closed. Nobody was there to welcome us. We milled about the prison's yard and talked while we waited for someone to let us in.

"Well, this is strange, prisoners desperate to get into prison," said Billy, knocking on the heavy wooden doors under the arched entrance. He rattled them and the padlock made a clanking sound. "The sign says it is a jail, but what do you think it really is?"

Guesses flew around us. One suggested this, and another that.

"You're all wrong," said a fellow by the name of Otto. "It's a factory for making a profit from rabbits; they're the main things they farm down here."

The idea caught on and caused a smile of grim jocularity to spread among the crowd as we mooched about waiting. As the minutes ticked by and nothing happened our mood darkened.

"What is the meaning of this, why can't we get in?" we complained to the Commandant.

Lieutenant Hinton shrugged his shoulders. "Nothing to do with me, I don't know what's happening."

When we realized we might be in for a long wait, we sat

under the trees and gave way to our feelings. I will not record our exact words but you may be sure they expressed great bitterness.

"What sort of a hole is this?" said Michael, taking off his shoes and examining the big blisters on the back of his heals.

Billy took a handkerchief from his pocket and wiped the dust off the case of his viola. "The administration is very bad."

"In Germany, you would be sent to the Eastern Front for such inefficiency," I said. I stood up and pulled on my coat before sitting down again, for by now the shadows were getting long as the day grew into early evening. "This coat was a nuisance to carry but I am glad of it now, the night will be cold."

"I hope we are not going to spend it out here," said Michael, spitting on the ground disdainfully, before easing his socks and shoes on.

We were all afraid of that unpleasant possibility, but after about an hour someone arrived with the key and unlocked the gates. Then still grumbling, we marched into the jail. After passing through the gatehouse, we found ourselves in a narrow yard that ran between the outer wall and a long building, which I found out later was the Services Building where the laundry, cookhouse, and mess hall were.

Billy cast his eyes over the dreary yard and derelict building. "It's obvious the jail has been empty and unused for some time."

I nodded. "It looks like they have made a few hasty preparations for us; the windows, doors, and roof have recently been repaired."

Michael snorted and pointed to the end of the building

The Spot The War Forgot

where the rafters and beams lay exposed to the weather.

"Not all of it. I hope they don't expect us to sleep in the end where there is no roof."

But he had nothing to fear, for (like the gatehouse) our pathway ran through the building, not into it. When we came out the other side we found ourselves in a large yard facing a massive stone building with a centrally positioned tower. The cell blocks radiated from the tower to form a T configuration. We congregated in front of the horizontal stroke of the T, our eyes flitting anxiously over the stairs that led into the tower and the third cell block hidden behind it.

"I've never been in a jail before," I said, as my eyes roamed over the two-storied cell blocks looming above us.

Billy stared at the long observation platform running along the top of the southern wall. "Neither have I."

"Of course you haven't," said Michael, impatiently. "None of us have." He pointed to a small weather-beaten hut beyond patches of weeds and discarded timber. "The commandant and his staff don't have much of an office."

"How do you know that is their office?"

"Because of the sign over the door."

While we looked, the door opened and the commandant and an officer came out and stood before us.

"LINE UP BEHIND YOUR CAPTAINS," barked the commandant, holding the knob of the riding crop tucked under his arm, "I want to see which men belong together."

"*Stell dich hinter deinen kapitanene auf,*" translated the officer.

We shuffled about and eventually, several rows of men stood before him. Michael stepped behind us, so only one man stood alone.

The commandant strode over to him. "Well, what ship do you belong to?"

The man glared at him with the expression of pent-up rage.

"I am not connected with the merchant marines or even a German. I am here by mistake. I am, Paul Machotka, a Bohemian, trained in horticulture and this…" he snatched the hat off his head and jabbed his finger on the enamel emblem on the brim. "This yachting cap is a souvenir from the ship I took passage on when I travelled from America to Sydney. The officer I normally report to was not at the Victoria Barracks this morning, and the new officer mistakenly thought I was a German mariner because of this hat."

"Why did you not show your papers?"

Machotka put his hat on and reached into the inside pocket of his coat.

"Here!" he thrust his passport and papers at the commandant. "I tried to show these to the officer (for I have a wife and three children in Sydney) but the fool would not look at them. Instead, I was hustled back to the others and ordered to 'fall in and stop creating a disturbance.' So here I am."

The commandant handed his riding-crop to the officer before taking the passport and the papers. We stood silently as he inspected them. At last, he slung them at Machotka and took his crop back.

"Well, I didn't bring you here, you brought yourself. I will take you back to Sydney tomorrow and see what I am to do with you."

Machotka's neck turned red and his eyes narrowed at these words. He was about to protest over the unjust accusation, but the commandant held up his hand and gave him a quelling look. Then he turned his attention back to us.

"As you will have seen by the notice in the front yard, this is Berrima German Concentration Camp," he said, as he paced back and forth before us slowly. He spoke loudly, pausing after each sentence for the officer to translate.

"During your time here fraternizing with the guards is forbidden. A field officer will call the roll at 7.30 am and 6.30 pm. A bugle call is sounded fifteen minutes before parade times. You are confined to the barracks at night, during which, the jail is locked and sentries posted. However, because you are mostly merchant seamen, not soldiers, you are free to roam a two-mile parole during the day. This parole area includes the village. You are free to use the bank and purchase things from the shops, but you are not permitted to fraternize with the locals-ESPECIALLY THE WOMEN."

He paused to let the last three words sink in.

"If the need for medical or dental treatment arises, permission to go further than the two-mile parole may be requested from the camp commandant, which will be granted or denied as he sees fit."

He pointed his riding crop at us.

"ANYONE breaking the parole boundaries will be confined to the barracks for as long as the commandant wishes. And if anyone ESCAPES, the ENTIRE camp will be confined to the barracks until the escapee returns voluntarily or is captured. IS THAT UNDERSTOOD?"

We nodded and shuffled our feet slightly, hoping he would finish speaking so we could get something to eat and drink.

The commandant tucked his riding-crop back under his

armpit and continued:

"The daily paper is allowed every morning. You may NOT send letters privately through the local post office, but you may send and receive letters and parcels through the Field Officer, provided the letters you send are written in ENGLISH and no longer than one-hundred-and-fifty words. Letters in any other language will be confiscated. We have provided accommodation but the responsibility for the detailed arrangements for the running of the camp IS YOUR RESPONSIBILITY. You will each receive two blankets, straw, and ticking, to make a mattress. In addition, we will supply food. Bread and meat will be delivered daily from the local baker and butcher, but YOU are responsible for the preparation of it. The Field Officer and the Regimental Officer will attend all meals to see that the food is evenly distributed. The Field Officer will also inspect the barracks daily. He will shortly issue you with a tin plate, a mug, a knife, fork and spoon and tell you what to do next. THAT IS ALL."

He dismissed us, and shortly after we heard the gates clang shut.

"I don't like the sound of that," I said, my heart plummeting as the key rattled in the lock.

Billy shuddered. "I feel trapped."

"Plates and cutlery are over there," shouted the Field Officer, mercifully breaking our train of thought. "Take one of each and line up at the kitchen in the Service Building."

At this, our spirits rose and we wasted no time forming a queue. Keeping to our custom we let our captains go to the head of the line and watched with hopeful expectancy.

"I hope it is beef stew," I said, as I shuffled behind Michael

The Spot The War Forgot

and Billy.

"It makes no difference to me," said Michael, "chicken or pork, it is all the same, so long as it is piping hot."

But it was not beef, chicken, pork, or even stew. For when the captains passed us on their return, we were horrified to see that all they carried was a mug of tea and a gigantic slab of bread and butter with marmalade scraped across the surface.

"*Ach komm schon*," burst out Michael in disgust. "I can't believe it. Is that all we are getting after our long march? Have they forgotten we have had nothing to eat and drink for hours and hours?"

He looked at Billy and me, expecting us to agree indignantly, but the whole room had fallen silent. For worse than our disappointment over the food, was the grotesque sight of our proud officers stripped of honour and strength. Like the other men of high rank, Captain Kühlken's despairing face was red with embarrassment and shame. I averted my eyes as he passed so he would not see my pity. When at last I received my allotment of food, I looked around for somewhere to sit.

"You can search for a table and chair all you like," said Billy, "you won't find either. The building is empty."

"And the floor is too grimy to sit on," said Michael, "even though my feet are killing me, I'd rather stand."

"Actually, the whole place is filthy," I said, staring at the long cobwebs dangling from the ceiling and the rubbish littered about. I bit into my bread savagely. "It's a pity it isn't a factory for rabbits. A factory for rabbits would be cleaner! I am dreading going inside the cell blocks. This is a castle of doom."

"Castle Foreboding-Ahnenscholss, *ja*, that is a good name

for this miserable place."

"Ahnenscholss," the name rumbled through the room like grumbling thunder. I think Michael spoke for us all when he said:

"It would be a relief to find an Australian head to smash in."

But there were no Australians, so we could not indulge ourselves with that comfort. We were mainly Germans, with a smattering of Austrians and Hungarians; all captains, officers or engineers of merchant steamships, and of course, the seven crew of the SMS Emden. In addition, there were a few businessmen, a sprinkling of ship's musicians, and three military officers (all titled men with von in their names.) Once we had finished our tea and bread, we felt a little better.

"It is obvious Captain Kühlken is beyond giving commands," said Billy, glancing over at our captain slumped against the wall. "We'd best find our accommodation by ourselves."

We nodded, and after washing our dishes in a large tub of cold water, we followed him up the short flight of steps that lead into the central tower. The stairway to the tower rooms was roped off so we turned left and passed into a long corridor lined with doors. At the end of the passage was a metal grating.

"It's rather grim," said Billy, "but it is better than spending the night outside." He glanced at the men crowding into the corridor behind us. "We'd best lay claim to our rooms if we want to stick together."

We nodded and Michael pointed to three cells close to the grill. "What about those?"

"They will do." Billy hastened down the passage and pulled open a heavy door fitted with huge iron bolts.

The Spot The War Forgot

"I've never seen doors as thick as these before," said Michael, taking the next cell. "They must be at least three inches thick and solid cedar."

I repressed a shudder and stood hesitantly with my hand on the last door. "I suppose they passed food through the small opening under the peephole," I took a deep breath before swinging the door open and stepping into the room.

My room (like all the other cells) was small and empty. High up was an unglazed window fitted with bars through which the cold night air blew, and in the corner were two filthy blankets swarming with fleas.

"Your room is as bad as mine," said Michael, coming into my cell.

"*Ja*, I thought we would at least get some sort of bed, but there is not even a rough camp stretcher. It is shameful that they expect us to sleep on a stone floor with filthy blankets."

"It is worse than that," said Billy coming in, "I've just heard from the fellow in the next room, our luggage has not arrived and won't be here tonight."

"No luggage!" I kicked the wall. "A fool is in charge of this camp. If I had my bag I could at least put on extra clothes and make some sort of a pillow."

Billy looked at the darkening sky and frowned. "What's more, there is no electricity so we'd best get ready for bed before we lose the light."

My mouth dropped open and I echoed his words like a parrot. "No electricity? Does this mean there is no lighting?"

"That's right."

"Castle Foreboding-Ahnenscholss, how well we have named this place," said Michael.

W.E. Hamilton

"It is a good name for a bad place," said Billy. "But we have faced worse things at sea, at least we don't have to worry about the place sinking or waves coming in through the window."

I spread my bundle of straw into a thick line, folded the mattress ticking in half, and laid it on top. "True. At least we have straw."

"You forget the best part."

"What?"

Billy flicked his head towards the dungeon-door. "No one is going to lock us in our rooms."

"*Ja*, that is the best part."

By now darkness was rapidly falling. I could see the moon creeping above the edge of the open window, so we bid each other goodnight. Then (leaving the door ajar) I wrapped my long overcoat tightly around my body, lay down on my makeshift mattress, and shivered my way through my first night in prison.

The Spot The War Forgot

March 1915
**British Navy Imposes Total Sea Blockage on Germany
Prohibiting all Shipping Imports Including Food**

The First Day

To our enormous relief, Captain Kühlken was greatly restored in the morning. He was almost back to his normal self when he called us together at the break of day. We stood before him unshaven and rumpled, shivering and blowing on our cold hands as he addressed us.

"The captains met last night and have decided that until something more permanent is organized, the crews of each ship will take it in turn to produce the meals. Our crew is on kitchen duties today." He laid a hand on the shoulder of the stout man next to him. "The ship's cook is in charge, take your orders from him."

"*Jawohl*" we said saluting.

We marched behind him to the services building and into the kitchen. The kitchen was very basic. A row of primitive woodstoves, a few enormous pans, some cooking utensils, and a couple of large kettles and teapots.

"There is not much here," said the captain, looking at a wooden shelf running along the wall where two large tins marked TEA and COFFEE sat. Beside them were smaller tins of jam and condensed milk. "I see the tea and coffee but not much else."

"The first thing, is to clean up and get the fires going," said the cook, as he wiped the dust from a ladle with the corner of his apron. He straightened and pointed at the men closest to him. "You, you, and you look for firewood and coal. The rest of you scour the benches, pots and pans. Billy, Wolfgang, and…" he squinted at Michael, "Whoever-You-Are, scout around for food. The commandant said there were provisions so they must be here somewhere."

While the others scrubbed and piled wood into the stoves, we searched in cupboards and dark corners. But by the time the fires blazed, and the benches and pots were clean, all we had found was rat droppings and oily dust. Then Billy opened what he thought was a cupboard door hidden in a dark corner of the kitchen and discovered a tiny windowless room.

"It's in here! This must be the pantry. There are gunnysacks of potatoes, carrots, and oats, a sack of sugar, and a bag of salt."

I went to look but the cook pushed past me and waddled into the room. While he was inspecting the provisions, Billy found a note pinned to the back of the pantry door.

"Here's a menu."

"Let me see that," said the cook, taking it from him. He pulled a pair of glasses from his apron pocket and hooked them over his ears. This is what he read:

The Spot The War Forgot

"Breakfast: Porridge.
Lunch: Meat (in various forms) and fresh local vegetables.
Dinner: Bread and jam.
The following is an allowance of food per man.
Oats
Bread 1 ½ lbs
Meat 10 oz
Tea ½ oz
Pepper ½ oz
Vegetables (mixed) ½ pound
Condensed milk ½ of a lb tin daily
Sugar 2 ozs
Salt ½ oz
Jam 2 oz
The local butcher, Alfred Taylor, and Henry Allen the baker will deliver fresh meat and bread every morning."

When he had finished reading, he took off his glasses and put them back into his pocket.

"It's not fancy, but at least we'll not starve. Bring the bag of oats, Billy, and, What's-Your-Name, I'll need salt and two of the biggest pots." He handed me a bucket. "Wolfgang, go out to the well in the yard and get me some spring water."

I hesitated. "Where is the well?"

"*Schnell, schnell.*" He waved me out with his hands. "You'll find it. We must hustle to feed everyone before rollcall."

I did find the well, and we did hustle, but is not easy feeding eighty-nine men under such conditions, nevertheless, by the time the bugle sounded at 7:15 am everyone was fed to the Field Officer's satisfaction, and large tubs of hot water stood ready for each man to wash his plate, mug, and eating utensils. At

W.E. Hamilton

7:30 am, we gathered in the assembly area as we had the night before. Then the Field Officer called out our names and we shouted "HERE," one by one. When everyone had answered, we were reminded that evening-rollcall was 6:30 pm. Then the barracks were inspected and we were dismissed for the day.

As soon as the big gates swung open we surged out, eager to escape Castle Foreboding and anxious to find some way to make our lives more comfortable. At the gateway in the picket fence, we scattered. Some turned right, towards the village. Some turned left, towards the large house on the hill. The rest of us turned the corner by the brick villa and walked past the imposing courthouse and down the hill. At the bottom of the hill was a river with white sandy banks. On both banks as far as the eye could see, was heavily wooded land. As seafaring men, the sight of water did much to lift our spirits.

"At last, something good in this terrible place, it is not the sea, but even a little river is better than nothing," we said to one another, for the stress of the last twenty-four hours had the effect of welding strangers into instant friends. We gathered in a knot and discussed the possibilities.

"Do we have any ship's carpenters in our midst?"

Three men stepped forward and gave their names as Harold Leyffer, Anton Gallwitzer, and Captain Jertrum. Nobody showed any surprise when Leyffer said he was a carpenter, or raised an eyebrow at Gallwitzer's claim to be a cabinet maker. But when Captain Jertrum said: "I make fine furniture," his crew looked at him in astonishment. Captain Jertrum, seeing their faces chuckled.

"You did not know I had such a hobby, did you?"

We gave them a few minutes to express their surprise

The Spot The War Forgot

before turning our attention back to the river and the bush. Harold Leyffer was the first to speak.

"Those tea trees will make good beds. A wooden frame with sacking or rope stretched across it is much better than a cold stone floor."

Anton Gallwitzer nodded. "Blue gums make fine furniture," he said, pointing at the tall eucalyptus trees that grew in abundance.

"They do indeed," said Captain Jertrum. "I once made a lovely tray out of blue gum."

"Perhaps you three men could give us tips on constructing beds," said Captain Kühlken, "they are our priority."

"*Ja*, of course."

"We need rope and sacking."

"And axes."

"And saws."

Billy volunteered to go to the village to buy as much rope and sacking as he could get, and someone found a couple of saws and an axe lying about in an abandoned house nearby. Then we went into the bush, and after the three men showed us the trees most suitable for our purpose, we set about hewing down a number of tea trees. When a group of sailors put their mind to something, they get a lot done. Before long we had gathered a large pile of logs (the thickness of a man's arm.) Then Captain Jertrum, Gallwitzer, and Leyffer, showed us how to build a bed frame on stumpy legs.

"And once you get your frame finished, you wind rope back and forwards across it like this," said Leyffer, as he wove the rope into a taut grid.

"Or stretch sacking over it," said Gallwitzer.

"I've got string and a few big sacking needles," said Captain Jertrum, "those of you using gunny will need them."

Like the other men, I was eager to make my bed for I did not want to spend another night like the last one. I chose short logs, long logs, four stumps, and got started. I was only half done when Captain Kühlken gave the order for our crew to go back to the kitchen.

"What a pain," I said, as we trudged up the hill. "I wanted to finish my bed."

"You can do that this afternoon while the other crews make furniture for the mess hall," said Captain Kühlken overhearing my grumbles.

"*Jawohl*," I said, feeling my face go red.

When we got back to the jail, two horse-drawn carts were in the courtyard by the kitchen door; one was loaded with bread and the other with meat. The good-quality meat looked fresh, but the misshapen bread lay tumbled on the grimy floor of the cart, exposed to dust and flies.

"Good morning," we said in our best English.

The butcher tipped his hat. "Good morning," he said with a smile.

But the baker, scowling, spat on the road and continued to move bread without looking at us.

"Help these men unload," said the cook coming to the door. "Put the bread on the bench in the pantry, and hang the meat off the hooks on the wall.

"Yarbol."

We ferried food in awkward silence, intensely aware of the baker's disdain. When we were done, the cook got us peeling potatoes and carrots. Nobody said a word until the rumble of the carts and the sound of the horse's hooves faded into the distance.

"That baker hates Germans."

"*Ja*, that is true. Perhaps the whole village hates us."

"How did they treat you at the General Store when you bought the rope, Billy?"

"At first they were suspicious, but after I tipped my hat and spoke to them in English, they were polite."

"I don't know why they were surprised you could speak English? "We are mariners and most of us can speak enough English to make ourselves understood."

"I don't think they thought of us as mariners or even human beings until I spoke to them in English."

"I expect a fistful of money helped them see your humanity."

"I expect so, but hate is a powerful emotion, a sack of money will not change the baker's heart."

At this, we felt sad until Billy started singing a catchy tune which made the job swing along.

After yesterday's lack of food and our busy morning, the men were very hungry when the cook banged the dinner-gong at midday. Their faces split into big smiles when they smelt the hearty stew we had for them. Our captains and high-ranking officers looked very different from the night before, and it did our hearts good to see our leaders striding about with their laden plates, their heads up and their shoulders back. They stood in a group apart from the rest of us as they ate, and during the meal, formed a committee responsible for overseeing and organizing the smooth running of the camp. That afternoon our captains put together a daily and weekly routine for our health and welfare. Meanwhile, my mates and I finished our beds while the other crews made rough tables and chairs for the mess hall.

"I'm not looking forward to another night in here, but at least we don't have to sleep on the floor again," said Billy, as we jiggled my bed through the cell door.

I nodded. "This is the worst bed I have ever owned, but I am proud of it."

"I feel the same way about mine," said Billy, as we put it down and pushed it next to the wall. "It is because we made them ourselves."

I looked at the straw and ticking lying on the floor. "It won't be much good without a mattress to cushion the rope. I wish I had my luggage. I could sew this together easily if I had my sail-mending kit."

The words had barely left my mouth when, with clattering hooves and rumbling wheels, horses pulled a wagon into the courtyard, and moments later, someone ran past the cells shouting:

"The luggage has come. Our luggage is here!"

We rushed outside and milled around the loaded cart. Then two fellows leapt onto the tray and, shouting out the names on the luggage tags, passed the bags down. I waited patiently in the dwindling crowd until at last, I heard:

"WOLFGANG SCHMITT."

"*Ja*," I shouted, grabbing the handle of my suitcase.

Once I had my needles and thread it was short work to sew the ticking into a bag and stuff it with straw. Nevertheless, I had only finished sewing the opening closed when Michael stuck his head around the edge of my door.

"The captain says 'report to the kitchen for duties.'"

The Spot The War Forgot

I hastily shook my mattress and laid it on my bed.

"Righto," I said, rolling up my mending kit before stowing it away in my bag.

Dinner was much less work than lunch. Even so, my arm was tiring by the time I had buttered eighty-nine slabs of bread.

"All done," said the cook, as the bugle sounded. "Put the big kettles on the fire so they'll be boiling by the time rollcall is over.

The meal the second night was more comfortable than the previous ones because now we had tables and chairs. It was not fine furniture, the chairs were wobbly and the tabletops merely rough slabs of timber, but they were sturdy and did the job well, which was all that mattered.

After we had eaten and cleaned up, we were milling around unsure what to do, when the sound of harmonious singing drew us outside once more. A small group of men were singing well-known songs from home. I leaned against the stone wall and listened to the beautiful music, waves of homesickness washing over me. A man nearby picked up a sharp stone and scratched his name on the wall while he listened, and I, (inspired by him) scratched 3/3/1915, Wolfgang Schmitt, of the Pfalz beside it. We lingered there until the shadows lengthened and the moon showed pale in the sky. Then because the light was fading the singers stopped, and we drifted off to our cheerless cells.

W.E. Hamilton

March 1915
Russians Capture 120,000 Austrians at Przemtsl in Galicia

Clean Ship Day

The next morning the sky was a brilliant blue, and despite being early autumn the day promised to be hot. Immediately after rollcall, Captain Jepsen, acting as the spokesman of the Camp Committee, stood before us and announced:

"Today is Clean Ship Day. I know it is not the traditional day for cleaning the ship, but it is necessary to do it a few days earlier. Yesterday the Camp Committee purchased buckets, brooms, mops, soap, and disinfectant, to clean this place from top to bottom. You will work as teams, and each captain is in charge of his crew as usual. Dismissed."

Our crew gathered around Captain Kühlken and he dispensed chores among us, along with buckets and brooms. Some went to sweep the floors, walls, and any ceilings they could reach, while others followed them with hoses, scrubbing brushes, and disinfectant. The rest of the men threw the filthy blankets into huge steaming tubs of soapy water and rubbed

The Spot The War Forgot

until all the grime and fleas were gone. Michael and I drew the short straw.

"Report to the Field Officer for sanitary service," said Captain Kühlken.

We did not know for sure what Sanitary Service was, but we guessed correctly it was toilet cleaning when the field officer led us to the latrines.

"Clean these," he said handing us buckets, and scrubbing brushes.

We did our best, but no amount of carbolic or disinfectant can stop latrines from stinking.

"This place is very primitive," I grumbled as I scrubbed. "No electricity, no glass in the windows, and no water-closet toilets."

"It is," said Michael.

Despite our grumbling, the day passed quickly, and that night we were rewarded for our labour by improved living quarters. It was still very basic but at least nothing was dirty. My blankets smelt of sunshine and fresh air as I spread them over my bed, and the walls were clean enough for pictures. I pinned a photograph of my family next to a small painting of a sailor sailing on a smooth patch of sea in the eye of a raging storm. At the bottom of the painting, penned in a curly script, were the words; May God keep you safe through storms. It was signed, Hilda Schmitt; the name of my sister. That night, as the Milky Way twinkled through the bars of my window, I did not feel so bad. I did not like being a prisoner, but Castle Foreboding was not so bad. And the next day softened me more, for now the housekeeping was organized into a roster, the Camp Committee turned their attention to ways of keeping us fit and healthy. After morning rollcall Captain Wilhelm Niemann stood up and addressed us.

"The Camp Committee has set aside some of the cells in the central tower as an infirmary and decided for the health of the camp, every man shall keep active. Young and old will have their own teams, and compete at appropriate levels. Tennis is very good for the body and mind. Other sports are also good. But tennis is very good. You will find a list of sports and activities on the noticeboard. Put your name down for anything you are interested in, but come and see me if you are excellent at tennis. Dismissed."

The crowd surged forward but Billy, Michael, and I leant against the prison wall waiting for the mob around the noticeboard to thin.

"Captain Niemann is very enthusiastic about tennis."

"He loves it, his crew say he plans to make tennis courts with ant bed construction."

My eyebrows shot up. "Ant bed construction?"

"*Ja*, they say when you crush termite mounds and mix the powder with water, it sets like concrete."

"*Ach komm schon.*"

"I have heard it is true, they make huts out of it in Africa."

By now the crowd had thinned and fewer men were gathered around the noticeboard so we sauntered over.

"Captain Niemann will be happy, tennis is popular," said Billy, writing his name at the bottom of a long column.

"So are gymnastics, wrestling, and athletics," said Michael.

I nodded as I wrote, Wolfgang Schmitt, under Swimming.

The Camp Committee was not long in sorting us into teams. That afternoon I followed the swimming captain down the hill

The Spot The War Forgot

to the river. The prison wall reared above us as we picked our way through eucalyptus trees, scrub and wattles as we tramped along the water's edge. Across the river, at the top of a steep bank was flat ground. Treetops shimmered and wobbled from the blows of many axes as men cleared an area for the sports fields and tennis courts. On our side sailors sang and whistled as they sank poles into the ground and bound bundles of brush into simple bathing huts, while the 'Tennis Court' teams smashed huge termite mounds to pieces, grinding them into power before shovelling them into sacks. As we followed the river downstream the singing and whooshing thumps of falling trees faded, and by the time we got to the deepest part of the river the only sounds were kookaburra cackles and the raspy screeches of cockatoos. At length, the river turned a corner, and the deep stretches of water thinned into shallows as it passed over a flat rocky shelf. Here, the captain called a halt.

"The plan is to dam the river across here." He pointed to the spot he had in mind, "and in so doing, raise the level of the waterhole into a lake. I want a row of rocks (two boulders high) in a straight line from here to there. Once you have the big rocks in place, fill the gaps with small stones.

"Yabol," we said saluting. Then we rolled up our trousers and carried large stones into the ankle-deep water.

There is nothing like working together to build friendships. Among the dam builders were many men I had not met before, but as we worked we struck up an easy comradery. The heroes of the group were Walter Bergien, Otto Mönkedieck and Karl Müller, who were in the battle between the SMS Emden and HMS Sydney.

"Tell us about the legendary Emden?" we said, as we laid

W.E. Hamilton

our stones side by side.

"She was a fine ship," said Bergien, "three thousand-six-hundred tons, lightly armoured, carrying torpedoes and ten mounted guns." He lobbed a big rock into the water as if it were a torpedo.

A faraway look entered Mönkedieck's eyes as he rolled a rock down the edge of the bank. "Four-inch calibre guns, firing thirty-six-pound shells."

"She was built in 1906 and part of Germany's Pacific fleet," continued Bergien.

"We were quartered at Tsingtao off the coast of China," broke in Muller, jumping out of the way as a rock fell into the water with a splash.

"Tell us about Captain von Muller," we said, without pausing in our job of placing stone upon stone.

"The captain is every bit as brave and gallant as the newspapers say he is," said Bergan.

"*Ja*, that is so," the other two nodded in agreement.

"He was good to us and chivalrous to all the prisoners we captured," said Muller.

"He treated the prisoners we took with courtesy and accommodated them as comfortably as possible under the conditions."

"Not like the captain of the HMS Sydney," said Mönkedieck, throwing a rock into the water with force. The faces of all three men darkened.

"*Ja*," said Bergain, "He shelled our beached ship and left us stranded and wounded for twenty-four hours before taking us to the hospital."

Nobody knew what to say other than, "The swine," so I

The Spot The War Forgot

said, "Tell us about the last battle." I said this to change the topic, but it was not a good choice.

There was a sudden silence as the three men hastily shifted their full attention to the stones at our feet. Finally, Muller spoke. "One-hundred-and thirty-six of our comrades were killed that day."

We could see none of them wanted to talk about it so we asked no more about the last battle. But they were happy to talk about their glorious exploits in the first three months of the war. During the next few weeks as we built a sturdy dam, they told of the battles where they captured and sank twenty-three Allied merchantmen, and destroyed a Russian cruiser, and a French destroyer. By the time the last stone was in place, and the waterhole upstream had expanded into a lovely wide lake, we were all firm friends, proud of what we had accomplished.

While we were building the dam the other groups had not been idle. Small bathing huts were dotted along the edge of the water, and two diving boards projected from tall rocks. The sports fields were almost completed, but the three tennis courts were far from finished. Many men swarmed over a square patch, spreading, watering, and rolling, layers and layers of crushed termite mud. Despite the huge effort they were expending, we could see it would be some time before the beds of the courts were deep and hard enough for tennis. And it was not only the river and the countryside that was changing. Inside the jail along the southern wall of the prison, was a long bowling alley for skittles and bowls, and in a sunny sheltered corner, the garden club diligently tended a flourishing patch of vegetables. Even the courthouse across the road had a reading room, and a library was springing up as men shared the books their friends posted to them. Moreover, the windows of our cells were glazed, and now that the wind was blocked, and sacks carpeted the floors, our rooms were not so bad.

"It almost feels homely," I said to Billy, as he helped me carry the small table I had just finished making, into my cell. "Now I have a table and a chair, a bookcase and a kerosene lamp I can read in the evening."

"*Ja*, but not tonight, you don't want to miss the choir."

I nodded. "The reading must wait. I expect the performance will be good, Karl Mehne accepts nothing less than excellence."

Billy nodded. "He is tough, but he is turning that little group of singers into a first-rate choir. Tonight, there is an extra surprise."

"What do you mean?"

Billy tapped the side of his nose. "I'm not saying anything more."

After dinner, I stood in the assembly yard with the other internees full of curiosity. The surprise turned out to be a short musical recital by three men; Billy on the viola, Meinert Horstmann on the mandolin, and Fritz Theiessen on the zither. The cheerful music bounced off the stone walls and filled the prison yard with hope. We clapped and whistled when they had finished, and that night as the choir sang under the gas lamplights, the old castle was much less foreboding; it was almost beautiful.

The Spot The War Forgot

April 1915
British Troops in Mesopotamia Defend Basra Against a Large Attack by Turks

The Village

The struggling little village of Berrima was an odd mixture of grandeur and poverty. The public buildings were almost magnificent, and a few Georgian styled houses were excellent. They rose regally from the midst of make-do slab and bark huts and tumbling down stone cottages. Across the road from the jail was an elegant boarding house, and crouching beside it were the general store, the butcher, and a sweet shop. Surprisingly, the shops were neither grand nor derelict. The general store was a simple wooden building with gable ends and a veranda that ran the full length of its front wall. Metal buckets swung in the breeze from the overhanging veranda, while washboards and axes leaned against its outside wall. Above the washboards hung softball bats.

"It's hard to believe this decaying village was one of the busiest towns in the state," said Billy, as we crossed the sleepy road and made our way towards the General Store.

"Who told you that?"

"Herr Davis from the General Store."

"That explains the buildings of grandeur among the hovels." I twisted and pointed to the courthouse behind us. "Look at those imposing columns, that's the sort of building you expect to find in a thriving city."

"William Davis said Berrima was once a large market centre, a posting stage, and over a dozen inns flourished."

"I wonder what happened?" I said, looking towards the huddle of shops again.

"Ask Davis yourself, he is a mine of information on the history of the town. I could hardly get away when I went there for rope the other day."

We pushed the door open, disturbing a little bell that announced our arrival by a tinkly jangle.

William Davis looked up from his ledger. "Hello Gentlemen, what can I do for you today?"

"I'd like a washboard and a bar of soap," I said.

"We have the standard board with wooden corrugations," said Davis, putting a bar of yellow soap on the counter, "or we have the new and improved board. The ones with the glass insert are more expensive but they last longer because the glass doesn't wear over time."

"I'll have the cheaper one," I said, handing him some money. "I don't need it to last long. The war will be over soon."

"I hope you are right," said Davis, handing me a wooden board before writing the price down in his ledger.

"And I'll have a packet of cigarettes," said Billy.

My friend tells me you know all the local history," I said.

The Spot The War Forgot

"I wouldn't say I know it all," said Davis, making another mark in his book and handing Billy his cigarettes, "just the interesting bits like the man accused of forgery. During his trial, he tried to avoid prosecution by snatching the evidence and eating it."

"Did it work?"

"No," said Davis, taking Billy's money and handing him change. "He had trouble swallowing the cheque because of the pin in it. A constable lost a fingernail when the prisoner bit his finger as he hauled Exhibit A from his mouth."

Billy and I burst out laughing, and Davis (gratified by our reaction) hooked his thumbs in his apron's waist and leaned back in a friendly manner.

"And then there were the convicts who were convinced China was about one-hundred-and-fifty miles south of Sydney."

"China!"

"Yes, China. That was a widely held belief among the convicts. In fact, that's how Berrima was discovered. So many of them tried to run away to China, Governor Hunter sent four convicts and four soldiers, along with John Wilson and John Price on an official trek to prove China was not there. After a few days, the convicts got fed up and went back to jail with the soldiers.

"What about the other men did they go back too?"

"No, they pushed on and passed through Berrima. When they returned, they gave such glowing reports of the countryside a bloke in Sydney called, Major Mitchell, decided to make Berrima an important administrative centre for the county of Camden and the southern districts."

"When was that?"

W.E. Hamilton

"Way back in 1829."

"Is that why the village has a grand courthouse?"

"Sure is. Mitchell visualized an English county capital and planned the town around the marketplace."

"Is that the green square by the church?"

Davis nodded. "Mitchell expected this to grow into an important city, and for a time it looked that way. In the jail's heyday, six-hundred-and thirty wagons a week passed through here and there were thirteen hotels."

"Big hotels?"

He pulled a face. "Of varying standards. The better ones like White Horse Inn and the Bergin's boarding house are still standing, but the Surveyor General is the only licensed hotel left."

"What happened?"

"The railway expanded south and unfortunately it went through Moss Vale instead of Berrima. Once the traffic dropped off the inns began to close, the tradesmen left, and the jail shut. Over time the population dwindled from six-hundred to the eighty locals who live here today."

"One-hundred-and-sixty-nine locals, you mean," said Billy, grinning. "You forget there are eighty-nine of us."

Davis smiled and slapped his hand on the counter. "You're right. I don't care what Henry Allen says, you are good for the village. I've sold more washboards and axes in the last few weeks than I have in the last ten years. I remember back in 1901…"

"*Danka* for your time, Herr Davis," said Billy hastily. He nudged me with his foot. "We must be going."

"Oh, oh, *ja*," I stammered, scooping my soap and washboard

The Spot The War Forgot

off the counter.

"Call again boys," said Davis, "it has been a pleasure talking with you."

We raised our hats and nodded, before opening the door and stepping outside.

"I wouldn't mind buying some sweets," I said, pointing to the lolly shop adjacent to the butcher.

"Good idea," said Billy.

We were about to bypass the butcher's shop when the door flew open and a woman, wearing a bloodied apron around her enormous girth, bounced in front of us.

"Guten morgen."

Our eyes flew open at this welcome to Berrima.

"You speak German?"

"Only a little. I'm Annie Taylor, daughter of German immigrants. I understand German but can't speak it because I was raised in Australia." She wagged a bloodstained finger at us roguishly. "So don't say uncomplimentary things about me in German."

All the time she spoke she inched backwards, so without knowing how it happened, we stepped over the gutter that ran with blood, and into the shop. By now the sun was high in the sky and the heat was rising. The stench from the carcasses hanging from the hooks on the walls and the sawdust strewn floor was overpowering. Billy's face went the colour of old cheese while, I, pretending to blow my nose, kept the handkerchief bunched against my nostrils. The woman, oblivious to our discomfort, rolled her sleeves over her elbows and reached up.

"I can make *bratwurst* sausages for you if you like?" Her biceps bulged as she hoisted a mutton carcass off its hook and whacked it down on the stump of a gigantic tree trunk. She picked up a meat cleaver and lifting it above her head brought it down with a mighty thwack and the carcass (neatly severed down the backbone) split into two. "I season them the traditional way with ginger, nutmeg, coriander, or caraway."

Normally the idea of ginger or caraway *bratwurst* made my mouth water, but the blowflies crawling over the uncovered meat made me feel sick at the thought.

"If you order some now," Annie put down her cleaver and slung half the mutton onto a bench. "I can have them ready by tomorrow morning."

"Who is the butcher who delivers the meat to the prison?" said Billy, saving the day by changing the subject. "I thought he was the local butcher."

"Oh, that's my husband, Alfred." Annie picked up a razor-sharp knife and turned back to the meat on the chopping block. "He still does the deliveries but nowadays he is too busy for butchering because of the limestone quarry he's leased at Marulan. And my son Arnold works in a shipping and coal business in Sydney. My daughter helps out, but most of the time she runs the lolly shop next door." Annie's vast stomach wobbled as she sliced between the ribs with surgical precision. "Don't mind the flies. The meat is fresh. How about some nice chops?"

"What are the villagers like?" I mumbled through my hankie.

"The Davis's are alright, and so is John Izzard who owns the Livery and Bait Stable. His wife, Rose, is a treasure. She is the local midwife. A real good sort, kind as they come. If you have any health problems go and see her, she is better than the doctor. He's useless."

"I'll keep that in mind for the next time I have a baby."

Annie snorted with laughter and gave Billy such a hearty thump on his shoulder it almost knocked him over. "You're a right one, aren't you? Silly me, I forgot to mention she is also the district nurse."

She picked up a smaller meat cleaver and with a series of skilful chops severed the ribs from the backbone before scooping them into a pile and dumping them on the bench.

"Then there is the Harper family. They are the leading family in the area. James and his wife run the Surveyor General and their daughter, Ada, is the local postie." Annie picked up the big cleaver again and guillotined a leg off with two blows. "She's a pretty girl. You'll see her riding her bike around the village with a bag of letters. They were very rich once. Used to own the mansion on the hill before they fell on hard times. Now it belongs to the Catholic Church and a bunch of nuns live there." She paused in her labours and looked hard at me, the cleaver in her upraised hand."Are you Catholic or Protestant?"

I gripped my washboard with sweaty fingers and took a step back. "Ah, I'm not sure, my mother is a catholic and my father a protestant."

"You have a choice then. In this town there a sharp division between the Church of England 'sheep' and the Catholic 'goats.' Take my advice," she waved the cleaver at me as her eyes narrowed, "if you want to mix with all the small-minded people who are considered somebodies, go to Holy Trinity Church; that's where the elite of English birth and all their bootlickers go. But if you want amusement," (the cleaver came down with a bang) "go to St Francis Xavier's Church, for the

Irish Catholics are more entertaining."

"Really?" I said, faintly.

"Father Martin is the embodiment of Friar Tuck. He's big, burly, and earthy. After he's driven his horse all the way from Moss Vale, he's in no mood for nonsense. One look at his red face as he descends from his buggy and you know there will be fireworks."

"What kind of fireworks?"

"Jim Murphy had a mongrel pup he took to church each Sunday. The pup used to lie quietly at his feet until the Elevation of the Host. As soon as the bell rang the dog howled. This went on week after week until one morning it got too much for Father Martin. Pointing his finger at the dog he bellowed, 'Jim, take that dog out and kick him, and kick him hard.'"

Billy and I laughed because Annie expected us to.

"And in winter, that stone church gets very chilly. On frosty mornings Father Martin gallops through the service and breathes an unholy sigh of enjoyment as he sips the wine."

"What about the baker?" I said, curious to hear the gossipy woman's opinion of the man.

"Henry Allen!" The cleaver smashed down and the sheep's neck catapulted across the room, landing in the sawdust. "You'll have trouble with him! A more prejudiced man I never met. Watch out for him and the schoolmaster Thomas Packer. Packer is an elderly Englishman, conservative to the bone. He knows nothing of history and regards anyone who speaks anything other than English with the utmost suspicion. The man is as rigid and unbending as the bamboo wand he canes the children with."

"What about the farmers?"

The Spot The War Forgot

"They are too busy milking and working at the railway station in Moss Vale to bother you. The only one who might be a problem is a chap called Row and only because he is friendly with Allen. How about a nice roast," she said, hacking off the foreleg and holding it aloft?

"We don't have an oven to cook it in," said Billy, hastily, "I was hoping to buy a liquorice strap in the shop next door."

Annie beamed. "Oh, here's me jabbering away wasting all your time. Off you go. My daughter will get you fixed up with the best sweets south of Sydney." She winked at us. "She is unmarried and has no boyfriend. Sweets from the sweety."

Billy got us through the awkward moment by raising his hat.

"*Danka*, for a most interesting conversation."

I followed his lead and, wading through the flies that erupted from the floor, we made our way to the door and out into the street.

"Whew! I blew out a short puff of air as I put my handkerchief back in my pocket. "Have you ever met anyone like her before?"

"*Nein*, she is original."

"I would not like to meet her in a dark alley if she was angry."

Billy lit a cigarette. "She is alright, a rough diamond. I like her."

"So do I. I wonder what the daughter looks like? Probably hideous."

"We are about to find out," said Billy, pushing the door of the lolly shop open.

The lolly shop was everything the butcher was not. There

were no flies, no grisly carcasses, no blood, and no sawdust. Instead, there was row upon row of glass jars full of brightly coloured treats. I did not need to block my nose in this shop for it smelt of cinnamon and aniseed, mingled with peppermint. I was contemplating the toffees and barley-sugar sticks when a young woman stepped out of the back room.

"Can I help you?"

Billy and I stood with our mouths open. It was hard to believe this dainty vision of loveliness, with the trim waist, and luxuriant hair was the butcher's daughter. Billy recovered first.

"I'd like a bag of liquorice straps," he squeaked.

The girl turned gracefully and lifted several long black strips into a small paper bag.

"Beauty and the Beast," I whispered.

Billy nudged me with his elbow. "Shut up."

"We've just been talking to Annie," said Billy, he sucked on his cigarette and little wisps of smoke leaked from his nostrils as he added, "she seems a very pleasant person."

"Mum is the best," said Beauty, twisting the corners of the bag into little cow's-ears, and taking the money he handed her. "She is very excited about Germans coming into the village. For once she won't feel like an outsider. It's been tough on her living in such a small-minded community. You can be here thirty years, and they still think of you as a foreigner." She dropped the money in the cash register before turning blue eyes on me. "Were you wanting anything?"

I felt my face go red as I stammered: "A penny's worth of toffees."

She lifted a jar off the shelf and shook toffees into the scales

The Spot The War Forgot

sitting on the counter. When the hand pointed to the right spot on the dial, she scooped them into a bag and twisted the top into a paper fountain.

"Here you go," she passed the bag to me. "Will there be anything else?"

"That will be all for now," I said, handing her a penny.

After that, there was a silence that grew heavier as the seconds passed, for unlike her mother, Beauty was more of a looker than a talker. Then as there was nothing to keep us there any longer, we thanked her and went back to the jail to do our washing.

———

W.E. Hamilton

April 1915
ANZACs, French and British troops land on Gallipoli Peninsula

Snakes, the Unlikely Peacemakers.

Easter had come and gone with little to mark the event. On Good Friday and Resurrection Sunday the Catholics were entertained at St Francis Xavier's Church by Father Martin, while the protestant's suffered through a prim and proper meeting at Holy Trinity. The rest of us were content with the captains reading a service which they did every Sunday, as was their custom at sea. Although the weather was cooling, it was not cold enough to stop us from playing sport and swimming every day. The bathing huts were a huge success, so much so, building fever gripped us all. Many huts were springing up along the edge of the right-hand bank of the river, as in ones or twos, men built daytime abodes of brush and bark. One man was more ambitious than the rest of us.

"Why do you not build something stronger," said Paul

The Spot The War Forgot

Pann, watching me lie sheets of flattened bark on the roof of my hut. "Clearing the sport's fields has left many logs lying about."

"What is the point?" I said, fastening a sapling over the bark, "if you go to too much trouble the war will be over before the door is hung."

"I hope you are right, but even if I am wrong, I'm going to build a log cabin. It will remind me of the Black Forest."

We thought he was a dolt and wasting his effort, but the huts had a way of becoming all-consuming, and before long we were adding verandas, windows, and even an extra room, to our bathing huts. Those who kept their huts simple teased us.

"You have built a five-pound bathing booth," they laughed.

By now the villagers were no longer shadowy figures hidden behind curtains. They stared at us openly as they wandered alongside the river looking at the huts, lake, and sports fields.

"The dam is good," they said, nodding with approval at the expanded waterhole. "We've wanted the river dammed for a long time but the Council never got around to it. You blokes are doing a great job."

"*Danka*," we said smiling.

We were breaking the rule of 'no fraternizing with the guards or locals,' but we did not care. Despite the villager's initial suspicion, friendships were growing. Moreover, our English was improving and every day we spoke a little better, for the Camp Committee had ruled English lessons were mandatory. Only Henry Allen the baker, his farmer friend, and the schoolmaster, persisted in their hate for us. Henry Allen even lobbied the council to close the jail and send us away.

W.E. Hamilton

"I do not understand this baker," I said to Michael as we returned from a hike in the countryside, "he makes a lot of money from us, but he still wants us gone."

"War sets men against one another," said Michael, turning off the road and onto a common path that cut across a field.

"You are right, but it does not make it any easier. If I could get baked goods anywhere else, I would never set foot in his shop again."

"*Ja*, me too."

A young woman on a bike rode towards us, her front basket bulging with letters and parcels.

"Good afternoon gentlemen," she said, as we stepped out of the way.

"Good Afternoon, Frauline Ada," we tipped our hats moments before she rattled past.

"Sorry, I can't stop, the mail must go on."

"Why can't Henry Allen change his mind about us like Frauline Ada? "She told the newspaper 'we are not amused,' when they reopened the jail, but now she is very friendly."

"It is a mystery," said Michael, slashing a stick at the tall grass at the side of the track.

We pondered the question as we continued walking, and at last, we came to the bridge by the Catholic church.

"Do you think it is worth braving the lion in his den for an iced bun, Michael? I jingled the loose change in my pocket. "I'll treat you to one if you like."

"For sure, I'm not afraid of that loud-mouth."

We walked over the bridge, across the green, and along the road to the bakery on the corner opposite the lolly shop.

"Here goes." I pushed open the door and stepped inside.

The Spot The War Forgot

"Good afternoon," I said, tipping my hat to Allen and his friend who was leaning against the wall talking to him. "I would like six iced buns please." I placed the correct coin on the counter.

Without replying or looking at me, Henry Allen took my money, slapped the buns in a paper bag, and slung them across the counter.

The man by the wall straightened up and glared at us. "Keep off the path that goes over my land, do ya hear."

I tipped my hat. "I am sorry Sir, *Fraulein* Ada said it was a common-path, and I have seen many people walk over it."

The man stuck out his chin and clenched his fists. "Australians may use it, but not Huns. Tell your friends I'm setting mantraps along there, so watch out."

I took my bag of buns, tipped my hat once more, and we walked out.

"Surely it is a big lie," I said, as the door clanged shut behind us. "Mantraps are not allowed in this country."

"From him, I believe anything. I will not be walking over his land again. He and his friend the baker are bad. I wish there was another bakery."

John Izzard's buggy diverted our attention.

"Herr Izzard must be going to the train station," said Michael, looking at the large bag of mail in the back.

I nodded, following the horse with my eyes. "The Livery and Bait Stables have good horses. I would like to hire that nice horse for a day."

"I have heard there are some very pretty spots around here for a picnic," said Michael. "The guards are friendly and lenient; we should ask permission to go beyond the two-mile parole."

"*Ja*, that is a good idea, when I have finished building my hut I will."

The bakery was not far from the jail, Michael and I crossed the road and walked past it, down Oxley Street and onto the riverbank. There we sat under a tree and tucked into the buns. We had just finished eating when the local policeman rode up to us.

"Do either of you men know how to catch snakes?" he asked, reigning his horse in. "A big brown one has got into the Izzard's stables."

"For sure, I have caught them before," said Michael.

"This is not a little garden snake, Australia has the deadliest snakes in the world, and brown ones are aggressive, they will have bitten you five times before you raise your spade if you are not careful."

"*Ja*, I know, I worked on a farm in Victoria before I came here."

"Go around to the Livery and Bait Stables then, and get rid of it for Rose Izzard."

"*Ja* sir," said Michael, scrambling to his feet. He looked at the many sticks scattered about and picked up a sturdy one with a forked end.

I thought catching a snake sounded an interesting way to pass the time, so I went with him. When we arrived at the Livery and Bate Stables, Frau Izzard was pacing anxiously outside one of the stable doors.

We tipped our hats.

"Good Afternoon," Frau Izzard, said Michael. "I have come to kill the snake."

The Spot The War Forgot

"Oh, thank you, thank you, he's in here." She swung the door open and pointed to the back corner. "It's over there, you can just see the end of its tail sticking out of the straw."

"I see it." Michael advanced cautiously into the stable.

Frau Izzard and I hung back while, Michael, holding the stick in his left hand, crept forward with his right hand outstretched. Then crouching slightly, he leant forward and with lightening-speed, grabbed the snake's tail and slid it out from under the straw. The snake writhed and coiled as it tried to strike, but Michael, leaping out of its way, lifted its tail high in the air. The snake dropped into a long line and dangled from my friend's hand as if it were a fat leather belt. But only for a moment. With huge strength, it twisted its head upward like a hook on a fishing line. As it rose, Michael took his stick and slotting it around the base of its head, swiftly pinned it to the ground. Shortly after, he emerged carrying the headless snake.

"Thank you, thank you," said Frau Izzard clapping her hands together. "I don't know what I would have done without you. My husband has gone to collect the mail and I was afraid the snake might get into the other stalls and bite the horses."

"It is good it chose the empty stable," said Michael, wiping his pocket knife on a tuft of grass.

"It certainly is. If it had bitten Prince it would have been a big loss."

"*Ja*, he is a valuable horse," I said, thinking of the fine animal I had seen by the bakery.

Frau Izzard nodded. "And smart too. He can open stable doors and gates. Many nights he lets himself out for a midnight stroll. By the way, my name is Rose, and if there is anything I can do for you, please let me know."

Michael, coiled up the snake. "It was nothing, it was my pleasure to help."

"I was a lot more than nothing. What about some garlic to ward off the ghosts of the jail. I have some in the garden?"

I raised an eyebrow. "Ghost's, I've not heard of any ghosts."

"Really? I am surprised. It is only a matter of time before you do. That has been a grisly place. It was built by convicts fettered in irons and chained together and was considered the most brutal jail in the whole country. Men went mad in the underground solitary confinement cells. They say there are flickering lights, cold spots, and ghosts walk there."

"For sure, the whole place is cold but I have not seen ghosts, and any lights will help, for our kerosene lamps are not strong."

Rose shook her head. "You won't be so brave if you see Lucretia Dunkley, the woman who murdered her husband. She is buried within the walls of the prison," Rose leaned forward and whispered, "buried upright and headless so she cannot rest in peace."

While Rose was talking a woman sidled out of the bushes behind her. At the name, Lucretia Dunkley, she rushed forward with her hands clasped; her face was white, and her long red hair cascaded over her back as she looked towards heaven and cried:

"Let them out, let them out, I see the prisoners, I hear their chains; their faces are despairing, they call to me to free them."

Michael and I jumped, but Rose was untroubled by this strange outburst.

"It's all right dear, it's alright, the men are long gone."

"But I hear them, the jail is full of voices. Let them out of solitary confinement!"

"It's all right, deary, nobody's in solitary confinement." Rose stroked the woman's arm as she turned to us. "The poor soul has had a nervous breakdown," she whispered. "The brutal history of the jail preys on her mind and she thinks you are the convicts of old."

"We will go."

Rose nodded, "it might be best if you did. Take care, and remember, if you change your mind and decide you want some garlic to hang around your neck, come and see me." She gave a little wave before putting her arm around the red-haired woman. "Come inside with Nurse and have a nice cup of chamomile tea, Lovey," she said, propelling her away gently.

Michael carried his trophy home, and the snake was the talk of the camp that night, and we were not the only ones talking. The story of the Izzard's snake flew through the village, and thereafter, women often called us to get rid of snakes. In this way, we got to see inside many of the houses. Some were models of neatness but most were not, as slopping pigs, milking cows, and chopping the heads off chickens, left little time for housework. The more cluttered the house was, the more difficult it was to get the snake. While I had seen many disorganized dwellings, one stands out in particular. The kitchen was monumental chaos. A large room, it contained a huge wooden table laden with clutter. Dirty dishes, old food and shallow pans of rising cream lay strewn between jars of jam, mending, and laundry. The woman of the house pushed a straggling lock of hair out of her eyes. She was probably in her twenties but overwork made her look much older.

"He's in here somewhere."

Billy and I swapped horrified glances. There was so much stuff on the floor I did not think anyone could dig through the accumulation to the floorboards, let alone find a snake.

"Where did you last see it?"

"By the fire."

We looked towards the cavity where iron kettles hung over glowing coals. Nearby several cats and a dog lay slouched over old clothes, slumbering, while chickens pecked at scraps on the floor.

"Surely the animals would be making more of a fuss if it was still over there."

"It went in the parlour, Mum, said a small boy munching a piece of bread and treacle. "I saw it go in there when you went for help."

"Oh, Danny! I told you to stay outside!" The woman gave her son a small shake. "You could have been killed."

"No, I wouldn't have."

"Don't be a fool, boy. The cemetery is full of people who died of snake bites. Next time do as you are told."

"Where is the parlour?" I asked the question merely as a polite way to get on with the job and out of the house as soon as possible, for almost everyone had a parlour, though they were seldom used. It was always the best of the two front rooms and kept for entertaining visitors.

"This way," said the woman, cautiously picking her way down the hallway. She stopped by the front door, and huddling close to the wall, pointed into the room on the right. "In there."

Billy and I, following her, threaded our way through piles of boxes leaning against the walls and entered the room warily. We clutched our long, forked sticks as our eyes roamed about.

The Spot The War Forgot

This room was tidier than the rest of the house and stuffed with memorabilia from a more prosperous time. I crouched down and stared under the horsehair couch and balloon back chairs, stiffly arranged around the walls.

"I don't see the snake," I whispered.

"Perhaps he is in the corner behind the table. You pull it out from the wall and I'll try to get him with my stick."

"Take the china and the shells off the table before you move it," hissed the woman, poking her head through the door. She pointed to the grim woman in the heavy picture frame on the wall above the fireplace. "Grandma will turn in her grave if you break them."

We nodded. Then Billy carried the tray of teacups out to the hallway while I followed with a dusty dome, filled with exquisite shells.

"And bring the vases, too," said the woman, as she took our burdens from us. "I don't want peacock feathers and dried flowers scattered about if there is a chase."

We did as she said. Then leaning forward, I lifted the small table and leapt back. I only glimpsed a fast-moving shadow before Billy lunged into the corner with his stick, and shortly after, he held the headless snake aloft.

"It's alright, you can come in now, I've got him."

The woman slumped against the wall, rolled her eyes back, and patted her chest with little repetitive movements. "Oh, I am so grateful. I would have died of fear if I had to spend the night in this house knowing a snake was slithering about." She let out a long sigh of relief and straightened up. "Come and have a cup of tea and a piece of bread and jam."

Billy and I exchanged stricken glances as we followed her

back to the filthy kitchen.

"That is very kind, but we must get back to the jail. We have things we have to do."

"Very well, suit yourself." She shooed a black and white bird out of the back door. "Watch out for the magpies, the cheeky things will steal anything shiny."

We touched our hats politely before stepping out into the fresh air.

"I don't care what anyone says about you," said the woman, standing on her threshold and putting her hands on her hips, "you blokes might talk funny, but as far as I'm concerned, anyone who gets rid of snakes is a bit of alright."

The Spot The War Forgot

April 1915
Germans Gas French Africans in Ypres.

Moonshine and a Fugitive

One day Billy, Michael, and I were returning from a successful snake hunt when we passed the Surveyor General Hotel. The hotel was a handsome two-storied building with a long low veranda, under which tables and benches sprawled. It was a hot day and the shady retreat looked inviting.

I halted in front of the hotel and sighed. "It is very hard that we are not allowed in there."

"*Ja* the weak beer they let us have is worse than dishwater," said Michael, pulling a face.

I nodded. "I understand why the Post Office is out of bounds, but a small schnapps now and again would not hurt."

"Perhaps the guards are afraid of drunken riots."

"Perhaps so."

While we were pondering on this question, Captain Jepsen

entered the large boarding house run by Thomas Bergin and his family. Captain Jepsen's wife lived there and the Captain visited her during the day.

"Captain Jepsen is a lucky man having a wife near," said Michael, shifting his attention from the hotel to the boarding house.

"A wife is not possible as there are no German fraulines about," said Billy, rubbing his chin thoughtfully. "But we could get a house."

"What do you mean?"

Billy spread out his arms in a sweeping movement. "Look around, there are many empty houses in the village, we could rent one. I have seen a house in Oxley Street I am thinking of renting. There are others nearby, you could take one too."

"Wouldn't that cost a lot?"

"*Nein*, not if you go in with others. Gerhardt Paradis and Max Adam are interested in sharing with me. We are still being paid by our shipping company and even if we drop to half-pay, the rent split between the three of us is alright."

"I will think about it," said Michael.

"What about you Wolfgang?"

"*Nein*, I like to be close to the river. I am happy with my bathing hut."

That afternoon Billy and his two friends leased the house. And they were not the only ones interested in houses as the jail was increasingly crowded with new prisoners arriving weekly. I still had my small cell to myself but I guessed it would not be long before I had to share with a roommate. Within a short time, all the empty houses in reasonable condition were tenanted by prisoners wealthy enough to afford a day-house.

The Spot The War Forgot

One day Billy and his friends invited Michael and me to afternoon coffee. Their house was a modest weatherboard cottage of four rooms with a fireplace in the front room and a woodstove in the back kitchen. The back veranda led to a dusty backyard with a few scraggly native flowers, while the front veranda faced a row of houses, behind which the prison loomed. Michael pushed open the gate in the tall picket fence, and we walked up the front path and knocked on the door.

"*Komm herein*," said Billy, opening the door.

"This is nice," I said, as he showed us about. "Much more homely than the cells and plenty of room."

"Your carpentry skills are getting better," said Michael.

"For sure." Billy pointed at a chunky chair by the woodstove. "Sit here, you will find it quite comfortable I think."

"What are the flour sacks filled with?" I said, sitting on one of the cushions and settling the other against the back of the chair."

Billy slid a kettle of simmering water from the back of the hob to the plate over the firebox. "Chaff, works well doesn't it."

A stack of newspapers lay on a rough table nearby. I picked up the top paper and frowned. "I want Germany to win the war but this business of the poisonous gas at Ypres is bad."

"Don't bother with that paper, you can't believe what you read in an Australian or British newspaper, they are all biased and misleading." He pulled up a loose floorboard and took three ragged newspapers from the cavity below. "They make it sound like Germany is a monster. Here read these."

I took them in astonishment. "An American, Dutch, and Swiss newspaper! How did you get them?"

W.E. Hamilton

"This is not a question we ask. You may take them and pass them on when you have finished reading them if you wish."

"*Danka*," I said smiling. "But now I am puzzled, why do you keep all the Australian newspapers?"

"They are not for reading! I keep them for a man who is building a hut with them."

"How is he doing that?"

"He stacks them on top of each other. The walls are already knee-high. Keep your papers for him and your jam and milk tins for Karl Wirthgen."

"Wirthgen? I've heard that name before. Is he the marine engineer for the steamer Cannstatt?"

"That's him."

"What is he saving them for?"

"He fills them with clay and is building a hut with them. He has the foundations laid and the walls grow higher each day."

"I haven't seen it."

"It is not close to the river like the other huts, it is on the left bank far up the slope below the sports ground." Billy scratched his head. "I can't understand why it's so far from the water."

"He plays the zither. Maybe he doesn't want neighbours. Maybe he and his three friends want to practice where no one will tell them to be quiet."

"Perhaps. The metal walls will make the music sound most beautiful I think," said Billy, glancing at his viola case. "The quartet is very good."

A scrawny cat wandered through the open door and rubbed up against his legs. "*Guten tag*, you have come to visit me again." He took a jug of milk from a ventilated safe on the wall of the kitchen. "Here you go, Sebastian."

The Spot The War Forgot

"Whose cat is he?"

Gerhardt, who was lounging on a couch softened with cushions of straw, looked up from his book. "He thinks he is ours."

Billy poured milk into a saucer on the floor. "He is a stray and now that we feed him, he thinks he belongs to us."

"I saw a man with a pet wombat the other day, and Richard Peytsch has a puppy," said Gerhardt. "One fellow even has a tame goanna in his cave. Pets are good for us, I think. They take our thoughts away from the war."

"I wouldn't like to spend my day in a cave. That would be as cold as Castle Foreboding. Why doesn't he make a hut?"

Gerhardt shrugged. "Perhaps he does not like company, or perhaps he is lazy."

A strange odour wafted through the open door. Michael sniffed the air with a puzzled look on his face.

"What is that?"

"I have smelt that smell coming from the still in my father's barn," I said.

"For sure," chuckled Max. He pointed out the window to a dilapidated cottage nearby, which (judging from the patches of kerosene-tin on the roof) had recently been repaired. "The marine engineer who has opened a cobbler's shop in the front room has set up a still in the back. If you want your boots repaired go in the front door, if you want a bottle of schnapps, go around the back."

"Why doesn't he keep his still in the bush like the others who are making grog from their jam rations?"

"The guards find too many of them. He doesn't want them to take away his still. Besides, it's hard to hide a still as big as his."

"But it is risky doing this outside the camp. What if the policeman catches him?"

Gerhardt put down his book and stretched. "The cobbler hopes the policeman's nose and eyes are not good." He took a packet of cigarettes from a torn paper package and handed them around as Billy poured the coffee. "These came in the post, have one."

I took a sausage from my pocket and peeled the wax paper from it. "I brought us a little treat also."

"German sausage! Where did you get that?"

"Same place your cigarettes came from, my mother sent it from Berlin," I said, putting it on a plate on the table.

Michael pulled a bag of sweets from his pocket. "Try one of these."

"The postman brings very good things," said Max taking one.

"These didn't come in the post, I got them at the new canteen."

"Is it finally open? The Camp Committee has been working on it for so long I thought it would never open."

"*Ja*, it is open, and they have all kinds of German delicacies. It is wonderful."

"Do they have kuchen?"

"No, cake is too hard to transport from Sydney. But they do have German sausage, jars of sourcrout, and even clothing."

I put the cigarette in my mouth and was about to light it when a loud commotion down the street interrupted me.

"What was that," I said, plucking it from my lips and putting it in my shirt pocket?

The Spot The War Forgot

We rushed out the front door and peered down the road.

"It seems the policeman's nose and eyes are better than the cobbler hoped," said Max. "That's his horse standing at the gate."

"We hung about curious to see the drama unfold, but when the policeman came out, he was alone.

"That's strange," said Gerhardt, watching him go into the next house, "I wonder where the cobbler got to?"

His curiosity was quickly satisfied because shortly after, we found the cobbler crouching behind the kitchen door.

"Quick hide me."

"How did you get here?" said Max.

"When I saw the policeman coming down my path, I ran out the back door and climbed over your fence."

"You can't hide here," said Billy looking out the front window, "the policeman is searching all the nearby houses. He will be here soon, and he will find you for sure, for there is nowhere to hide."

At this, the cobbler's face crumpled into despair. "What shall I do, they will send me to jail?"

"We are already in jail."

"A real jail, with criminals. I don't want to be locked up during the day with dangerous men."

"I know," I said. "Go down to Wallaby Rocks and hide in one of the caves down there."

"That'll work," said Max. "When you hear a kookaburra laugh, it will be us bringing you food."

"Go quickly," said Billy. "The policeman is coming this way."

"I sliced a chunk off the sausage and thrust it into his hand.

"Here take this with you."

"*Danka*," said the cobbler, before disappearing out the back door.

We hid him for two weeks. Fortunately, we did not need to save portions of our camp rations to feed him. Annie's meat was cheap and the gardening club generously gave us plenty of vegetables, which was all we needed, as by now almost every hut had an outdoor fireplace. On the day it was my turn to feed the cobbler, I bought a dressed rabbit from the internee who snared and sold them, and placed paper and kindling in the fireplace by my front door. The flames flared as I touched a match to the dry sticks and before long the metal plate was too hot to touch. I laid pieces of rabbit on the grill and crouching down, fed the fire until it burned steadily.

Michael sat on the bank beside me, smoking lazily. "I'm glad the Camp Committee has put a stop to the crews cooking," he said, looking at the sizzling rabbit.

I poked another stick into the fire and nodded. "I was getting very sick of sea pie and ship fare. It is alright to eat such a diet when at sea but on land, there should be more."

"It is good they sent Mathew Schmid, he is a fine German butcher who knows just the way we like our meat."

"Annie does too, she is more German than Australian."

"She may know the cuts we like, but she doesn't cook it," said Michael. "Schmid, Sellin, Fischer, and Becker, are worth the sixpence a week they charge each of us."

"*Ja*, you can tell by their food they are professional cooks."

I stabbed a fork in the slabs of rabbit and turned them over. "It is nice to cook for ourselves sometimes."

"For sure." Michael, blew a perfect smoke ring. "I like a

change, and some days it is too much bother to go back to the Castle for lunch; especially now it is so crowded."

The aroma of steak mingled with the smell of rabbit every time a gust of wind blew in our direction because many men felt the same way. Once the meat was done, I piled it onto a tin plate while Michael doused the fire with sand. Then we wandered down the riverbank until we came to a deep gorge dotted with sandstone caves.

"Ha ha ha," I laughed.

"That doesn't sound like a kookaburra's laugh."

"If I sounded too real, the cobbler wouldn't know it was us."

"For sure he will know that laugh is us, but so will the policeman."

I rolled my eyes, "*ach komm schon*, the policeman is miles away."

"Then we did not need a signal."

I flicked my head towards the cobbler creeping cautiously into the open. "It doesn't matter, either way as he has heard us."

I put my loaded plate on a large flat rock, and after greeting each other, we sat on nearby boulders and ate the rabbit with our fingers. When we had finished the tasty meal I piled the bones onto my plate and was about to bury them, when the cobbler stopped me.

"Save them, I'll give them to the man in the next cave, his goanna will eat them."

"There is not much meat left on them."

"Meat or no meat, it will still eat them. I once saw the outline of a shoulder of lamb progress through the creature's neck and stomach."

"Uhh!" I pulled a face before scraping the bones onto the rock. "All right, here you are."

"How are you getting on," said Michael, changing the subject.

"This cave makes my cell in the Castle look very warm and nice. I think the money I made from my schnapps was not enough for this."

"Why did you do it," I asked, "it was almost certain you would get caught?"

"It is alright for you Hansa and Lloyd men, you are still on full or half-pay, those of us from smaller vessels have to survive on the Government allowance. Thirty shillings doesn't go far. I am lucky I can also mend boots. Others make-do by cleaning the toilets and peeling vegetables."

"They say some of the profits from the canteen will be used to help out the men such as yourself."

"That's nice but it is too late. Is the policeman still looking for me?"

When Michael and I nodded, the cobbler rubbed his hand over his eyes in a gesture of despair. The awkward moment was broken by two men striding down the riverbank towards us. The cobbler, seeing them, leapt to his feet and was about to scuttle into his cave but I said:

"It is alright, it is Gerhardt and Max, and they look like they have some news for us."

Sure enough, they did. We huddled around them expectantly.

"There is a man who lives in a village a safe distance from here, who is willing to hide you," said Max. "Leave tonight as soon as the stars come out and follow them south until you

The Spot The War Forgot

come to a farm at the edge of the bush. The man who owns it is the one who's willing to hide you."

Gerhardt handed him a bag of food. "Take this and eat sparingly, for it will take a few nights solid walking to get there."

"*Danke schoen*" said the cobbler.

"Someone is coming," I said, as a villager with a picnic basket strolled into view.

"We'd best be going," said Max. "Good luck for tonight."

With that, the cobbler scuttled into his cave and we went back to the castle. It was many months before we found out what happened to him.

W.E. Hamilton

May 1915
German Submarine Torpedoes U.S Tanker Gulflight.

A Boat a Bridge and a Mystery

Billy was the first to make a boat. Most of the camp thought it was a stupid idea.

"How are you going to build a boat? There is no shipyard here, and what would you make it from, kerosene cans?"

"*Nein*, sailcloth spread over a wooden frame and waterproofed with oil paint." Billy took a piece of paper from his pocket, unfolded it and held it up. "See my plan," he said, pointing to the diagram on the paper.

"That won't work you dumme person," said one.

"Call it the Titanic," said another.

"*Nein*, the Titanic hit an iceberg, this one will not need an iceberg to sink."

At this, there was a great roar of laughter.

Billy jerked his head towards the newly finished tennis

The Spot The War Forgot

court on the other side of the river. "You will stop laughing when you have to walk through the village and all the way to the bridge to get to the sports fields while I row across the lake," he said, folding up his plan and putting it back in his pocket. He looked at me. "Do you want to help, Wolfgang, or do you also think it's not going to work?"

"I do not know if it will work or not but I would like to try."

"I am happy you feel this way, my friend," Billy said clapping me on the shoulder.

The evening bugle call sounded, and out from the bush and every hut, men appeared, and together we moved towards the Castle like a swarm of ants. That night as we ate our slabs of bread and jam Billy and I calculated how much sailcloth and paint we needed. In the morning we went to the General Store to purchase our supplies, and that afternoon we got started on building our boat.

"I think it is best to keep it simple," said Billy, "just a small rowboat to begin with. If it works, we can make a bigger one."

"*Ja*," I said, looking at the long spindly tea trees all around us. "There is plenty of wood for many boats."

Billy picked up two saws and handed me one. "If we choose young curved trees it will make the job easier."

I nodded and we set to work hewing down enough trees. Once we had those, it did not take long to bind the frame together, and covering it with canvas was not hard. The bit that took a long time was the many coats of oil paint required to waterproof it; especially as the paint was slow to dry because the weather was turning cold. The man who swam every morning before breakfast was the only one who braved the water now, and that was purely to cure his rheumatism.

Interest in our bathing huts was also waning as winter inched closer and south winds from the Antarctic blew. Nobody was building huts anymore, instead, those who already had huts were thickening the walls and roofs to make them warmer. I could see them hunting about in the bush for grasses and brush. The only other people by the river were a group of men from the Hansa shipping line. Some of them were examining the vegetation up the side of the bank, while others measured the depth of the water. Billy and I watched them day after day as we waterproofed our boat with layers of paint. When they began timing floating sticks, curiosity got the better of me, so I went over to them and said:

"What are you doing?"

"We are working out how high and swift the water will be in a flood for we are planning to build a bridge here."

"Good idea, that will save twenty minutes walking to the sports fields. But why not build it by the dam where it is narrower."

"*Nein*, too low, it will wash away with the first big flood."

"This is a dry country, perhaps it does not flood?"

"It does flood, see the flattened vegetation on the side of the banks?"

"*Ja*, now you show me, I see the water rises high. This will make it hard to build a bridge I think."

"*Nein*, it can be done. We will position it in line with Oxley Street and one end will start downstream from those large boulders over there."

I looked at the rock face that rose from the water of the Great Lake swimming hole, and nodded. "Where will it end this side?"

The Spot The War Forgot

"Over there, well back from the river on the higher ground behind us."

"That will make it very long and high."

"*Ja*, almost a hundred meters in length, and five meters above the normal water level. That way our hard work will not wash away with the first rain."

"When will you start on it?"

"When the engineers finish their plans." The man shut his notebook and put his pencil in his pocket. "And now I say *Auf Wiedersehen,* for I must get this information to them."

I waved as he left, and sure enough, a few days later I saw the Hansa men string a flying-fox cable across the river. After that, they made a working platform, which they hung on the cable so it could be hauled back and forth across the river. It was entertaining and watching them made our rather boring job much more interesting. The platform and our boat were finished on the same day. That morning, the Hansa men scattered into the bush to cut logs for the beams and supports for the bridge, and we named our boat Nelly.

"Now for the moment we have been waiting for," said Billy. "Let's try her."

I took one end and Billy took the other and we carried her the short distance to the river and set her gently on the water.

"Beautiful," I said.

"I knew she would float," said Billy, "all those who scoffed at the idea are the dumm persons now."

I handed the paddle to him.

"You go first, it was your idea."

Billy smiled, nodded, and was about to step into the Nelly when one of the guards marched up to us.

"Wilhelm Köster, and, Wolfgang Schmitt?" he said, flicking open the notebook he carried.

"*Jawohl.*"

"I need volunteers for the coal gang, the kitchen needs more coal for the stoves."

"We do not wish to volunteer."

"Then it will cost you threepence."

"How is this?" I said frowning, "you say it is voluntary."

The guard stabbed a line in the notebook with his finger. "It is nothing to do with me. The Camp Committee has put your names on today's roster." He held out his hand. "Pay up, and then I will find others to take your places."

Billy and I felt in our pockets. But all we had between us was a pocket knife, a ball of string, a couple of cigarettes, and a box of matches.

"It's no good, we will have to go," I said, picking up one end of the Nelly.

"Perhaps it is for the best," said Billy, picking up the other. "We will keep the success of the Nelly secret, and launch her on May Day as a surprise."

"*Ja*, that is a good plan."

We carried the boat into my hut, shut the door, and hurried after the guard who was walking back to the Castle. When we got there a dozen men stood around two horses hitched to a wagon. A guard sat on one of the horses and another guard leaned against a wagon wheel.

"That's the last of them, we can go now," said our guard, jerking his head towards us and shutting his notebook.

The guard by the wagon wheel straightened up. "Right O, let's get cracking, I want to get there before smoko time. Come

The Spot The War Forgot

on you blokes."

The waggoneer flicked the tip of his whip at the rump of the lead horse, and the wagon rumbled forward while we followed behind, talking among ourselves as we walked. A small distance from the village we turned west and followed an old road that led to an abandoned coal mine six miles away. The road wound through the pretty plateau, following a deep slice in the land. As we strode along, I could hear the river tumbling over rocks and boulders below us. When we got to our destination the waggoneer went as close to the mine as he could, and drawing to a halt on a flat grassy area, slipped the horse's heads into nosebags.

"Ten minutes smoko time," called a guard, sitting on a boulder and taking a packet of cigarettes from his pocket.

After the two-hour walk, we were more than happy to do the same. Within minutes the air was filled with the aroma of cigarettes, pipes and even cigars. All too soon it was over, the guards lit lanterns and then each man grabbed a pick or shovel, and a bucket. Then skirting around the scrap iron that lay scattered about, we climbed down the side of the gorge and into the mine. It was hard work digging coal, but when fourteen men set their minds and backs to do something, things get moved quickly. Within a short time, the wagon was full and we were on our way back. We were nearly home, and the talk was about what we would have for lunch when we saw a strange sight. A man shackled in irons and between two guards was entering the prison yard.

"Who is that man and why is he in irons?" I asked the guard near me.

"Don't ask questions and forget you saw him."

W.E. Hamilton

I was surprised by his curt answer for the guards were usually friendly and happy to chat.

Many others asked the same question as we watched the chained man disappear into a solitary confinement cell, but the three guards told us nothing. Naturally, the secrecy surrounding the man heightened our curiosity.

"Who do you think he is and what has he done?" we asked each other as we ate our meat and vegetables.

"He is a spy who has done wonderful work for Germany."

"He is a very important General."

"He is a dangerous murderer."

By the end of the day, numerous rumours circulated throughout the prison. It was five weeks before we learned the truth about the mystery man, and his story was stranger than anything we imagined.

The Spot The War Forgot

May 1915
Americans are Killed when German U-boat Opens Fire on the British Passenger Liner the Lusitania

Locked Up

The Hansa men cut strong beams and supports from the nearby timber for the bridge, and on the fifth of May 1915, they started work. It was a tremendous job. While men on the river bank hauled the platform back and forth across the river, other men sank heavy beams deep into the riverbed.

The next day was May Day, and what a strange May Day it was. There were no pretty *frauleins*, no maypole, and no flowers, and strangest of all, no spring. It was good Billy chose to launch the Nelly on May Day, for the sight of her in the water lifted our hearts. All the men cheered as he rowed across the Great Lake.

"I did not think it would work, but it does," I overheard many say.

I thought after the success of the Nelly, others would immediately start making boats, but this was not so. Only three men set to work, and that was on a canoe very different from our rowboat. Instead of a light frame and sailcloth, they chopped down an enormous tree five meters long and half a meter wide. Then they stripped the bark off and dug out the centre.

While they worked, the rest of us were busy making stoves from stone or scrap-iron to heat our cells, as, even with the glazing in the windows, the night temperatures dropped below freezing. I had only finished collecting stones and cans to make my stove when the big escape happened.

Nobody noticed the two men slip into the bush. And even if we had, we would have thought nothing of it, for we were free to roam over many acres. The first we knew of it was when they failed to turn up at evening rollcall. The commandant waited a few minutes, thinking they were merely late. But when there was still no sign of them after ten minutes, he ordered an officer to lock the big gates and said:

"You will be confined to barracks until the men return or are captured. If anyone knows where they are, step forward and save yourselves a lot of trouble."

Of course, nobody stepped forward, because the runaways were not foolish enough to tell anyone they were going, and even if they had, we were not traitors; no one would inform on his comrade. That night there was a lot of shouting and thumping of fists on the table over dinner, for we were angry at suffering for other men's sins. But as the days rolled on and the men failed to return, the shouting fermented into grumbling and discontent.

"How long do you think they will keep us locked up if they don't find the men?" I asked Michael, as he helped me make a chimney for my kerosene stove, "it's been five days already."

Michael cut the bottom out of a jam tin, snipped the edges, and slotted it into another tin. "I don't know, but I am very tired of being shut up."

I piled stones on top of each other to form a primitive stove. "At least it is not as bad as when we first arrived."

"*Ja*, it is almost cosy now." Michael eyed the chimney thoughtfully. "I hope we have punched enough holes to let the air through."

"We will soon know," I said, putting the wick in place.

"Captain Pahren's cell looks like a real captain's cabin," continued Michael, jamming the chimney on top and wriggling it so it pointed towards the ventilation gap in the wall.

"So I have heard, but I have not seen it."

"I have not either, I wonder what it looks like?"

"Perhaps he has a desk for navigation charts," I said, pouring a small amount of kerosene into a cigar tin before popping it inside the stove.

"*Ja*, maybe. You can buy almost anything at the canteen now, perhaps he has a globe of the world."

"Maybe not, but for sure he has a wine wrack, a cigar box, and a tin of German sweets."

"But only bottles of two per cent beer in his wine-wrack and the sweets cost him half a week's wages," laughed Michael.

"Some things are a bit expensive," I smiled, but it is good we have the canteen during this time. Small treats make lock-up a little better."

"*Ja*, the canteen is making a big profit; it made over six-hundred pounds last month."

"*Ach komm schon*," I rocked back on my heels and shook

my head disbelievingly. "Who told you that?"

"Ernst Dannemann."

I pulled a face of wonder. "Then it must be so, for he is the treasurer."

I turned my attention back to my heater. "Let's see if this works," I said, striking a match and lighting the wick.

To our delight it did. Within a short time, the room felt almost warm. The sound of many voices singing in harmony filtered through the thick door and stone walls.

"Karl Mehne will be pleased about the lock-up," said Michael, holding his open hands over the warm air flowing from the chimney. "Lots more men have joined his choir."

"*Ja*, it is not all bad, the watercolour painting and carpentry clubs have doubled in size, and the captains have started classes for junior officers who want to continue their studies. I think I will sign up for that class."

"Good idea." Michael's face brightened and then fell. "But I am sad we can't go to the Star Cinema this week."

"Why? The cinema isn't very good, the parish hall is cold, the village children noisy, and the English films are dreadful."

"For sure, everything you say is true, you even forgot to say the filmstrip keeps breaking, but I still liked going out, it was something to look forward to each week."

It seemed Michael was not the only one disappointed about the Star Cinema, for that afternoon Otto Pahanke posted a sign in the assembly yard, announcing the newly formed theatre or the DTB was giving a concert after dinner.

"What is the DTB?" I said.

"The Deutsches Theatre Berrima," said Billy, who always seemed to be in the know.

The Spot The War Forgot

"I've never heard of it," said Michael.

"That is hardly surprising, it's only been recently formed."

"Another product of boredom," I said.

Billy snorted with laughter. "You may be right."

We gathered in the assembly yard that evening, full of curiosity.

"Pahanke and his friends have been busy," said Billy, as we made our way through the expectant crowd.

"*Ja*, I did not expect a stage," I said, looking at the small raised platform at the end of the courtyard.

"I hope it doesn't fall," said Gerhardt, stopping by the prison wall. "It doesn't look strong."

Max leaned against the sandstone and pointed to a sheet of corrugated iron spanning two towers of stone blocks, one on either side of the platform. "At least the curtains will stay up, it would take more than a wind to knock those supports down."

The performance that night was little more than several tableaux, a few poems, and ballads, but we were happy for any entertainment and clapped until our hands smarted.

The theatre was not the only fruit of boredom, by the time the escapees where caught (eighty-miles south of Goulburn, on the Breadalbane Plane) many new clubs were formed. Nevertheless, it was a good thing the escapees were immediately isolated and confined to the barracks for a spell, because theatre or no theatre, many of us wanted to punch them in the head.

As soon as the big iron gates opened wide, Billy, Gerhardt, and Max rushed over to their cottage, and I wandered down to the river to watch the progress of the dugout canoe. It was slow hard work hacking out the middle of a log, but the men making the canoe kept at it day after day, and at length, it was finished. A crowd gathered at the Great Lake to watch its launching. After the success of our boat, nobody dared call this canoe the Titanic. But they should have; for the Ajax sat on the water for a few minutes before sinking like a stone. Not willing to lose it, the owners of the canoe rushed into the chilly water and hauled it out.

"What went wrong?" we asked scratching our heads.

Several engineers, carpenters, and Anton Gallwitzer the cabinetmaker considered the problem and agreed the trouble lay with the timber.

"Eucalyptus wood is dense with sap when newly cut."

"*Ja*, that will be your problem."

"Try drying it out and installing buoyancy tanks."

So, we made a bonfire and when it died down, we suspended the canoe over the embers on a wooden frame; turning it every so often until it dried. Then, with empty kerosene cans lashed to the canoe's sides, we launched the dugout again. By now it had become a community project. We held our breath while it was lowered onto the water, and cheered as it smoothly slid across the Great Lake. Even the Hansa men (fixing supports to the bridge beams) paused their labour to wave and whistle. It was only one small boat but it had a big impact on us. The Ajax and the Nelly showed boat building was possible and opened the way for many more to follow.

The Spot The War Forgot

May 1915
Italy Sides with Allies and Declares War on Austria-Hungary

A Gala for the Hansa Bridge

Frau Jepsen hosted little afternoon teas in the lounge of the boarding house where she lived, and Billy, Michael and I had been lucky enough to receive an invitation. At that time, the bridge was close to completion and the subject had arisen in genteel conversation.

"We ought to have a social event to mark the occasion," said Frau Jepsen, bending over a low table and pouring black coffee into little cups. "After all, a hundred-meter bridge, is a real accomplishment." She handed me a cup and I took it gingerly, afraid I might spill coffee on the Bergin's best floor rug.

"Marvellous idea, my love," boomed Captain Jepsen, leaning back in his armchair expansively.

He and his wife were the only relaxed people in the room,

for although Frau Jepsen was a middle-aged matron, buxom to the point of stout, we mixed with so few women we felt nervous in her presence. My friends and I sat rigidly upright as, plates on laps and all fingers and thumbs, we tried to eat Black Forest cake without dropping crumbs.

A woman walked past the door, and Frau Jepsen seeing her, waved to attract her attention.

"Mrs Dibbs, come in here for a moment."

The woman altered her course and we scrambled politely to our feet as she entered the parlour.

"This is Mrs Dibbs the commandant's wife," Frau Jepsen said, by way of introduction. "She's in the room next to me." She turned to the woman. "And Wilhelm Köster, Wolfgang Schmitt, and Michael Becker. You know my husband of course."

We bowed and Mrs Dibbs said: "How do you do?"

"Where is your son?" said Frau Jepsen, craning her neck towards the door.

"He is with the nanny, having an afternoon nap."

"Oh good…I mean, that is nice for you to have a little break. Toddlers are so tiring. Would you care to join us for coffee?"

"That would be very nice," said Mrs Dibbs as we sat down.

"I was just saying to the men," said Frau Jepsen, pouring out another cup of coffee and sliding a slice of cake onto a china plate, "I think we should have some sort of event to mark the opening of the Hansa bridge."

"Good idea," said Mrs Dibbs, taking the cup and plate Frau Jepsen handed her. "My husband is always looking for ways to foster goodwill between the villagers and the internees."

"Is that why the Guard host dances in the Masonic hall

every couple of weeks?"

"That's right. Perhaps we could invite the villagers to attend some sort of gala. They too will benefit from the bridge."

Frau Jepsen beamed. "Why not! We'll tie a ribbon across the end of the bridge on the left bank, and, you, as the commandant's wife, could cut it and declare the bridge open."

"Then the choir could sing," said Michael.

"Yes!" Mrs Dibb's face became animated. "I have a silk gown that's just the thing for such an occasion."

"And I have the perfect hat," said Frau Jepsen.

"Then there could be a procession across the bridge," said Mrs Dibbs. "Ada, Fanny, and Annie's daughter could lead it."

At the mention of the butcher's beautiful daughter, we sat up straighter and took an active interest.

"They could wear ribbons in their hair and dance across the bridge shaking tambourines," said Frau Jepsen. "It would make up for the dismal May Day."

"What about an arch over each end of the bridge?" I said. "We could weave them from wattle and pine boughs."

"Ooh yes," nodded the ladies.

"There has to be some sort of water carnival," said Billy.

"A couple of boats won't make much of a carnival, and it's too cold for swimming sports," said Michael.

This was so true we all sagged a little.

"It doesn't matter," said Captain Jepsen. "The advantage of a sleepy little town where nothing happens, is you don't need much to stir up excitement. An eel catching contest is just as good as swimming competitions." He licked his lips. "I could go a smoked eel."

"Quite right, my Love," said Frau Jepsen.

From then on, the conversation diverged along two paths; the ladies continued talking about the gala, while we discussed smokehouses. In this way, the afternoon passed pleasantly, until a harassed young girl carrying a howling toddler dragged her feet wearily into the parlour.

"I can't quieten him, Mam," she said, plunking the fattest child I had ever seen on the floor. "And the neighbours are complaining.

"Come to Mama, Sweetheart," said Mrs Dibbs setting down her plate and cup before opening her arms.

The child, however, spying the cake, stopped his bawling and (ignoring his mother) rushed over to the low table where he thrust his pudgy fists into the middle of the remaining cake. We watched in frozen horror as he squished chocolate and sponge into his mouth.

That was the end of that. The moment was ruined along with the cake.

"*Danka*, for the coffee, Frau Jepsen," we said standing. "It has been a most enjoyable afternoon."

"Very productive," said Frau Jepsen. "A gala is a wonderful idea."

"I shall speak to Owen about sending invitations to the villagers," said Mrs Dibbs, trying in vain to extract her child from the centre of the cake.

We raised our hats and left. A few days later the villagers each received a card that said:

'Lieut. Owen Dibbs, the Members of the Berrima Guard, and the Berrima Internees request the pleasure of your company at a gala to celebrate the opening of the Hansa bridge on July the 18th.'

The Spot The War Forgot

Almost everyone came.
Frau Jepsen wore the perfect hat.
Mrs Dibbs, dressed in silk, cut the ribbon.
The choir sang.

And the pretty girls led a merry procession under an archway of pine and wattle boughs.

It didn't matter there were only two boats, for the young women were more interested in flirting with the young men than looking at water sports.

The boys and fathers were more interested in the eels.

And the mothers were more interested in the local gossip.

A reporter came from the Southern Mail, and three weeks later this article appeared in the paper.

To commemorate their internment at Berrima, the German prisoners have erected a footbridge over the river near the cricket ground.

"I'm very happy with how the gala turned out," said the commandant, when Michael, Billy and I met him in the street one day. "As I hoped, it has fostered tremendous goodwill between the villagers and the internees. I am grateful to you chaps for your involvement." He jerked his head towards the boarding house. "I'm on my way to have afternoon tea with my wife. Come and join us as a thank-you."

We were about to accept his kind invitation when the sound of loud bawling and howling floated through the door.

"That will be my son, bless him," said the commandant, smiling indulgently. "He's a strapping boy with a healthy set of lungs."

"I'm sorry but I have a letter to write," said Michael, hastily.

"I can't, I have to practice for the concert," said Billy.

W.E. Hamilton

"Oh dear, I'm rostered on woodchopping this afternoon," I choked out.

"Some other time then," said the commandant.

"Some other time," we agreed. And tipping our hats, we fled.

The Spot The War Forgot

> *July 1915*
> **Chronic Supply Shortages and Declining Morale Weaken Russian Army**

The Mystery Man tells his Story

The mystery man stood in the mess hall with a mug of tea in one hand and a slab of bread in the other, uncertain where to sit.

I nudged his elbow as I passed him. "Come and sit with us, *freund*," I said, over the din of many voices. He smiled and followed me. As we slid our cups and plates onto the table, the men on the long bench beside it squeezed up to make room for us.

"I'm, Wolfgang, and this is Billy, Gerhardt, Max, and Michael.

"Hello, I am Paul Schmitt." His voice sounded dry and croaky and he spoke hesitantly. "Sorry my voice sounds so strange," he pulled a wry face, "I think it has gone rusty."

"It is not surprising," said Max. "You have been in solitary confinement for five weeks."

"Is that all, it felt like five years."

"Why were you in there?"

"It is a long story you don't want to hear it."

"*Ja* we do."

Paul finished eating his bread and drained his cup. Someone handed him a bottle of beer and another passed him a smoke. After he had drunk a few mouthfuls, and blown a smoke ring, he put his elbows on the table, leant forward and started his strange story.

"I was a mariner from German New Guinea. At the beginning of the war, I was interned at the Holsworthy Camp. A couple of months ago things got bad there. [1]*The commandant of the camp gave an order that the internees be put to work. From then on, every morning those on work detail were marched out by soldiers with guns and bayonets and compelled to dig ditches, erect fences, or chop wood. Elderly professors, priests, clerks, and businessmen, (who had never done manual work, and many in poor health) were forced to go with the others. If they lagged behind the Aussies did not hesitate to stick their bayonets into them.* We stood this for a few weeks before the feeling of resentment grew to such a pitch, the whole camp decided on a campaign of passive resistance and went on a hunger strike.

I was not the ringleader of the riot, but for some reason, the Camp Commandant thought I was. One morning at breakfast I was seized.

'You are under arrest for stirring the camp into a rebellion,' said the Camp Commandant.

---

1   Taken from Edna Machotka's diary.

The Spot The War Forgot

'I don't know what you are talking about. I am not the ringleader.'

'Do you know who the ringleader is?'

I did not want to lie so I said, 'yes.'

'Who is he?'

I would not say, for I am not a traitor, and my silence angered the commandant and the guards. They shouted and threatened me for some time, but when they saw I would not be moved, the Commandant in a towering rage, pushed his face close to mine and shouted:

'You have twelve hours to reveal the name of the ringleader or suffer execution by firing squad.' He turned to the guards. 'Put him in solitary confinement so he can reconsider his stubbornness.'

Of course, I was very troubled by this idea, but to betray a comrade would be worse than death, so I decided I would die rather than speak. In the small hours of the morning, I was taken before the commandant.

'I ask you for the last time, who are the men who instigated the strike?'

I stood silent.

'Tell me the names or be shot.'

I stood straight, looked him in the eye and said, 'I will die rather than betray my comrades.'

'And so you shall. Take him out and have him shot at dawn.'

I was taken back to my cell and a priest was sent to prepare me for death. At dawn, the commandant had me handcuffed in front of the whole camp and marched out with an armed platoon carrying picks and shovels. When we were out of sight, they made me dig my grave.

'Who are the troublemakers, who is the ringleader,' they kept shouting at me as I dug?

Again, and again I replied: 'I do not know who the troublemakers are, and I will not tell you the name of the ringleader.' At last, the grave was finished and because I still refused to name the man, they blindfolded me and positioned me against a tree. I thought the end had come when I heard the commandant say to the firing squad: 'Get ready and I will give you the signal to fire.'"

The cigarette in Paul's hand trembled, and for several minutes he was unable to continue speaking as he remembered the moment. We waited patiently until he was calm enough to continue his story.

"A volley was fired but to my great astonishment, I was not hurt. When my knees stopped shaking it dawned on me, I was the victim of a great hoax. Then the commandant commanded the soldiers to take the blindfold off, and when that was done, he said :'You are a very brave man Paul Schmitt, because of your bravery I will pardon you.' Then they rewarded me by clapping me in irons and bringing me here."

"Why did they put you in solitary confinement?"

"I've had plenty of time to think about that. I don't believe they really meant to execute me. I think they wanted to scare the men in the camp by making it appear I was shot. That is why they did it out of sight but within earshot."

"And the reason why they hid you for weeks," finished Max.

"For sure. They did not want the word to leak out that I was still alive. To the men in the Holsworthy camp, I am a tote man buried in a grave outside the prison walls."

The Spot The War Forgot

Nobody spoke after Paul finished his story because we realized we were in the presence of a hero. I did not know if I would be so brave in the same situation and judging from the expressions of the faces around me, the others felt the same. The silence was on the brink of awkwardness when Michael saved the day by saying:

"We should call you Tote Schmitt because you are a dead man."

At this, we all relaxed and laughed. The nickname stuck and Paul remained Tote for the rest of the time he was at the camp and became a very good friend.

W.E. Hamilton

August 1915
Austro-Germans Take Warsaw

The Hurtzigs arrive from Enoggera

We knew something unusual was up because activity was happening in the empty house by the south-east corner of the prison. The sandstone building was a handsome two-storied dwelling set behind a row of large pine trees, and guards were going in and out of the doors that opened onto the veranda.

"I wonder who is moving in?" said Michael, swinging a stick idly as we wandered past. "The villagers say that house has been empty for six years."

"Maybe a new detail of guards is coming and they have decided to shift them in there."

"*Nein*, they are always changing the guards and they never go to that much trouble."

In the background as we chatted was the sound of approaching vehicles, and shortly several cars came into view.

The Spot The War Forgot

They chugged along the main road and came to a stop not far from where we stood. The backdoor of the first car opened and a guard and a man helped a heavily pregnant woman out.

"I thought we would never get here. This is the backwater of nowhere," whined the woman.

"Never mind, *Liebling*, we are here now."

"Come this way, Frau Glintz," said the guard, ushering the couple down the path.

While we watched, a well-proportioned fellow of middling height, got out of the second car. He had dark hair, a prominent forehead, a moustache, and a small pointed beard.

I turned to speak to Michael but before I could say anything, he gave a start of recognition. "It is Captain and Frau Hurtzig from my old ship the Prinz Sigismund! "he shouted, throwing his stick in the air and running over to the car.

"Michael, is it really you?" said the man, his face lighting up."

"Jabowl," Michael said, his face splitting into a wide smile as he saluted.

Captian Hurtzig reached out and grabbed his hand. "So good to see you. My only sadness is we should meet under such circumstances."

As they greeted each other a slim angular woman and two little girls emerged from the depths of the car.

"I thought I would never see you and your family again," said Michael. "Welcome Frau Hurtzig," He turned to bow to her, but she rushed forward and hugged him.

"It is very good to see an old friend," she said, smiling warmly.

"This is, Wolfgang," said Michael, turning to introduce me

as I drew near.

"*Guten morgen*," I started to say but once again my words were cut short.

"This way Captain Hurtzig," said a second guard.

Frau Hurtzig clutched Michael's arm. "Don't go, come inside with us, when the guards have gone you boys can tell us about the camp."

Michael nodded and we fell in with the group moving up the path.

By now Herr Glintz, his wife, and the guard had reached the steps of the veranda.

"I only see one house," the woman said, in a loud petulant voice. All eyes switched to her. "Who gets this house?"

"There is limited accommodation you will have to share until a cottage comes available in the village," said the guard. "Each family may have a room for their private use but you share the kitchen, dining room and toilet."

At this, the faces of all the newcomers sagged.

"I want my own house," said Frau Glintz, flushing red with anger. "It's bad enough my husband has to spend every night in prison without having to share a house. I'm sick of sharing a house with other people."

"I'm sorry Madam, nothing can be done about it, I am only following orders."

"I shall die, buried in the country with no house of my own," shouted Frau Glintz, throwing a hand to her forehead, her breath coming in little pants.

Michael, I, and the guards shuffled uneasily, not sure what to make of this outburst. I glanced at Captain Hurtzig but he merely shrugged while his wife rolled her eyes.

The Spot The War Forgot

"Come, come, *Schatz,* don't fret." Herr Glintz put his arm around the hysterical woman's shoulders. "It is better than in Brisbane where we had to share with nine other people."

But Frau Glintz was not willing to be comforted. "If I can't have my own house I will die!"

At this, her husband snatched his arm away and shouted back at her: "What do you expect me to do about it? I am not God."

Frau Hurtzig stepped forward. "You may have first pick of the house, Frau Glintz, which room would you like?"

Frau Glintz switched off her dramatics. "I don't know which one I want. I will tell you when I have seen through the whole house. Come, Fredrich." With that, she stomped through the front door. After an apologetic smile to the rest of us, her husband followed.

The guard mopped his head and blew a sigh of relief as they disappeared inside.

"What is upstairs?" Frau Hurtzig asked him.

"It is empty. We are keeping it in reserve just in case headquarters sends us more families." He turned and spoke directly to Captain Hurtzig. "After you have gathered your belongings from the cars, you and Herr Glintz may stay here until nine tonight to help your wives settle in. But from tomorrow onwards report to the jail by five. Rollcall at 6:30. Fifteen minutes before rollcall the bugle will sound a warning. Make sure you are not late."

As the guards left, one of the little girls tugged at her mother's hand. "Can Lore and I look around the house, Mama?"

"Not yet, Hanna *Liebling*, wait until Frau Glintz has chosen her rooms. Come and help carry our things in from the car. The girls nodded and trotted alongside their parents.

Frau Hurtzig plucked anxiously at her husband's jacket as they walked. "Gust, I do not know how I will put up with that woman's tantrums! If only they had put us with the Wallners instead."

"Perhaps they put us with them because you are a saint and will put up with more than most women, Lulu."

"I'm far from being a saint, and I fear I am not up to her ferocious quarrelling. Remember the two days she fought continuously with her husband and railed against us all."

"That was only once, Lulu."

Frau Hurtzig pulled a face. "One big fight between hundreds of smaller fights."

Captain Hurtzig nodded. "She is a difficult woman. I feel sorry for her husband, he is a good-natured man. If she stopped confronting him, he would be no trouble."

"For sure." Frau Hurtzig sighed. "I hope there is someone like Pastor Truez here to help me through the trial."

By now we had reached the cars. While the girls scrabbled about looking for their dolls, Captain Hurtzig pulled out two camp stretchers and gave them to Michael. Then he put a saucepan, two spoons, a fork, and a couple of billies into a tin washbowl, and handed them to me. Frau Hurtzig, meanwhile, picked up two lamps, and as we walked back up the path she asked:

"Is there a Lutheran church here?"

"No, there is not. There is the St Francis Xavier's Church at the end of the village on the other side of the bridge. Father Martin rides a horse out from Moss Vale on Sundays, and the Catholic interns join in with the locals. The Hungarians and Austrians have no trouble with the language because the services are conducted in Latin."

"What about the Protestants?"

Hanna and Lore came running up behind us as Michael answered:

"There's Holy Trinity Church. Unfortunately, the Pastor does not speak German, but as most sailors are not very Godfearing, and the captains continue the custom of reading a service on Sundays, it is enough."

Frau Hurtzig's eyes sprang open and the lamps in her hands wobbled. "No Lutheran church! This is a barbaric place indeed!"

"Why did they send the Glintz's down here? The guards told me this is a camp for mariners, but Glintz is a butcher," said Captain Hurtzig, striding up with feather quilts bulging over his arms.

"I can answer that, sir," I said, climbing the veranda steps. "Although this is a camp for sailors, they have brought in a few men to help maintain the camp. There is a tailor called Paul Golich, a bootmaker, several cooks, and a barber called Jules Muler."

"Jules Muler has set up shop in the cell reserved for condemned criminals," said Michael, with a chuckle. "He calls himself Sweeny Todd."

"The demon barber from the penny-dreadful, The String of Pearls?"

"*Ja*, that is right."

Frau Glintz clumped out a French door that opened onto the south end of the veranda, and the conversation stopped abruptly as she appeared.

"I have decided to take the left side of the house," she said, in a hollow voice.

"As you wish," said Frau Hurtzig, nodding graciously.

"You'll have to go outside and around to the backdoor, to get to the kitchen, dining-room, and toilet," said Frau Glitz, her tone lifting in triumph. "The door, between your room and the main house is jammed and cannot be opened."

"It is not ideal," said Frau Hurtzig, with a sigh. "Let's see what it's like."

Frau Glintz returned to her side of the house while we went through the French door to the right of the front entrance.

"Better than I expected," said Frau Hurtzig. "A bit dusty but with a good clean it should come up alright. At least the walls are smooth and painted. I feared they might be rough yellow stone like the outside."

"And linoleum is so much easier to scrub than wooden floorboards," said Captain Hurtzig, scraping the heel of his boot in a semicircle over the floor.

"Wolfgang and I can cut you a load of wood for the fire," said Michael, picking a dead bird out of the grate.

"Thank you, that would be wonderful." Frau Hurtzig chaffed her hands together. "The girls and I can sleep in this corner by the fire. She whirled around. "Oh Gust, I nearly forgot my hot water bottle."

"It's leaking," said Captain Hurtzig, walking out to the veranda.

Michael threw the bird into a bush as we walked down the steps and moved towards the rear of the house.

"I shall stick a plaster over the hole," said the little woman, unperturbed. "Which reminds me, the first aid kit and the

The Spot The War Forgot

washtub still need to come in."

"I'll get them," I said. "You carry on looking at the house."

Frau Hurtzig nodded gratefully, so I turned around as they continued on their way to the back door. I went down the path to the cars still parked in front of the house, collected the forgotten items and carried them back to the veranda. I was wondering where to put them when the Hurtzig family and Michael returned.

"Thank you, Wolfgang," said Frau Hurtzig, "Leave them on the veranda for the time being and I will sort everything out tomorrow after I give the house a proper clean."

Hanna, patted her mother's arm to get her attention.

"Can Lore and I look around the garden, Mama?"

"Alright, *Liebling*, but stay in the front yard and don't go into the Glintz's side of the house."

"*Ja*, Mama," they said, skipping away.

Frau Hurtzig picked up an old broom lying abandoned on the floor, and Michael and I set about assembling the camp stretchers. I was sliding two of the side poles together when there was a knock on the door and Captain Jepsen and his wife arrived.

"Hello Luise," said Frau Jepsen, as the two women hugged. "It is strange we should meet again in this way."

"The world has gone mad," said Frau Hurtzig. "What is it like here?"

"Not too bad; things could be worse. I'm staying in the boarding house where the lieutenant's wife, her toddler, and the child's nanny live." Frau Jepsen rolled her eyes. "The boy is obese. I can't believehow much they feed him. Watching him eat at in the communal dining-room makes me glad I have never had children."

"I fear Lulu, you will find it dull here after your busy social life in Brisbane," said Captain Hurtzig.

"For sure, I miss all my German friends and the neighbour already. The old woman over the back fence had a granddaughter about Eva's age who Hanna and Lore played with." Frau Hurtzig's eyes watered and she dabbed them with a handkerchief. "Dear Eva, what harm is this long separation doing to her?"

"Is she not with you?"

"No, we didn't want to interrupt her schooling. This was supposed to be a nice little holiday. I would never have left her behind with my parents if I had suspected this could happen."

"*Nein*, we would never have come at all if we had known we would get caught here and lose the ship," corrected Captain Hurtzig, "we would have stayed in Germany."

"I heard about your brother," said Frau Jepsen, patting Frau Hurtzig's shoulder. "I am so sorry. He was a good man."

"It was a terrible shock." Frau Hurtzig's voice trembled. "We did not know Otto was fighting on the Western Front until we got the telegram saying he had been killed in action. At least we are comforted by the knowledge we will one day meet again in heaven."

"The Wallners were at the hotel with us last night, and are on their way here," said Captain Hurtzig, changing the subject abruptly.

"Ludwig Wallner, who sailed with me on the Germainia?" Captain Jepsen's eyebrows shot up.

"*Ja*, after we were captured, we shared a house with him and his wife, the Glintz's, and three older men."

The Spot The War Forgot

"Captain Madsen off the freighter the Cannstatt, is also coming," said Frau Hurtzig, "not today like the Wallners, but sometime soon, I am told."

"*Wunderbar*," said Captain Jepsen, his face splitting into a wide smile.

"It will be nice to see Captain Madsen," Frau Jepsen paused before continuing, "but we will not be associating with Frau Wallner, of course."

"Why not?"

"I do not know why you look so surprised, Luise; her husband is only a third officer. As captains' wives, it is beneath us to mix with her socially."

"In this time of war, we should not make these petty distinctions," said Frau Hurtzig. "We must band together and show one another kindness."

The tension was rising in the room. I exchanged nervous glances with Michael.

Frau Jepsen's top lip elongated and her nose rose into the air. "If you choose to demean yourself Luise that is up to you, but war or no war I will not let the standards slip."

"I am sorry to hear you speak this way. I think as Germans we should live like Christians and set a good example for the English to follow."

"To maintain proper order among the ranks is a good example," said Frau Jepsen unmoved.

"We are old friends, let us not quarrel," said Frau Hurtzig, as the girls came skipping in, "especially in front of the children."

"You are right, Luise," said Frau Jepsen, her face softening. "You have come with the group from the Enoggera Camp. Did you have to stay in the camp?"

"No, fortunately. When I thought Gust was going there, I decided to go with him for I could not bear the thought of being separated. But I saw at a glance it was not possible, for the tents were the size of an umbrella. Eventually (after much argument) the authorities agreed that wives and families should receive an allowance of money instead of military rations, and the captains and senior officers were granted the right to live out (provided they report to the camp once a week.)

"Yes, it was the same with us," said Frau Jepsen. "After the ship was taken, we lived in our house in Sydney until they brought us here."

"Ah, the poor Prinz Sigismund, our lovely ship," said Frau Hurtzig. "How sad she no longer sails under the German flag."

"Did you have to leave the ship immediately?" asked Captain Jepsen.

"No, we didn't go until October the first," said Captain Hurtzig. "Almost all the passengers were allowed to leave but the Chinese and Indonesian servants had to stay on board." He smiled at his wife. "Lulu loved the luxury. At dinner, we had a servant behind every chair."

Frau Hurtzig sighed wistfully. "I felt like a princess, especially when the oil lamps replaced the generators to save fuel; it was so romantic it was hard to remember we were at war. Every day I walked in the botanical gardens and we had afternoon coffee and cake."

"And Lore and I walked over the gangplank to Captain Madsen's ship to listen to his gramophone records."

Frau Hurtzig frowned at her daughter. "Do not interrupt an adult conversation, Hanna," she said, before turning back to the Jepsens. "On Sundays, Pastor Treuz came to conduct a service and in the afternoon, we listened to the band recitals in the botanic gardens. It was a nice life, but the uncertainty and the rumours we were going to be moved into tents, cast such a shadow over everything I was almost relieved when they came to get us. We hastily packed enough for a few days, and Gust stowed all our treasures into lockable cupboards and drawers which the officials said they would guard."

"I even had two lockable chests made up for our more valuable possessions," said Captain Hurtzig. He looked around the bare room. "When our belongings arrive things will be much more comfortable."

"If they arrive, you mean," said Frau Hurtzig, "I am not even sure the large trunk I had to leave at the hotel this morning will get here, let alone the things left in storage. I do not trust the English."

"My dear, I keep telling you, they are Australians."

"They are all English to me," said his wife with a toss of her head.

"Where did you go after you left the ship?" said Captain Jepsen.

"The men were taken to the Enoggera Camp," said Frau Hurtzig, returning to the main thread of the story. "But nobody had given any thought to the women and children. We stood in the yard in the heat for over an hour until an officer came with a dogcart and took us to the People's Palace; a Salvation Army hostel. We spent the night there and they gave us breakfast. Pastor Treuz and his sisters were a big blessing. They offered their house for our daytime use until the authorities allowed us to rent our own place."

"What happened to you when the war broke out, Jepsen?"

said Captain Hurtzig.

"We docked in Sydney during the last week of July and the crew were enjoying weekend leave when a group of civilians boarded the ship and tore down our flag."

"Why did they do that?" broke in Frau Hurtzig. "We were not at war with Australia at that time."

"Something to do with Germany declaring war on Russia," said Frau Jepsen.

"*Ja*," said Captain Jepsen. "That is what Wilhelm de Haas told me when I complained to the German consulate. At first, I was pleased when guards were sent to protect the ship. But on the following Wednesday, the guards were given orders to seize the ship, and I have since heard the Germania is now refitted and sails under the name Mawatta."

Everyone sighed and the room went quiet. In the sudden silence, the muffled background noise of Frau Glintz's peevish voice magnified.

"*Nein*, you dumm person, you have forgotten one of the bags. Go and get it before the cars leave."

The tension in the room rose as heavy footsteps stomped onto the veranda.

"I don't think we need this open," said Captain Hurtzig, striding across the room and shutting the door."

"Who closed the door? What are you whispering about?" boomed the peevish voice.

The Jepsens and the Hurtzigs exchanged glances.

"While you are waiting for your things to arrive," said Frau Jepsen. "Come back to the boarding house with us for coffee and cake and stay for dinner. The boarding house has a reasonable menu, and after dinner, I have some German sweets

The Spot The War Forgot

the girls will like."

"I know they are talking about me." The peevish voice had grown into shouting. "Make them leave the door open, Friedrich."

"How can I?" (now two people were shouting.) "It's their side of the house!"

"I have some fine cigars for you to try, August," said Captain Jepsen raising his voice above the commotion.

"That will be very nice," said Captain Hurtzig.

They bid us goodbye and left. Michael and I lingered so we could finish putting the camp beds together, and then we chopped a load of wood, left a pile by the fireplace and stacked the rest of it in the back yard. When we were done, Michael picked up his forgotten stick as the cars drew away from the curb.

"I suppose the cars are going back to Moss Vale to get the Wallners," he said, swinging his stick idly.

"I expect so."

And continuing our interrupted walk, we wandered over to Billy's house to tell him about the new arrivals.

W.E. Hamilton

August 1915
Hoping to Break Stalemate at Gallipoli, British Renew Offense

I Get a Cell mate

The night the Hurtzigs arrived Michael had another surprise awaiting him; for at the dinner table was his close friend Hermann Josenhans.

"What are you doing here?" said Michael, slapping him on the back with joy.

"The same thing you are doing. I'm waiting for the war to finish."

"Have you got a place to stay yet?"

"*Nein*, there are no empty cells."

"You can share with me."

"Captain, I have room for you in my cell if you don't have anywhere to stay," said Billy.

"That is very good, Wilhelm, I thank you," said Captain Hurtzig.

I bit into my thick bread gloomily, knowing I ought to

The Spot The War Forgot

extend hospitality to Herr Glintz. But, happily, fate intervened when the man seated next to him invited him to bunk in with him. I whistled as I wandered back to my cell delighted by my lucky escape. But the surprises of the day were not over, for when I pushed open my door, I found a man lounging on the top tier of a bunk, smoking a cigar.

"Szia, I mean hello," he said, twisting and raising himself onto one elbow. "You must be Wolfgang, the others said this was your room."

"*Ja*, who are you, and what happened to my bed?"

"I am Captain Poszisch of the steamer Turul, but you may call me Julius. I apologize for this intrusion. Unfortunately, it was necessary to make a few adjustments in your absence. You will see your bed is still here, but now it has another one above it."

"I suppose it had to happen someday." I sat on the wobbly chair by the small table. "What nationality are you? I don't recognize your accent."

"I am Hungarian, and as you are so generous to share your cell with me, I shall show you something magnificent." He pulled a photograph from his shirt pocket and handed it to me.

"Very pretty," I said, looking at a woman in Hungarian folk costume.

"Very pretty!" Julius's face tensed and the veins on his neck rose. "Marcella is not merely very pretty! She is a glorious goddess. Hungarian women are the most beautiful women in the world, and the ones from Budapest are the best of all."

"*Ja*, she is magnificent," I said hastily.

Julius sat up swiftly and swung his legs over the edge of the bed. "Do not be getting any ideas about her," he said, glaring at me and snatching the photo from my fingers. "She is my girlfriend and I will kill any man who dares look at her disrespectfully."

I spread my hands wide and shook my head. "*Nein*, I would never do that."

"Good, I am happy to hear that," his face cleared into a sunny smile. "Have a cigar," and plucking a good quality one from his pocket he handed it to me.

I took it warily, not sure if I would unwittingly offend him again. But his mood remained friendly as he lay with one arm bent under his head puffing away.

"I saw the huts down the river this afternoon. Do you have one?"

"*Ja*." I lit the cigar and leant so far back the front legs of my chair lifted off the floor. "Just a small bathing hut made of bark."

"I have decided to build a hut as a token of my love for Marcella. When does the post come?" he said, switching the subject.

I blew a plume of fragrant smoke. "Monday to Friday usually after lunch."

"It will be an agony to wait for my beloved Marcella's letters. She writes the most beautiful letters." He felt under his pillow and pulled out an envelope. "Listen to this." He opened a folded page. "My dearest, most handsome, Julius." He stroked his thick blond hair. "Isn't that both beautiful and true?"

I made a vague, mmm, noise.

He folded it and put it back under his pillow. "That is enough for now."

The Spot The War Forgot

I could not agree more. I was beginning to think Herr Glintz was preferable to this volatile man with his strange mood swings. But within a few days, I realized his cries of joy or bouts of gloom, and the odd extravagant gesture were the worst of his flaws. Much of the time he was good company, it was when the post came that anything could happen. The day Michael got a letter from his sister, Maria, Julius was wailing with frenzied jealousy.

"Marcella mentions another man's name! How could she do this to me?"

Michael continued reading quietly while Julius tore at his hair.

"It is probably nothing, just like all the other times," I said, sighing. "Tell me the bit that troubles you."

"Alright, but it is shocking." His voice trembled with emotion as he read aloud: "My brother came home for the weekend and he and his friend, Jon, went for a long bike ride." Julius smacked the page with the back of his hand,. "See my Marcella taunts me with this Jon."

"*Nein*, it is not so, you are worrying about nothing. Marcella did not even go with them."

Julius studied the page closely. "That is true," he said, breaking into a smile, "you make me very happy my friend."

"Maria writes to say she and her friend Elsa are coming here for a visit," said Michael.

"That is marvellous," said Herman, turning red and running a finger around the inside of his collar. "I should like to see Maria again. Your sister is a fine girl."

Michael rubbed his forehead. "I am happy she wants to come but where will she and Elsa stay?"

W.E. Hamilton

"That is a question for my wife," said Captain Hurtzig, putting a pink envelope in his pocket and getting up from the table. "I am going to see her now. She will be down by the river, come with me if you like."

"Good idea," said Michael, also getting up.

"I shall come too," said Julius, "I have found the perfect spot for my Villa Marcella. I shall show it to you, Wolfgang."

So, we all walked down to the river. When we got there, Frau Hurtzig and Frau Jepsen were seated on a blanket while the children (a little distance apart) dug in the sand.

After we greeted them Captain Hurtzig introduced Julius to the ladies.

"You are most beautiful ladies," said Julius, bowing and kissing their hands. "And your children are most beautiful too." He swept his hand towards the four little girls piling their sand into castles.

"Oh, they are not all mine," said Frau Hurtzig, "only the two smallest ones. The other children come from the village." She smiled. "It is so nice to see them playing together happily. Hanna and Lore need friends." She sighed. "They miss their older sister."

"I have a surprise for you, Lulu," said Captain Hurtzig, pulling the letter from his pocket and handing it to her. "This came in the post."

Frau Hurtzig snatched it from his fingers and held it to her heart. "It is from Eva!"

"Before you open it, perhaps you might be able to help Michael. His sister and her friend wish to visit, perhaps they could stay a few days with you."

Frau Hurtzig pulled a face. "You know Gust I would love

The Spot The War Forgot

to have them stay, but it is not possible. Frau Glintz is very difficult and her baby is due any day."

"I can help," said Frau Jepsen, looking at Michael. "Tell her they can stay at the Bergin's boarding house. It is comfortable and I can get them a room if they are willing to share."

"That is a wonderful idea," said Michael, beaming.

"*Ja*, that will work," said Frau Hurtzig, pleased. "Now for my letter!" She slit open the envelope and unfolded the paper carefully. But before she read the first word, Hanna and Lore ran up to her crying.

"What is the matter lieblings?" she asked, standing up and gathering them to her skirt.

"That man says we are dirty Germans and the village children are not to play with us," sobbed Hanna, pointing at an elderly man ushering the other children away. "But my hands are clean and I have a bath every Saturday."

"Don't listen to him, lieblings," said Frau Hurtzig, holding them close and rocking them. "A man who cannot tell the difference between clean and dirty, deserves our pity. We must pray for him."

"It is the schoolmaster Thomas Packer," I said, in a low voice to Captain Hurtzig. "He and Henry Allen the baker make trouble for us whenever they can."

The Captain frowned. "The war has stirred up hate everywhere. Are there many in the village who feel this way?"

"No, only those two, and a small farmer who threatened us with mantraps if we walked on his land. The rest of the villagers are friendly and see us as people, not enemies."

"I am so sorry, Luise, it is sad when people drag children into the fight," sighed Frau Jepsen.

"It is indeed."

"Wolfgang says the man is the schoolmaster. Lulu,"

"For shame!" Frau Hurtzig's eyes widened and her hand flew to her mouth. "A man like that has no business teaching children."

Captain Hurtzig looked sad. "I fear our little ones will have trouble making friends here. That man has the power to turn all the village children against our girls."

Frau Hurtzig sucked in her breath sharply and nodded. Then she threw her shoulders back. "Sit girls, we will forget that nasty man," she said, sinking down on the blanket. "I have a letter from Eva. You will like to hear what she has to say."

"A letter from Eva! Read it, Mama read it," they chorused, flopping down and leaning against their mother.

As Frau Hurtzig slid the letter from its envelope, Julius turned to me and said:

"Come, Wolfgang, see the spot I have picked out for Villa Marcella."

We tipped our hats to the ladies and wandered downstream to a pretty area where a creek inlet joined the river.

"Is this not a pleasant place?" he said, pointing to a spot on the other side of the bank.

"It is indeed."

"The river here is narrow. I shall build a bridge to Villa Marcella. And here, at the beginning of the bridge," he waved his hands above his head. "I will build a Transylvanian lucky gate so Marcella will always be mine."

"What is a Transylvanian lucky gate?"

"Transylvanian lucky gates are often mistaken for Japanese tori gates, but they are much more powerful. Marcella will

The Spot The War Forgot

never go off with another man once I build the lucky gate. I will put the side poles where we stand and the crossbar will sit on top. Do you have an axe I can use my friend?"

"Yes, when do you want it?"

"Now," his face grew dark. "I need a lucky charm to send the brother's friend away."

As I went to get the axe, I was troubled. I did not have much faith in the lucky gates but I hoped he was right; for if Julian tore his hair over an innocent bike ride, what might he do if Marcella really did break up with him?

W.E. Hamilton

September 1915
Bulgaria Enters War on Germany's Side

Two Lovely Visitors

Rumours of us had spread, and young women were flocking to the village, so much so, it took all Frau Jepsen's powers of persuasion to get Maria and Elsa a room.

"Next time book well in advance, especially if you wish to stay over the weekend," she said after she greeted them. "It seems all the single girls in Sydney know there are many nice young men here."

"*Ja*, the guards are very busy in the weekends," I said. "They have orders to keep the girls from chatting and laughing with the internees."

Maria slid a swift glance at Herman and bit her fingernail.

"Don't look so worried, Sis," said Michael, putting Elsa's bag down by the arrival desk. "It is a hopeless job. There are only twenty-four guards and we are free to roam over a large area; most of it covered in trees. There are many places to slip away."

The Spot The War Forgot

"How about the six of us go on a picnic tomorrow," said Billy. "We can show the girls some of the pretty spots around here."

"That's a wonderful idea," said Herman, putting Maria's suitcase beside Elsa's bag.

"I suggest you have Mrs Bergan make up a picnic basket, and meet the boys at the edge of town," said Frau Jepsen. "The guards might get suspicious if they see men with a picnic basket."

We nodded.

"*Ja*, that would be best," said Michael,."We will bring blankets to sit on and a book of English lessons, then if we are caught, we can tell the guards we are going into the woods to practice our English."

"We can also bring a billy and tea, the guards would think nothing of that."

"I expect you girls are tired and want to freshen up after your long journey," said Frau Jepsen, pinging the small bell on the counter. Mrs Bergan will be here in a minute to show you your room."

Maria and Elsa nodded. So, after arranging a rendezvous point, we bid them goodbye and left.

Although it was still early August, the weather the next day was mild, and everything went smoothly. We met the girls without a hitch, Herman took the basket from Elsa and we walked to a pretty little spot in the bush. Then we made a fire, set the billy on it, and the girls set the food on plates. After lunch, we lounged about talking.

"Tell me, Sis, are you still driving horses?"

"Every time I get the chance."

"I didn't know you could drive, Maria," said Elsa.

"*Ja*, when I stayed with the Schilgs on their farm in Burrumbuttock…stop laughing, it is a real place," she said, pretending to hit us. When we had quietened down, she continued: "They taught me to ride a horse and drive a sulky."

"The first thing I knew about it was when she met me at the station and drove me home," said Michael. "I am sure she kept it a secret just to surprise me."

"*Nein*, I only drove because nobody else could be spared from the farm."

"Tell the truth, you loved it, you don't fool me."

Maria laughed. "I was excited they trusted me to go. It was the first time I'd driven unsupervised."

"Remember that funny little station?"

"How could I forget? There was nobody there, only a little red flag and a sign that said: 'wave flag to stop the train.' So, when the train came in sight I waved frantically, and sure enough, it slowed down. But to my surprise, a flag waved back at me."

"Who was it?" said Elsa.

"It was me," said Michael.

"He was the only passenger to get out and we fell into each other's arms laughing. Tell me, brother, do you like being a prisoner more than a farm worker?"

"*Ja*, strange as it sounds, I do. I get to do as I wish during the day and in the evening there are many stimulating conversations about politics and culture."

"We also have a choir, a theatre, all sorts of sporting activities, courses on foreign languages, navigation, water-colour painting, and much more," I broke in. "And of course our talented Wilhelm Köster often gives us viola recitals."

"Not just me, Meinert and Fritz play the mandolin and zither with me. Do not let him fool you into thinking we are the only musicians in the camp, fraulines, there are many others."

"Tell them what your latest interest is, Billy," I said.

Billy stretched and lounged back on the blanket. "Photography; I've ordered a camera from the General Store. It is coming from Sydney and I'm hoping it will be here by the time the Grand Slippery Slope is finished. I want to get pictures of its official opening."

"What is the Grand Slippery Slope?" said Elsa.

"A water chute like the American ones," said Herman. "A large seat slides faster and faster down a set of rails until it hits the end, then it shoots you into the water like a pebble from a slingshot."

"That sounds great fun, I should like to see it."

"There is not much to see at the moment but by the end of the month we expect it to be finished. We have got an old carriage seat and some of the framework is up, but we still need to cut lots of saplings for the rails."

"And joining them end to end so the seat runs down them smoothly will be difficult," said Billy.

"What a pity we have to go back to Sydney so soon," said Maria. "I should very much like to ride the Grand Slippery Slope."

"It would be fun."

Herman looked directly at Maria. "You shall have to come again."

Maria smiled and nodded. After that, the topic was all about ways and means for the girls to return. The school holidays in early September seemed the best time as Elsa taught conversational German at Normanhurst Girls College. The time flew and all too soon it was time to pack up the hamper and head back to the jail. I did not see the girls again until their next visit, for the following day Julius wanted me to help him build his hut, and I did not have the heart to refuse him.

The Spot The War Forgot

September 1915
British Use Poison Gas Against German 6th Army in the Artois

How Hugo Bahl was Captured

Spring was around the corner and a lot was happening. The new internees were busy making huts, and now we could get to the other side of the river easily, lots of rustic little buildings were popping up on the left bank. Paul Pann and Hugo Bahl both started building proper log cabins (as good as you would find in the Black forest) but nobody said, "you won't get the door hung before the war is over," anymore. The united feeling was the war was going to last longer than we hoped, so we might as well make ourselves comfortable. Because of this attitude (and our steady paychecks), the General Store was kept busy with many orders for odd things. On the day Billy's camera was expected we walked to the store with Hugo Bahl and Captain Hurtzig.

"Seeing as they can get you a camera, I expect they can order me a small window for my cabin?" said Hugo, as we neared the shop.

"For sure," said Billy, "they can get in almost anything."

"If they are cheap enough, I might even order two windows, said Hugo. He entered the shop jauntily and greeted William Davis cheerily. The mood of happy anticipation stayed upon him until the sight of a row of sturdy boots and a barrel of straw filled with china plates stopped him short. "Ah, my poor wife," he said, his shoulders slumping, "I wonder how she is getting on with our little son?"

"Is he your first?" said Captain Hurtzig.

"Yes," he sighed deeply, "eight months old and who knows what age he will be before I set eyes on him?"

"It is very hard. Did you hear Herr Glintz's wife has given birth to a girl?"

"Very nice."

"*Ja*, it is. My wife loves babies. Frau Glintz and Louise have been getting on much better since baby Ursula has arrived, which makes the mood of the house much nicer."

Hugo picked up a blue willow-patterned plate, sighed again, and put it back into the barrel. "I brought a fine ninety-six-piece dinner set as a present for my wife, and a pair of sea-boots of real Russian leather (that would have lasted thirty years) and the whole lot are at the bottom of the ocean."

Michael and my eyes shot open and we were glad when Captain Hurtzig asked:

"What happened, Hugo?"

"Before the war, I was the first officer on the HAL freighter

The Spot The War Forgot

the Markomamnia, said Hugo, leaning his elbow on the side of the barrel. "It was early July and we had just spent several days in Vladivostok, (where I bought my sea-boots) and were on our way to Nikolayevsk to take on a cargo of salted fish. When we got there we loaded up, and on the last night, Captain Faahs invited the military governor of the town to dine with us. The governor arrived with three very pretty Fraulines. He was a trim older fellow who spoke good German and we had an enjoyable dinner and liked him very much. But when he took his leave, he said:

'Gentlemen, [1]*we have enjoyed ourselves and agreed on so much it is very wrong that we will soon be enemies.'*

Hugo put his hands on his hips and rocked forward onto his toes. "What do you think of that?" he said, looking at us fiercely.

"What did he mean?"

"That is exactly what we wanted to know." Hugo relaxed his stance and spread his hands wide as he continued his story. "'I don't understand, what are you saying?' Captain Faahs said to him, and the governor replied, '[2]*The key to Constantinople lies in Berlin, and we must have it.'* Of course, we were all shocked by his words for it had not crossed our minds we would soon be at war with Russia."

"What happened then?"

"We started on our way home to Hamburg but on August the first, just out of Tsingtao, we noticed a lot of activity in and around the harbour, and being unaware Germany had a few hours earlier declared war on Russia, thought it was a naval exercise in progress. To shorten a long story, we were

---

2   Taken from Hugo Bahl's diary.

pressed into service as part of Germany's Pacific fleet. They took our cargo of salted fish and filled every nook and cranny of the Markomannia with coal. Then at five in the afternoon on August the sixth, Captain von Muller came aboard…"

"Captain von Muller from the Emden?" said Billy, his eyes growing wide.

"*Ja*, he and his first officer von Mucke had selected our freighter to be the collier for the Emden. After nightfall (and without lights) we and the Emden followed the Prinz Friedrich Eitel through the protective minefield at the mouth of the harbour."

"Once you were out at sea did you all stick together?"

"We did at first. The three ships moved as a convoy until two days out from Tsingtao the Markomannia received orders to alter course." Hugo looked over his shoulder at William Davis standing by the counter and spoke in German. "So, we separated from the other ships, and on the 13th of August we arrived in a large bay on the southern shore of Pagan."

"Where is that?" I asked in German.

"The Mariana Islands." Hugo crouched down and drew a semicircle in the dust on the floorboards. "We sailed in here," he drew a line into the mouth of the curve, "*[3]and I was astounded to see the entire Eastern Fleet peacefully at anchor in the bay, including the Emden and nine merchantmen all laden with coal.*"

"That must have been an amazing sight."

Hugo nodded, picked up a small pebble lying on the floor and stood up.

"What happened then."

---

3   Taken from Hugo Bahl's diary.

The Spot The War Forgot

"The Emden was separated from the fleet and ordered to operate as an independent raider in the Indian Ocean, while we followed with the coal to keep her going. We got to the Bay of Bengal without any trouble and won our first prize on September the ninth.

"What was it?"

Hugo threw the pebble in the air and caught it. "The Pontoporros, a Greek steamer. Although the ship was neutral it carried a cargo of contraband coal so it was alright to take it. The plan was to use the coal and then sink it, but the captain of the Pontoporros (with quick thinking and fast-talking) struck a bargain with Captain von Muller and joined the Emden's entourage as its second collier. To make sure the Greek Captain kept his promise and did not run off, a prize-crew from the Emden were put aboard the Pontoporros and I found myself suddenly promoted to captain of our new Collier. I packed my bag, took my new boots, and all ninety-six pieces of my dinner set, and boarded the Pontoporros as Captain Bahl. It was an honour but I felt like Blackbeard for we led the life of pirates. We hunted down enemy ships and looted them of coal or anything else that was useful, we even took the soap from the bathrooms, and if the ship was of no further use, we sunk it."

"Did you sink them all?"

"*Nein*, Captain von Muller was chivalrous towards his captives. We used some of the ships to accommodate prisoners as comfortably as we could, then we stopped empty colliers from neutral countries and filled them with prisoners; that way the prisoners were taken to a harbour and set free within days."

"I thought you were on the Markomannia when it sunk?" said Billy.

W.E. Hamilton

"I was, I'm getting to that." Hugo fingered the pebble absentmindedly and a faraway-look entered his eyes. "One day the officers were transferring most of the remaining coal into the Emden and we were swarming with prisoners when I was ordered to the island of Simeulue where I was to idle just outside the boundary of the Dutch territorial waters awaiting further orders. If I had heard nothing by the tenth of October [4]*I was to steam to Sabang, land with my men from the Emden and set the Pontoporros and the prisoners free.* We set off alone that night and arrived at Simeulue on the afternoon of September the twenty-third. I had hoped to slip in unnoticed but that was impossible, the Dutch had seen us. For two weeks six Dutch warships watched we did not cross into their neutral zone as we steamed back and forth. At last, on the morning of October the seventh, we saw the smoke of an approaching ship and I was relieved to see it was the Markomannia. My new instructions when she arrived was to coal her then free the Pontoporros and her original crew. This I did, and once I and my prize-crew were on the Markomannia, we started for Java tasked with the job of purchasing provisions for the Emden."

"But you never got there."

Hugo shook his head as he threw the pebble in the air and caught it. "The terrible day was October the twelfth. We saw a Dutch ship approaching, but as they had been patrolling past us for two weeks, we were more interested in the flag than the ship. It was an extraordinarily large flag; so large it hid a ship."

"What was the ship?"

"It was the destroyer HMS Yarmouth. By the time we saw her, it was too late; we were too slow to cross the boundary into

---

[4] Taken from Hugo Bahl's diary.

The Spot The War Forgot

neutral waters. Both ships were stopped by the destroyer and BOOM, BOOM," Hugo threw the pebble out the door with force, "the poor Markomannia was sunk within the hour. It was horrible watching her slip beneath the water, knowing she was taking my good boots and fine dinner-set to the seabed." He sighed again and stared forlornly at the barrel of china.

"What happened next?"

"We were taken to Singapore and held as prisoners until they shipped us to Australia. Most of the crew went to the Holsworthy or Trial Bay camps, but Captain Faahs and I were sent here, so it is not all bad. I like being a prisoner better than being a pirate," his face brightened into a jolly smile and he switched back into English. "If they can get me a window, I will be very happy."

Davis spoke from across the counter. "Did I hear you are wanting a window, sir?"

"*Ja*, I certainly do," said Hugo walking over to him.

"What sized window?"

"A small square one, about this big." He held up his hands and marked out a space in the air.

Davis opened a thick catalogue and flicked to a page. "maybe something like this?" He stabbed his finger under a picture. While Hugo discussed windows the storekeeper's wife came out of the backroom carrying a small leather case.

"Mr Köster, just the person I wanted to see, your camera has come," she said, handing Billy the case.

Our glazed eyes refocused as our minds switched from Bahl's story to smaller matters.

"I thought it would be bigger than that," I said.

"You are thinking of the huge old ones," said Billy, sliding out a thin rectangular camera. "This is a Kodac folding autographic camera."

"I have not heard of an autographic camera before?"

Billy swung the front panel of the camera down and the lens popped out like a jack in the box lying on its side. "It's the latest thing." He turned the camera around and opened a small door at the back. "You can write information directly onto the photograph so you have a description and the date recorded under the image."

While we examined it Mrs Davis turned to Captain Hurtzig. "And what can I do for you, Captain?"

"I need some aspirins for my wife please, she is laid low with a bad migraine."

"Is that why you were hanging out the washing this morning?" said Hugo, handing a wad of notes to William Davis.

"Yes, they are very bad and she suffers with them frequently."

"Does it not bother you that many of the men will have seen you doing women's work?"

"I would do this and much more for my Lulu. I am only sorry I cannot have the headache for her."

"You are a kind husband," said Mrs Davis, handing the Captain a small bottle of pills. She took the money he gave her, punched numbers into the enormous till on the counter and pulled the lever down with a loud ka-ching. Then she turned to Billy. "I expect you will get lots of good photos on the opening day of the Grand Slippery Slide."

"I hope to. Are you coming, Mrs Davis, the village is invited."

"I can't come for the whole day, but if we are not busy I'll

The Spot The War Forgot

come for a few hours. Oh, I nearly forgot, here is the box of film you ordered."

"I'm glad you remembered, I will not be getting any photographs without film."

When we had finished our business, we left the shop in good spirits. I had a nice new pocketknife, Captain Hurtzig had pills to help his wife, and Billy was very pleased with his new camera. Hugo Bahl, however, was the happiest of us all, because, in addition to ordering three windows, he had bought a willow-pattern gravy boat for his wife.

———

W.E. Hamilton

September 1915
Allied Troops Move through Mesopotamia to Capture Baghdad

Secrets

Billy, wandering about with his camera became a common sight. At celebrations, he spent most of his time taking pictures. On the morning of the inauguration of the Grand Slippery Slope, a dozen or so of the villagers turned up to the opening. Billy took snapshots of them as they stood on the bank watching us catapult out of the seat into the chilly water. He also got a good picture of the dugout-canoe paddling about on the Great Lake swimming pool. At the time, we thought the inauguration had been a grand day, but compared to later celebrations it was pretty tame, nevertheless, we enjoyed it and were admiring Billy's snapshots of the dugout one evening when someone (I don't remember who,) suggested we had a Venetian carnival in December. The idea fired our imagination and we got quite carried away with planning water sports and gymnastic displays until another someone said:

The Spot The War Forgot

"It won't be much of a Venetian carnival with only two boats."

We all realized the truth of this.

"I and my friends will make another rowboat," said Billy. "But this time we will make it bigger than the Nelly and call it the Attila. I challenge the rest of you to make boats as good as ours."

At this, friendly rivalry sprang up between the various crews and shipping lines, and the next day all those who had finished their huts were making boats. Despite their instability and tendency to sink, dugout canoes were popular. As we constructed the frame of the Attila, we could see groups of men stripping bark and hacking the centre out of long longs. Further up the river, another rowboat like ours was under construction, and two ambitious men were each attempting to make a paddlewheel boat.

"The one to watch is that fellow who says he is making a bicycle boat out of scrap metal and rubber tubing he found lying near the old coal mine," said Billy. "I can't see how he is going to get a boat out of that junk."

"I cannot either, but if he does, he might win the competition by sheer originality," said Michael.

"We could still win if we have some witty or striking point in our decoration," I said. "We could disguise the canoe to look like something different."

"Like what?"

"I don't know, maybe," I lowered my voice, "a Venetian Gondola?"

"*Ja*, that is very fitting for a Venetian carnival, we could extend the prow and stern easily enough."

"It will be a while before we are ready to do that," said Billy, "we have to make the boat first, but until the carnival, I think we should keep our idea secret and hide her in a hut when we start to change her into a gondola."

"For sure," we said nodding.

As December was still a few months away we had plenty of time to get the job done, and just as well, for we had barely put the frame together when Maria and Elsa arrived. After that, the boat was forgotten in a round of picnics and outings. By now it was apparent Hermann was very interested in Maria, but even so, we were caught by surprise when one picnic (over a bowl of pea soup) Hermann asked Maria to marry him and she said yes. We called at the Hurtzigs later that afternoon wildly excited, for an engagement under such circumstances seemed nothing short of miraculous.

"Oh, my dear, I am so happy for you," said Frau Hurtzig kissing Maria on the cheek.

"Congratulations," said Captain Hurtzig, shaking Hermann's hand vigorously.

"You must all stay for a celebratory evening," said Frau Hurtzig,."How wonderful I baked a cake today." She turned to Billy. "Run home and get your viola and we can have a little sing-along."

Billy nodded and nipped out as Frau Hurtzig scribbled a quick note. "And Hanna *Liebling*," she folded the letter and gave it to her daughter. "Pop across the road and give this to Frau Jepsen."

Soon Billy returned with his viola and Hanna and the Jepsens arrived shortly after. Frau Jepsen was in a flutter of joy.

The Spot The War Forgot

"To think I was part of bringing you together," she said, kissing Maria. "For I got you the rooms at the boarding house."

"This certainly is wonderful news," said Captain Jepsen, shaking Hermann's hand.

"I've been saving this for a special occasion," said Captain Hurtzig, pouring blackberry wine into glasses, "and I can't think of a better reason to celebrate. Heinrich Bartels said when he gave it to me, he had made it from blackberries and it was supposed to be brandy but something had gone wrong. Nevertheless, I think you will find the flavour is very pleasant."

It was pleasant. We toasted the happy couple until the bottle was empty. Then Frau Hurtzig made coffee and we all had a slice of rich German cake. And after that, we men smoked cigars while the ladies sang songs, right up to the moment the bugle sounded.

"Ah, the bugle, how I hate that noise," said Frau Jepsen, as Billy packed his viola away in its case, "the evening is barely begun and suddenly our time is cut short."

"You, Maria and Elsa don't have to go," said Frau Hurtzig, "I insist you ladies have dinner with me and stay the evening."

"*Ja*, I would like that," Frau Jepsen beamed. "We can talk more. To think if I had not found the girls a room this could not have happened," she repeated.

Captain Jepsen's face tensed. "Don't tell anyone you helped Maria and Elsa find a room, my love, we could get into trouble for this."

"Why?" Frau Jepsen's eyes grew wide.

"Because we are not supposed to fraternize with the guards or civilians; especially the women."

"Nobody follows that silly rule, not even the guards. They

chat with us every day and are very friendly."

"They even look the other way when men bring alcohol over the prison wall," said Frau Hurtzig.

"I know, they bend the rules all the time, but an engagement is not something they can wink at without getting into big trouble."

"Captain Jepsen is right," said Captain Hurtzig. "I think it is best if we keep the engagement a secret. The less people who know about it the better."

"The war spoils everything," said Frau Jepsen drooping. "It is very hard, but I agree. I will speak of this to no one other than the people in this room."

"Very good, my love," said Captain Jepsen, kissing her goodbye. "I will see you tomorrow morning."

And with that, we left.

Frau Jepsen kept her promise, nevertheless, word leaked out. Early one morning a fortnight later, Michael, Hermann and I were walking with Captain Hurtzig when his wife came running down the path.

"Thank goodness, you are here, Gust, something terrible has happened. Come inside all of you, this concerns Michael and Hermann as well."

Feeling anxious we hurried after her.

"Now, Lulu, what is this all about?" said Captain Hurtzig, sitting on the couch beside his wife. He put his arm around her. "You are trembling."

"Oh, Gust, it was horrible, last night after you had gone the policeman came and asked if I had permission to live here. I told him we were here by Official Authority. He wanted proof and I told him he needed to talk to you but as it was after

The Spot The War Forgot

the curfew hour he would have to wait until tomorrow. He was hunting for strangers and visitors, for he has asked all the women in the village the same question. I was so afraid he was going to send me away without you."

"Don't worry, my perle, he won't send anyone away."

"Oh, but Gust, he will. Frau Jepsen, Maria, and Elsa have to go. It seems he has found out about the engagement and knows Frau Jepsen had a hand in it."

She had barely finished speaking when the Jepsens, Maria, and Elsa arrived.

"I have to go back to Sydney," said Frau Jepsen, entering the room and bursting into tears. "And from now on I must get permission to visit Berrima, even for a day, and permission will be very hard to get."

"Oh Michael," said Elsa, running over to him, "we have five days to leave the area and then I will never see you again."

Michael put his arm around her shoulders. "We will think of a way around this."

At this, all the eyebrows in the room shot up, and Captain Hurtzig whispered to his wife: "I think there is more than one engagement in the wind."

"Come Hurtzig," said Captain Jepsen. "Let us go to the police station and sort this mess out." He looked at Maria and Elsa, "I'm sorry I won't be able to do anything for you girls. If it were up to me, I would let you stay, but without proper authority it is hopeless."

Frau Hurtzig put on her hat. "What about Hanna and Lore, Gus, they are playing outside?"

"Don't worry, we will keep an eye on them," said Maria, looking out the window.

"Thank you, my dear, that would be a big help."

"What we need," said Elsa, when the captains and their wives had gone. "Is someone in the village who is willing to smuggle us into Berrima."

"You wouldn't even need to come right into the village," said Michael. "The area is surrounded by bush. We could meet somewhere in the parole area."

"What about Rose Izzard?" said Hermann. "She is ideal, as she couriers the mail for the Walker girls at the post office. She drives her horse and sulky back and forth from Moss Vale every day."

"Yes," said Maria, her face brightening. "We could send letters hidden in food-parcels by her."

"That's a good idea, we could collect the parcels from the stables and nobody would suspect a thing."

"We can't even tell Frau Hurtzig of this," said Michael.

"Why not?" said Elsa.

"She is a good Christian woman and cannot be trusted to tell a necessary lie."

"*Ja*, that is true, she is very honest," said Hermann. "If the guards question her, she will tell the truth and feel bad about it. We can't involve her or Captain Hurtzig for they are such a close couple he might let the secret slip out."

"But will Rose Izzard be willing to do it?" I said, frowning. "She is always helpful but this is bigger than advice and kindness. She could get into serious trouble if she was caught."

At this the room went quiet, Elsa's bottom lip trembled and Maria wiped a tear away. As if she knew we wanted to talk to her, Rose Izzard came running up the path.

"Help, help," she cried, bursting in the door. "Prince has

The Spot The War Forgot

fallen into a large underground cistern and we can't get him out."

"Where is he," said Michael?

Rose pointed into the distance. "Over on that farm. My husband is trying to get Prince out but the water is deep and the sides of the cistern rise like a wall."

"If there is a tree near the cistern," said Hermann, as we hurried down the path. "We could adapt a bosun's chair and lift him out."

"A double chair," I nodded. I ran over to the rickety fence and ripped two palings off. "These will do for the planks."

Michael turned to Rose. "Have you got any rope?"

"There's lots in the tack shed."

"I'll come with you to get it," he turned to Hermann. "Get more men, I'll be back soon."

Hermann rushed off and I hurried in the direction Rose had pointed. Within a few minutes I came upon a group of men from the village crouched beside a large hole. As I got close, I heard splashing below me, and peering down I saw the dark head of a horse barely lifted above the water.

John Izzard ran a hand across his face. "I think he is done for, he has been in there all night and I don't think he can swim much longer."

"Don't worry, help is coming," I said, dropping the planks on the ground.

John shook his head. "I can't see how anyone can get him out."

"Don't despair, we are sailors and used to hoisting things up masts."

As I spoke Michael and Hermann arrived. Behind them

ran a crowd of internees, a couple of guards, and the village policeman. Rose, clutching a horse blanket and a bucket of oats, watched as a couple of mariners were let down into the cistern. Above them, another sailor scaled the nearby tree, while still others lowered the planks, slung ropes over branches and twisted them into knots and loops. The hard part was getting planks under the swimming horse, but once the men had both ends of him in a chair everything was straightforward. Then the villagers, the guards, the internees, and the policeman, grasped the rope and all heaving in unison, hoisted Prince out and lowered him on the ground gently.

"I can't thank you enough," said Rose, throwing the blanket over the quivering horse.

"Without your help, we would have lost him," said John, putting the bucket of oats before Prince.

Rose turned to Michael. "I owe you a debt of gratitude, he is our most valuable horse, if there is anything I can do for you, just let me know."

"Actually, there is something I need help with."

"Yes, anything."

"Come for a little walk with me," said Michael. And together they walked off to a quiet spot where they could not be overheard.

The Hurtzigs were already home when we got there.

"Maria and Elsa said you went to rescue the Izzard's horse," said Captain Hurtzig. "Did you get him out of the cistern?"

Michael smiled and nodded. "*Ja,* and after a rest, he will be fine."

I expect that is the end of his midnight adventures," I said. "Rose will padlock his stable door after this and not even a

The Spot The War Forgot

horse as clever as Prince can open one of those with his teeth."

"How did you get on, Captain?" said Hermann.

"We got it all sorted out and even Frau Jepsen can stay. The policeman was about to give her a long lecture on her sins but the Izzards horse cut it short."

"I got off with a quick warning instead," said Frau Jepsen.

"To think my first oath on the bible was, 'I will not raise arms against England,'" groaned Frau Hurtzig. "How appalling!"

"Never mind Lulu, all the other wives of internees had to swear too."

"How does that make it better, Gus?"

"Don't worry your head over it, my dear, it is not as if you could do anything against England even if you decided to."

"*Ja*, that is true. I am so sorry this has happened, girls, especially at this time."

"It will be alright," said Michael. "We can send letters and food parcels to each other," he said, turning and winking at Elsa and Maria.

"Was Mrs Izzard happy with you for getting her horse out,?" asked Maria, looking at him meaningfully.

"Very grateful," he nodded. "She said, she would help us *any way she could.*"

"It is alright then?"

"Yes, *everything is settled.*

"You are taking this very well," said Frau Hurtzig. "I don't think I would have been so brave in your place."

"Oh well, what we can't change we must endure," said Maria, leaning against Hermann. "Regular letters and food-parcels will be enough."

W.E. Hamilton

October 1915
Austro-Hungarians and Germans invade Serbia

Troubles and Disappointments

Our fame was spreading and by spring the bridge, huts, and our general activities were drawing large crowds of visitors. They came by horse, motor car, dray and omnibus, all anxious to see the 'Huns.' They admired the cabins, used the picnic places, rode the water chute, and left behind paper and rubbish. Some weekends a thousand people descended on Berrima. Most came to picnic and swim but some came to wreck and assault.

"I don't care if people stare at me, and I will pick up their rubbish," I said to Billy, one Monday morning, "but vandalism is too much." I gathered up the sheets of bark lying scattered around my hut. "This hole in the roof will take me all day to fix."

"At least they did not smash the Attila, if they had broken

her frame we would have had to start all over again."

"Sorry about your roof," said Michael, coming over. "They damaged some of the clubhouses too. The top is knocked off the turret of the Emden hut and one of the veranda posts is broken."

"What about Lloydhall?"

"It is alright, the NGL men are pleased the vandals left it alone."

"I suppose this is the price of fame," I said, pulling a face.

"I don't like it much," said Michael.

We were not the only ones concerned, the camp commandant and the guards were increasingly worried; especially once the assaults started. There were not many fights, just enough for the commandant to take action. In early October a new rule was posted on the noticeboard in the assembly yard.

During weekends and public holidays, curfew has been shortened from 6:30 pm. to 1 pm.

Hanna and Lore were playing on the sand and Frau Hurtzig was watching us stretch canvass over the Attila when Captain Hurtzig broke the news to her.

"You have to go back to the jail so soon?"

"Sadly, *ja*. Every Saturday, Sunday, and all public holidays, we have to return by one. It is for our safety."

Frau Hurtzig tossed her head. "I do not believe it. The English are bad losers and this is a petty spiteful way of getting back at us for the victories Germany has recently won."

"I do not think so, Lulu, The Southern Mail says it is a stopgap measure. The Department of Defence is considering banning civilians from our stretch of the river. They are worried about the eighty prisoners of war that arrived here the other day. They think some Australians might seek to avenge loved ones lost in the war, and a guarded stockade would be an easy way to protect us."

Frau Hurtzig put her hands on her hips. "Why are you reading that paper, Gust? You know it is hopelessly biased."

"Only about the war, *Liebling*, not local news. It says the Nattai Council is strongly opposed to the idea and the villagers are outraged. The letters to the editor are very hostile."

Frau Hurtzig sucked in her breath sharply and her hand flew to her mouth. "Hostile towards us?"

"*Nein, nein*, they are angry with the Department of Defence. Henry Allen has written to local members of both the State and Federal Parliaments demanding they support the villagers."

"I know where this will end," groaned Frau Hurtzig. "They will build a big cage and put us in there." She gazed down the river sadly. *"[5]All the lovely walks in the bush will be lost, and more than half the huts and picnic places made useless, with no freedom to go on long two-mile excursions."*

Captain Hurtzig tried to soothe his wife but she remained gloomy. Her pessimism was catchy and for a time we all felt nervous. But the wheels of bureaucracy move slowly; although protests and discussions continued past December, nothing more than the early curfew happened.

While Henry Allen kept stirring up trouble, we meanwhile, were engaged in much more pleasant tasks. As October rolled into November and the weather got warmer, we swam and dived and rode the water chute. When we weren't playing in

---

5   Taken from Frau Hurtzig's diary.

The Spot The War Forgot

the water, we worked on our boats for the Venetian carnival. Our team successfully extended the prow and stern of the Attila into the swan-necked gondola and rigged a canopy of brown and green cloth. We were putting the finishing touches to her the day before the event.

"The Attila is sure to win," I said, painting the last A in Attila before stepping back to admire her, "especially when they hear the mandolin playing. Nobody will be expecting that."

"For sure," said Michael, his arm moving vigorously back and forth as he sanded the gondola pole.

But, Billy, looking out the door of the hut, said, "Only if the weather stays fine. I don't like the look of those grey clouds."

"Neither do I," said Michael, dropping his pole and walking outside. "If we were at sea the captain would be preparing for a storm."

And indeed, we all felt the barometric pressure plummet and the wind suddenly rise.

"I think we'd best be getting back to the jail," said Billy, as big drops of rain spattered about spotting the ground.

This seemed a smart idea. I dropped my brush in a jar of water and (when everyone was out) shut the door firmly. Then we ran back to the jail. We had only got inside when the clouds burst and it bucketed down. It rained solidly for the rest of the day, and all night, and by the next morning there was still no sign of a letup. As the days passed and the river rose, we feared for the safety of the bridge as increasingly large clusters of sticks swept under it. When the deck sat only inches from the swirling brown water, we knew something had to be done to save it. The Hansa men were in charge of the operation of course. They organized teams of men to stand along the length of the bridge by the piles. Our job was to guide flotsam-and-jetsam safely underneath and not let big things hit the beams and supports. My shift started in the afternoon. As I scanned the water for debris, I marvelled at the change the rain had brought to the riverbank. The huts nearest the waterline were flooded or swept away, and the Grand Lake had swollen to such an extent it was barely recognizable as the location of our doomed Venetian carnival.

"I expected to use this," said Michael, clutching his gondola pole as he pushed a log away from the bridge supports, "but not in this way."

Crouching down I caught a big stick as it came towards me and hurled it over the other side. "I hope the Hansa engineers are right about the limit the river rises to."

"Don't worry," said Billy, using the oar of the Nelly to guide a dead sheep around a beam. "Those Hansa men know what they are doing."

And they certainly did, for although the water came almost level with the deck, it never went over it.

The bridge was not the only thing the torrential rain put pressure on. The jail had been overcrowded for months yet internees kept coming. Every cell had at least two men in it and some had three. Confined space was less of a problem on fine days because we spent most of our time outdoors. But in torrential rain, our huts leaked and the riverside was dismal. Inside the jail was dry but it was much less pleasant and, worst of all, the open pan toilets stunk and got horribly full. The married men and those with rented houses had a way of escape but the rest of us had to get along as best we could. Michael

The Spot The War Forgot

and Hermann were especially disappointed.

"The girls have to cancel their visit," said Hermann. He was sitting on his bunk reading a note he found in a salami.

Michael, sitting hunched on a bush chair, sighed. "It is for the best; it is impossible to picnic in this rain, and to meet anywhere else is risky." His elbow nudged the wall as he felt in his pocket for a packet of cigarettes. "If we get caught, they might send us away."

"*Ja*, then we would be in big trouble." Hermann nodded. "The guards say this is the nicest camp with the most freedom; and they would know, they get sent around them all."

"Have a cigarette, Wolfgang," said Michael, passing the packet over the tiny table between us.

"Thanks." I took one and lit it. "They call Berrima Camp a lolly stick and consider it 'a sweet cop' and 'no sweat' to be assigned here."

Hermann put the salami on the table without getting off his bed. "It's not surprising, there is little for them to do other than relax. The captains rule us as usual and life is as regulated as a well-run ship."

"Except we get more free time," said Michael, passing the cigarettes to Hermann.

"For sure, although it is not much use on a day like today."

"You could join the woodturners group. They have a lathe now and they are turning bowling-balls for the bowling club."

Hermann leaned down and turned the flame of the kerosine heater up, "my hands are too cold for that. Who would think only last week it was warm enough for swimming?"

"We could go to the library in the courtroom," I said, between puffs. "The rich titled men who live in the side rooms of the courthouse keep the reading room warm."

"I've read all the books that interest me."

"I bet you haven't, it's very well stocked now."

Michael nodded. "Wolfgang's right. When the Singapore internees came, they brought with them the entire library of their German club, including an extensive collection of classical and general works."

"Plus, the camp committee has purchased books relevant to all the subjects taught here," I added. "Billy got a book on photography the other day."

"Perhaps something good has come from this rain and disappointment, after all," said Hermann, swinging his legs over the side of his bunk and standing up. "I have re-discovered the library over the road."

"That is not all," I said, following him out of the jail, it doesn't matter how famous we are, nobody is coming all the way down from Sydney to gawk at the Huns in this weather."

The Spot The War Forgot

November 1915
Allies Attack Banyo in the Cameroons and Capture it

Christmas Preparations

The rain had finally stopped and the entire camp was buzzing with preparations for Christmas. Those not involved with the theatre or choir were industriously making toys for the Berrima and Bourke Camps. Berrima had only four children but Bourke had many because larger German families were interned there.

"We look like Santa's elves," I said, as I glued tiny shingles onto the roof of the dollhouse I was building.

Billy painted the funnel of a train red. "We do rather if you ignore our height, clothes, ears, and the fact our workshop is a derelict jail in Australia."

Nearby Captain Altneppen sat sewing a dainty doll's dress, his gnarled hands looking large as he threaded a fine needle through gauzy fabric.

"And Captain Altneppen is Santa Claus," said Hermann,

painting a smile on the face of a rag doll.

Captain Altneppen snorted. "I'm not fat enough for Santa and I don't have a beard."

"But you do have a luxurious handlebar moustache which does the job," said Michael, winding a string around a spinning-top, "and nobody would know you are bald if you wore a red hat."

"I am sure I was not so rude to my seniors when I was a young man," said Captain Altneppen, to Captain Hurtzig. He frowned as he stitched, pretending he was offended, but we saw the twinkle in his eyes.

Captain Hurtzig chuckled. "If they get too cheeky, Captain Altneppen, I will tell the Krampus to give them coal in their stockings." He held up the doll's pram he was making. "The woodturning club made a nice job of the wheels, he said spinning a wooden disk. The girls are going to love their prams."

"They will be excited when they see them on Christmas day," I said, pasting glue on a chimney before sticking it onto the roof.

"These are not for Christmas Eve," said Captain Hurtzig, screwing the hood of the pram in place. "I'm going to make them little chairs for Christmas, and Luise has brought them teddys and fixed up their old dolls and cot. No, these are for the Christmas concert. Herr Pahnke is to present all the camp children with something from Santa. My girls are getting one each. Baby Ursula and Gertrud Brauns are getting something too, but I am not sure what."

"Speaking of the concert, how is *A Springtime of Love* getting on, Billy?" I asked.

The Spot The War Forgot

"Most of the cast know their lines and the zither quartet sounds good."

"Has Herr Lüdeking finished making his cello out of kerosene tins?" said Captain Altneppen, tying thread into a knot and snipping the ends off.

"Yes, and it's a work of art. He's painted it to resemble old wood."

I pulled a face. "It may look good but does it sound good?"

"That is the biggest surprise of all," said Billy, "I heard him play it and it has a beautiful mellow tone. I asked him the secret to the sound and he said he filled it with wool. You shall hear it on Saturday and judge the quality of sound for yourselves."

"What time does the concert start, and who is coming?" I said. "Did the villagers get permission from the commandant to attend?"

"8:30 pm and not expected to finish until midnight," said Captain Hurtzig, moving the pram hood up and down experimentally. "The commandant said, NO, to the villagers coming; only the wives and children of the internees can attend."

"That's a pity," I said, adding shutters to the sides of the windows. "Annie and Ada Harper will be disappointed. "It doesn't seem fair because the ladies of the village have helped us out with clothes for the female parts.

"I'll give Ada a program," said Billy, painting the wheels black. "Then she and her friends will know when to sit on the veranda of the guard's house and listen from the other side of the wall. They gave me a hat with a large feather and a stripy skirt I look hilarious in. I'm going to wear it when our quartet plays our pieces."

Captain Altneppen shook out the dress. "There you go Hermann, this should fit your doll."

Hermann slid the dress onto the doll, taking care not to smudge the mouth. "Perfect. What do we do with the finished toys?"

"Give them to the Commandant and he and his officers will see they get to the children of the Bourke camp," said Captain Hurtzig. He lifted the finished pram. "But this one goes to Herr Pahnke." He started to walk away but stopped. "Before I forget," he turned and looked at us." My wife said to invite you boys to Sunday Breakfast and the lighting of the first advent candle."

Michael and Herman exchanged glances uneasily.

"That is very kind but Hermann and I can't come, we have made other plans."

"What kind of plans?"

"We are going on an early morning picnic to study English," said Michael, flushing at the lame excuse.

"English lessons," said Captain Hurtzig, pulling a face, "wouldn't you prefer to eat *Platzchen biscuits* than study English?"

"*Ja*, if that was the only thing we were doing," said Hermann, running his finger around the inside of his collar. "But we can't. Please tell Frau Hurtzig we are very sorry."

"What is the other thing you are doing?"

"Don't ask."

"Ah, I suppose it is like asking which of the villagers buy foreign newspapers, even though they only read the local paper, and why the post office girls have not informed on them?"

"Exactly."

The Spot The War Forgot

"What about you, Wolfgang? Do you wish to come on Sunday or are you involved in activities I should not ask about?"

"I would love to come."

"And so would I," said Billy.

"It is settled then." He looked at Michael and Hermann and sighed. "My wife will be disappointed you can't come. I wish I had a better excuse than English lessons."

Captain Hurtzig was right, Frau Hurtzig was astonished when she heard why Michael and Hermann were not coming. By Sunday morning she still hadn't got over it.

"English lessons!" she said, as we gathered in the Hurtzigs rooms. "I don't know what has come over those two lately. Why are they so anxious to study English?"

"Who could say," I said, spreading my hands. I looked around for something to change the subject. "Your place is transformed, I barely recognize it," I said, noticing the furnishings.

I could not have chosen a better topic. Frau Hurtzig instantly lost interest in Hermann and Michael.

"It feels more like home now," she said, smiling. "Once our familiar things finally came, they made all the difference." She pointed at items in the room. "The children's beds, the lightweight things, the doll's bed and rocking chair, my meat-safe, the table and chairs and so on, arrived the day of the picnic last week. I came home to find them outside. Herr Voges helped me move my treadle sewing machine into the kitchen for the men had to leave immediately. The trunks came a few days later on the freezing wet day that Captain Madsen and the others arrived. Poor Herr Hansen, the guards took the military overcoat the Government lent him. They could have let him have it one more night."

I nodded. "The first night is always the worst, for it takes time to get beds set up and learn tricks like putting newspapers between the blankets for extra warmth."

"What is done is done, I suppose, he has a new coat now and is no longer sleeping on the floor, which is all that matters. I sent Gust one of our stretchers with a mattress together with a small table for his new cell when our furniture came, for now we have beds we have no further need of them."

"He certainly was lucky to find an empty cell. Although the barracks we built along the prison wall have helped relieve things somewhat, we are still overcrowded. I suppose the man who vacated the Captain's cell had comrades in the barracks."

"Gust said it belonged to a man who went mad and was sent to a psychiatric hospital, but I prefer your idea."

Hanna sidled up to my side. "Papa and I set up a playroom in one of the storerooms, and Lore and I helped Mamma make the Christmas decorations."

Frau Hurtzig switched her attention to the festive decorations draped along the marble mantelpiece. Above them sat a lamp, a mirror, and several framed photographs of family members.

"The girls helped me collect the fur branches, and the store had a sale on red ribbon. I miss the holly berries but what can you do? The seasons are the wrong way around down here."

"It doesn't matter," said Billy, putting his viola case on the hearth next to the grate (filled with yellow wattle flowers.) "Everything looks so comfortable."

"My little Lulu is a born homemaker," said Captain Hurtzig, putting his arm around his wife. "Not every woman can make

The Spot The War Forgot

such a comfortable home under such circumstances."

Frau Hurtzig smiled modestly. "Come," she waved her hands towards the table where a pine wreath and four candles sat. "We will eat before we light the candle. Bring the marmalade and butter, Hanna, I'll get the brotchen.

We sat around the table while Captain Hurtzig put a fat cushion on a spindle-back chair and helped Lore onto it. Meanwhile, Frau Hurtzig bustled about in the kitchen and came back shortly bearing a large platter of hot rolls and a pot of coffee. Hanna, following in her mother's wake, placed a dish of marmalade and a pat of butter on the table. Once they were seated, Captain Hurtzig prayed a short prayer thanking God for the food, and the company, and the beginning of Advent. Then we tucked into the delicious breakfast as we talked about music and culture, the war and the upcoming concert. And after that, Captain Hurtzig helped Hanna light the candle while Billy played Stille Nacht. Then we sang a couple of hymns and ate crescent moon shaped *Platzchen biscuits*, and none of us realized it was the last time we would meet together in that room.

W.E. Hamilton

November 1915
Third Battle of Artois: Allied Offensive to Recapture French Territory from Germans Ends in Failure

Harmless Waves in the Sea of Romance

"How were Maria and Elsa?" I asked Michael and Hermann, on Monday as we walked down to the river.

"Very good."

"Did you have any trouble getting away?"

Michael pulled a face. "*Ja*, we did. The commandant saw us heading into the bush carrying rugs over our arms and sent a guard after us."

"We saw him coming," said Hermann, "but we managed to lose him in the scrub. We thought we would get away with it, but the guard recognized us and when we got back, we had to go and see the commandant."

"What happened?"

"We told him a touching story of how we wished to study

and practice the beautiful English language, but our comrades were a rowdy and uncouth so we desired a quiet spot in the bush to get away from them."

"Did he swallow it?"

"Like a fish taking the bait," Michael chuckled. "We were prepared for questioning. Elsa had written notes in the margin of our English books to make it more realistic."

"The girls also had a narrow escape at the Railway Hotel last night," said Herman.

"What happened?"

"The guests eat together at a long communal table, and a young man showed a lot of interest in Maria. She kept her mouth shut only answering yes and no so he could not hear her accent. Elsa tried to draw him away but it didn't work, and they had to take refuge in their room for the rest of the evening."

"But everything else went smoothly. Rose Izzard was marvellous. She picked up the girls from the hotel and they sat on the mailbags until she let them off in the bush not far from here. Then after the picnic, she took them back to Moss Vale with the outgoing post."

"I'm pleased it turned out all right."

Hermann nodded. "Are you coming swimming?" he asked, as we reached the edge of the water.

"*Nein*, not today, I promised I would help Julius with his hut. He is in despair this morning because Marcella said the man next door had a pretty flower garden."

"I suppose he thinks Marcella is going to elope with the neighbor."

I grinned. "Something like that. Have a good swim, I will see you later."

W.E. Hamilton

They waved and I wandered along the riverbank until I came to the lucky gates. By now a small bridge ran under them to a bark cabin with two little windows in the end wall.

"Ahoy there Julius," I called, striding over the bridge. "I've come to help you with the roof."

Julius appeared in the doorway, his shoulders slumped and his face a picture of dejection. "What is the use, my friend? You might as well go back." He thumped his chest with his clenched fist. "My Marcella is unfaithful to me. Why should I finish this token of my love when she forgets her faithful Julius?"

"*Ach komm schon*, it is not like that, a woman does not elope with a man because she likes his garden. Tomorrow's letter will say you are handsome and all will be well again."

"Do you really think so?"

"I am sure of it."

Julius stood straight and his melancholy expression changed to self-satisfaction. "It is true I am a handsome fellow." He clapped me on the back in a friendly manner. "You are right. Flowers cannot compete with my handsomeness."

"Let's get this roof finished," I said, picking up bark. "You've collected enough for us to get the job done by the bugle call if we both work hard at it."

Julius, scrambling onto the roof, burst into song as he pinned layers of bark under long saplings. I did not understand Hungarian, but I guessed from his intensity and Marcella's often repeated name, they were improvised love-songs. Down below, I flattened the bark before handing it up to him. Then after a lunch of potato pancakes (cooked on his outdoor fireplace), we swapped jobs and I worked on the roof while he

The Spot The War Forgot

sang over the bark.

"I knew we could get it done today," I said, tying a slender sapling across the last row of bark as the bugle sounded.

"Just in time," Julius put his thumbs in the crook of his back and stretched backwards. "I am glad to be finished, my back aches."

I shuffled to the edge of the roof, let myself down carefully, and dropping the last couple of feet, landed lightly.

"It looks good," I said, gazing at the completed hut. "It will keep the sun off and be reasonably waterproof."

"I shall ask Billy to take a picture of Villa Marcella so I can send it to Marcella. Then she will see a magnificent demonstration of my love and devotion," said Julius, as we walked across the bridge and under the lucky gates.

"I am sure she will be very impressed," I said, hoping my words were true.

We walked along the riverbank and merged in with all the other men swarming up the hill to the jail. As we passed the brick house at the corner of the prison wall opposite the Hurtzig's house, we noticed a lot of unusual activity.

"I wonder what is happening in the guard's quarters?"

"They will be changing the guards again, they are always changing the guards."

"They don't usually bother to clean it between regiments. This is something different."

We passed through the picket fence and walked under the tall trees towards the iron gates. It was eight months since we first arrived and sat under those same trees complaining bitterly. While our old castle was certainly not luxury accommodation, within its walls was friendship, culture, music, theatre, and all manner of interesting hobbies. I passed under the imposing archway without fear or foreboding and stood with all the other men until rollcall was over. Then when the gates clanged shut and the key rattled in the lock, we went in for dinner. As we stood in the queue, Captain Hurtzig marched past us clutching his mug of tea and plate of bread and marmalade.

I nudged Billy with my elbow as we shuffled towards the food-counter. "What's wrong with the captain? He looks down in the dumps."

"He has had a tiff with his wife. The commandant offered Herr Glintz and Captain Hurtzig the opportunity to swap houses with the guards and they agreed. At first, Frau Hurtzig was pleased because the house is divided into two separate apartments, but now she doesn't want to go."

"That was nice of Captain Stoddart. I thought she would jump at the chance to live separately to Frau Glintz."

Billy reached the head of the line and took his bread while the cook filled his mug with tea. "The house is dirty and things between her and Frau Glintz have been much better since the baby arrived," he said, moving to the side so I could get my food.

"I am pleased to hear that," I said, as we headed towards the table where Captain Hurtzig sat.

"Not half as happy as I am." Billy leaned close to me and said in an undertone. "It was not easy being the captain's cellmate when those women were fighting. I got sick of hearing about dreadful Frau Glintz and was relieved when the captain got a room of his own."

I pulled a wry smile as we walked the last few paces to the table and sat down.

The Spot The War Forgot

"Is everything alright, Captain?"

"*Nein*, but what can I do about it? I am not master of my destiny; I miss my ship."

"Has Frau Hurtzig got over having to shift?" said Billy.

Captain Hurtzig's face darkened. "*Women* who can understand them? She says she would never have agreed to move if I had told her how dirty the house was. I said, '*liebling*, the dirt will wash away.' Then she fusses about the curtains and Christmas decorations."

"Curtains and decorations?"

"I'm in trouble because I let her waste time decorating the house. But it was impossible to warn her, I did not know Captain Stoddart would offer to exchange houses. And as for the curtains, if they are a little bit short, she can add a bit to the bottom."

"Is there anything I can do to help?"

"*Ja*, there is," said the Captain in a heavy voice. "Help me clean and move our things tomorrow."

"Alright," I said, "I'll meet you at the house after morning roll call.

W.E. Hamilton

November 1915
German Submarine Sinks French Troopship SS Le Calvados off Coast of Algeria Killing 740 of 800 Aboard

Moving Day

In the garden of the guard's house was a large fountain with a cupid in the centre of it. I gazed at the cupid while I waited for the Captain to unlock the door.

"A rather odd choice for a prison's fountain," I said, giving it one last glance as the captain pushed the door open.

"No stranger than the picket fence the armed sentries stand by."

"True," I said with a laugh.

"*Ach komm schon*," words of irritation burst from the captain as he stepped inside. "They haven't taken everything out!"

I squeezed in behind him and looked at the cluttered room. Spread over the long table and desks were crockery, office equipment, files, paperwork, and a portable telephone. "This is obviously where the soldiers ate and worked," I picked up an

The Spot The War Forgot

old apple core and threw it out the door.

Captain Hurtzig stepped into a second bigger room with a fireplace and a nice bay window. "At least this one is empty." He banged the heel of his boot on the wooden floor and a hole appeared. "Dry-rot," he said frowning. "We will have to fix the floor before shifting in."

"The Home Help Squad could rip up the floorboards and replace them while we clear and clean the other room," I said, "some of the gang are at Billy's house this morning."

Captain Hurtzig's face changed from a frown to a smile. "Good idea. Run and get them while I start moving this stuff out."

The 'Home Help Squad' (as we were nicknamed) were the junior men of the NGL line. It was our job to help the families in any way we could, especially when they first moved in. There were eight of us Michael, Billy, Hermann, Euringer, Bahr, Mahler, Carstens, and me. It did not take long to run to Billy's house for it was only a short distance up the road and around the corner. As I expected, Michael, Hermann, and Ernst were having coffee with Billy when I arrived.

"The Hurtzig's need help, the floor in one of the rooms is rotten and needs replacing."

"Give us a few minutes to finish our coffee, then we will collect our tools and be there," said Billy.

I nodded and sped off. "They're coming," I said to the captain.

For the next few hours, he and I ferried things between each house, while the Home Help Squad replaced the rotten floorboards with better ones scavenged from a ruined cottage. When all the guard's stuff was in the stone house, and all the

W.E. Hamilton

Hurtzigs household goods were stacked by the cupid fountain, the captain and I started cleaning. He scrubbed the walls, windows, floor, and doors with soapy water, while I rinsed them off. Of Frau Hurtzig there was no sign as she had stayed behind supervising until the last things had been moved. Then together with a jug and lamp under each arm, she picked up a birthday cake and walked the short distance to the new house.

"Such a sight," she said, looking around in dismay. "What a day for Hanna's birthday. Wherever am I going to put this cake? There's nowhere clean enough to set it down."

"Put it in the meat safe under the trees, *Liebling*, it is empty."

"*Ja*, it will have to do for the meantime." She disappeared and came back empty-handed. "I told the girls to play outside," she said, tying on an apron and rolling up her sleeves. She inspected our work closely. "We will have to wash the walls, windows, and floor, a second time, the grime is ingrained." She picked a brush from a bucket of soapy water and started scrubbing at the smeary windowpane. "I hope I never have to clean up after a mob of soldiers again."

We scrubbed and rubbed and swept, while the others wrenched and sawed and banged. The room was almost clean and the floor was finished, when suddenly shrill screams ripped through the air and both girls came running in from the garden. Hanna had blood streaming into her eyes, over her nose, and into her mouth, from a cut on her temple, and Lore had a big lump on her head.

"What has happened?" said Frau Hurtzig, rushing to them in alarm. "Where is your handkerchief, August?"

Captain Hurtzig pulled a pad of fabric from his pocket and handed it to his wife, who used it to staunch the bleeding on

The Spot The War Forgot

Hanna's head. The child quietened as her mother pressed the hanky to her wound but Lore who was not so hurt screamed all the louder.

"Hush *liebling*," said her father lifting her up and rocking her. "Hush, it is alright."

"What happened?" repeated Frau Hurtzig.

"We were running around the fountain," said Hanna, calming into sniffs and little hick-ups, "when suddenly the fountain toppled over. The basin hit Lore, and cupid's arrow hit my head when he fell on me."

"What luck nothing worse happened," said Frau Hurtzig, gathering her daughter close. "The cut is deep but not extensive. Promise me, children, you won't run around the fountain anymore."

Both girls nodded and said, "I promise Mama."

"Bring in the sofa, Gust, and the girls can have a little lie down once I've taken care of their wounds."

I followed Captain Hurtzig outside (because carrying the sofa was a two-man job.)

"Put it over there," said Frau Hurtzig, pointing to the cleanest corner of the room as she finished bandaging Hanna's head. "Lie down girls and have a rest before Gertrude comes around for afternoon tea."

Now the crisis was over, the captain and I swept the floor and began bringing in the rest of the furniture.

"Would you like us to build a stove in the fireplace, Frau Hurtzig?" said Billy.

"For sure, that would be wonderful. It is quite marvellous what you men can do with a few bricks and iron," said Frau Hurtzig, nodding vigorously. "Will the metal bars and sheet of iron that Herr Jertrum and Herr Pahren used to make the stove in the stone house, fit this fireplace?"

"We can adapt it to make it work," said Michael, picking up a metal bar and some wire I had just brought inside.

They busied themselves with intricacies involving three roasting-bars, an oven, and a firebox with a sliding door, and by the time Frau Brauns and Gertrude called with curtains for Frau Hurtzig, and chocolates, plums, and radishes, for the birthday girl, it was done. Then Frau Hurtzig made coffee on her new stove, and after lighting the candles on the cake and singing happy birthday, the three girls had an afternoon tea party on the veranda while the women fussed around with curtains. Captain Hurtzig was hanging a large map on one of the marred walls in the front room when the evening bugle sounded.

"Ten more minutes, my love, how do you want me to spend it? Do you want me to move the furniture or hang the blanket and the Lloyd flag?"

Frau Hurtzig tilted her head to one side as she considered the effect of the map on the wall. "That map has made a huge difference. "Hang the blanket and flag, for the graffiti and discoloured patches are unsightly. I can get the girls to help move things around if I need to."

While he hung the flag, the Home Help Squad packed up their tools and we said goodbye. Partway down the path, I stopped beside the fallen fountain.

"Go on ahead fellas, don't wait for me, I have a little job to do."

"Alright, Wolfie, we will see you soon."

As they continued down the path and turned towards the

The Spot The War Forgot

jail I bent down and lifted the basin of the fountain and set it firmly back on its pedestal.

"I don't think you need to go back, fatty," I said to the cupid. I was about to put him in the bushes when Annie's daughter wandered past and we exchanged smiles. I watched her until she turned the corner and disappeared. "A man who lives in a camp of three-hundred men needs all the help he can get," I said to Cupid. And I put him back in the centre of the fountain facing the lolly shop.

W.E. Hamilton

December 1915
British Indian Forces Under Major-General Charles Townshend arrive at Kut on the Tigris

The Day Before Christmas

On the twenty-fourth of December, there were no signs of Christmas preparations in the village (other than crowds at the Hotel) because in 1915 the Australian's way of celebrating anything was bonfires and booze. As it was summer and scorching hot, the risk of bushfires reduced the festivities to booze and brawls. Therefore, the sight of a Christmas tree peeping from the window of the Hurtzig's house was homely and comforting. And it was not just me who felt that way. Almost everyone who walked past, found themselves treading reverently up the path and knocking on the door in the hopes of getting a closer look at the tree. Frau Hurtzig took it all in her stride and welcomed internees, guards, and villagers, without prejudice.

The Spot The War Forgot

"*Komm herein*," she said, as I knocked on the door. "I suppose you want to see the tree?"

I nodded, wiped my boots on the doormat, and trod carefully over to the tree in the bay window.

"Papa got the tree from the bush, and we planted it in a kerosene tin," said Lore. "Then Mama covered the tin with a sheet."

"It is very beautiful," I said.

"I helped Papa wire the candles on," said Hanna. "Usually, we have glass balls hanging on our Christmas tree and a pretty angel at the top, but we had to make do with biscuits, apples, and lollies this year."

"It is every bit as lovely as a tree with glass balls and an angel," I said, truthfully. "In fact, I like it better because you can't eat glass balls or angels."

Hanna and Lore giggled.

"Grandma sent us stockings and boxes of bonbons. And Auntie sent nuts and a Christmas cake. Did your Mama send you anything for Christmas, Uncle Wolfgang?"

"*Ja*, she and Papa sent me socks and cigars, and my sister sent me Moby Dick."

"I'm telling the Christmas story at the concert tonight, and Lore is going to recite a bible verse," said Hanna.

"And we are going to have a really rich Christmas dinner," said Lore, licking her lips. "Eggs and sardines, and rice with radishes, and…" she leaned forward and whispered, "Mama has bought Papa a bottle of real beer, but don't tell him because it is a surprise."

"I promise I won't," I whispered back.

There was a knock on the door and there stood Annie.

Without her blue and red striped butcher's-apron, her girth looked even larger.

Frau Hurtzig's face lit up and she hugged her.

"So lovely to see you, Annie. *Frohe Weihnachten.*"

"Merry Christmas to you too, Luise." Annie's big beefy arms reached back and she drew two small children from behind her tent-sized skirt. "Can these littlees look at your tree?"

"Of course," said Frau Hurtzig, ushering them in."

The children tiptoed shyly to the tree, their eyes wide with wonder while Annie wobbled behind them.

"Ah, it does my heart good to see a Christmas tree," she said, wiping a tear from her eye. "It takes me back to my childhood."

"Hello Annie," I said. "Who are the children?"

"Oh, hello Wolfgang," I was so busy looking at the tree I didn't see you there. They are my neighbour's children. I saw them standing by the gate so I brought them in."

"That's our Annie," I smiled. "We should call you Big Heart."

"Oh, go on with you," said Annie, looking pleased and giving me a hearty thump on the shoulder. "Big Waist, is more like it."

"Nien, I got it right the first time," I said, laughing.

Through the window, I saw people coming down the path, and not wanting to overcrowd the room I said: "*Danka* for letting me see the tree, Frau Hurtzig. Have a nice Christmas, Annie, and give my regards to your family." And with that, I bowed, put on my hat and went back to the jail.

In the assembly yard, men bustled about preparing for the

The Spot The War Forgot

Christmas Eve concert. Other than a coat of whitewash on the walls, the stage hadn't changed much, but the bleachers they were hastily installing, were a big improvement.

"Do you need any help?" I called to the man in charge of putting them together.

"*Nein*," he said, "if I have any more help, we will trip over each other." He jerked his thumb toward a man carrying a stack of folding chairs. "You could help Captain Pharen with the chairs for the guests."

"Righto." I moved towards the stage and picked up a chair. "Where do you want them, Captain?"

"In a long row right along the front." He dropped his load beside several other piles of chairs and wiped his perspiring face. "There, that should be enough."

"How many chairs do we need?"

"Just enough for the commandant and his wife, plus the married internees and their families."

I counted on my fingers. "That's two, pus four Hurtzigs, three Bruans, two Wallners, two Jepsens, and Herr and Frau Glintz (the baby doesn't count.) Have I forgotten anyone?"

"Fifteen, hmm," Captain Pharen's nose scrunched up as he thought. "I think that's them all. Put out a few extra seats just in case we have forgotten someone or the commandant brings extra guests."

"I'm looking forward to sitting rather than standing through the play tonight," I said, "as I opened the folding chair and set it in front of the bleachers.

The Captain put a chair next to mine. "Not as much as I am, your legs are young. The items the theatre put on in its early days were alright because they were short." He lifted a flattened chair off the pile closest to the stage and flicked it open. "Ten minutes at most for a poetry reading, skit or song. But as their productions have become more ambitious, it's been tough on my knees. I don't know if I could have stood through tonight's play."

I opened another chair and put it down next to the Captain's chair. "Even young legs would ache at the end of tonight if we had to stand," I said, turning back to the pile. "'*A Springtime of Love*' is a full-scale play. I've had a sneak preview, and tonight will be their best performance yet."

"I am certainly looking forward to it," said the Captain, pulling the chairs straight.

I placed my next chair at the end of the row, and the captain put one next to mine, and we continued in this manner until we were finished.

"There!" I said, straightening the last chair. "Is there anything else you want help with?"

"No, we are all done here, but you could go to the courthouse, they might still need a hand setting up the banqueting hall."

Like the prison yard, the courthouse was abuzz with activity when I got there. A horde of men were stringing masses of fur and eucalyptus branches all over the walls.

"You and young Bartel can set up the tables," said Captain Kulkhen, waving me over to trestles and boards leaning against the wall.

"How do you want them laid out?"

"Oh, I don't know, just juggle them around so that we can seat about a hundred-and-fifty. That's the number we are expecting for Christmas dinner tomorrow."

"You must be Bartel," I said, as a young man picked up a

The Spot The War Forgot

trestle. "I'm Wolfgang Schmitt."

"Heinrich Bartel pleased to meet you." He put the trestle down and held out his hand.

"What ship were you on?" I said as we shook hands.

"I was a junior officer on the Stolzenfels."

"The Hansa steamer?"

"*Ja*. What about you?"

Bartel picked up two trestles while I grabbed a couple of wide boards, and together we walked to the middle of the room.

"Ordinary seaman on the Pfalz. Captain Kühlken was the captain."

"What line?"

"NGL."

Bartel nodded. "I think I read of it in the papers. Didn't you draw the British Empires first shot? Or was it just Australia's first shot?"

"It depends on which history book you read."

"Perhaps we could put three lines of tables across here, parallel with the judge's bench," said Bartel, switching his attention back to the job on hand.

"We can get two along here, but three will be too much of a squeeze."

"Hmm, you're right." Bartel hooked his thumb under his chin rubbed his nose with his index finger. "What about turning the third line of tables on a right-angle?"

"And put it at the end of the other tables, in a sort of horseshoe? That would work."

We set to and soon had them laid out to our satisfaction.

"As soon as the men have brought in all the wattle flowers, spread these over the tables," said the captain, handing us each a stack of white sheets."

"Why can't we put them on now?"

The captain pointed at a man carrying in a huge armful of fluffy yellow blooms. "I don't want pollen all over the sheets. Wait until they've put them all on the magistrate's bench."

"What do you mean by it depends which history book," said Bartel, returning to our former conversation, as he leaned against the wall leisurely?

"There is a dispute over it," I said, my face going red. "Either way I was captured within the first three hours of war breaking out."

"It's not your fault. It's the old story of being at the wrong place at the wrong time. Most of us are here through inglorious circumstances."

"Not the Emden men."

"True, but there's only a handful of them."

"All the wattle flowers are in," shouted Captain Kühlken, breaking up our conversation, "you boys can set the tables now." He pointed to the witness-stand where posies of flowers sat in jam jars. "Table decorations over there, and salt and pepper shakers are on the juror's benches. And when you've finished, I need your help with the clean-up," he added, pointing to the carpet of foliage strewn about.

"Yes sir," we said, and walking back to the tables we started spreading the sheets over them.

With so much to do the hours flew and the evening came upon us quickly. At 8:30 pm, five husbands stood close to the entrance of the gatehouse, waiting to escort their wives into the prison. It was a big moment for us because this was the first time females had entered the walls of the jail. Finally, at the

The Spot The War Forgot

commandant's command, the iron gates swung open. Every head turned towards the archway as five ladies, three children, and a baby carriage passed into the yard.

"Guten abend, ladies," I said, tipping my hat, as they walked by me.

"Ah, Wolfgang, this is wunderbar," said Frau Hurtzig, beaming. "So many friendly German faces, some known, and some not yet known."

"This certainly is marvellous," said Frau Jepsen.

Ten-year-old Gertrude pulled on her mother's hand. "Look Mamma a real stage," she said, her eyes growing wide. Even Frau Glintz was in a mellow mood. She followed her husband to a chair without fussing and parked the baby carriage beside it. Frau Wallner sat in the next seat. When Frau Jepsen saw this, she stopped walking and turned to Frau Hurtzig.

"I'm not sitting next to her," she hissed, "it's not fitting that a Captain's wife should sit with the wife of a third officer. You go next, for you can put the children between her and you."

"*Ach komm schon*, don't be like that!" whispered Frau Hurtzig. "It is Christmas, and we are aliens in a foreign land. We must put aside pettiness and band together."

"Well then, you sit next to her," said Frau Jepsen with a small sniff.,"seeing as you are willing to mix with the riffraff."

"Aright, I will! Come children, follow me. And with that, she marched over to Frau Wallner and sat in the seat next to her.

Captain Hurtzig and Captain Jepsen, looking at each other, shrugged their shoulders and rolled their eyes before following their wives. Once the guests of honour were seated, the rest of us sat down, oozing excited anticipation. The night was still and the stars above twinkled as the curtain on the stage parted to reveal a tall Christmas tree lit with many candles. In the quiet hush Lore's shrill voice rang out:

"Look Mamma, a Christmas tree, it's even bigger than our one in the kerosene tin."

When the laughter died down, we sang 'O Tannenbaum' and Herr Pahnke gave a short speech.

"This is the bit I'm waiting for," I whispered, as Father Christmas came on the stage carrying a large red bag.

"Why?" said Hermann.

"I helped make the second pram and I want to see the girl's faces when they see them."

"Come children, come over here," said Father Christmas, sitting on the edge of the stage. "Let me see what's in my bag for you?"

Gertrude stepped forward shyly and Hanna, holding Lore's hand followed, while Frau Glintz carried baby Ursula to the stage.

Father Christmas rummaged in his bag, and pulling out a rag doll, handed it to Herr Pahnke. "Here you go Gertrude," said Herr Pahnke, handing it to her. "Merry Christmas."

Father Christmas felt in his lumpy bag once more and pulled out two doll's prams.

"A pink pram for Hanna and a blue pram for Lore," said Herr Pahnke, wheeling them to the girls.

Lore squealed with excitement, but Hanna flushed red with pleasure and remembering her manners said: "Thank you."

"I'm so glad they like their prams," I whispered to Michael.

But Santa was not finished yet. He put his hand into his floppy bag once more. It did not look as if there was anything

The Spot The War Forgot

in it, but to our surprise, he pulled out a small shank surrounded by wooden rings.

"And a rattle for Ursula to cut her teeth on," he said, handing the gizmo to her mother.

At this, the woodturner's club burst into rowdy whistling and clapping.

"It took several tries to make that," whispered Billy. "Captain Jertrum told me it's made from a single piece of wood and the rings were tricky to carve." As he spoke, the curtain squeaked shut in jerky bursts, and Father Christmas and the tree disappeared.

Once the children and Frau Glintz were seated again, Herr Pahnke spoke a few more words, and when he finished the cook carried in a huge cake. Then there was supper for everyone who wasn't in the play."

"Save me a piece, Wolfie," Billy called over his shoulder as he rushed off, "I've got to get into my costume."

"Alright," I nodded, taking two slices off the plate as it came past.

The small orchestra took their places and tuned up as we mingled and chatted. When they were ready, Herr Pahnke quietened us down and the curtain parted once more.

'The Springtime of Love' was a super play.

"The best so far," I said when we discussed it afterwards.

"For sure," said the others, nodding.

"And the orchestra gave a good performance."

"Absolutely marvellous," said Frau Hurtzig. "I almost cried when we sang Silent Night at the end, it moved me deeply it was so beautiful. And the dolls prams are wonderful. Did you know about them, Gust?"

"I not only knew about them, but I also made the pink one," said the Captain, hitching up Lore who was draped over his shoulder, sleeping.

"And I helped with the blue one," I said.

"Thank you so much," said Frau Hurtzig, "the girls will have endless fun with them."

A guard holding a lantern moved through the throng towards us. "It is past midnight and the other ladies have gone," said the officer, picking up the doll's prams by their handles, "I am here to escort you home Mrs Hurtzig."

"She nodded, and the Captain (without waking Lore) gently transferred her to his wife. Frau Hurtzig settled her slumbering daughter on her right hip, and, Hanna (almost asleep on her feet) leant against her mother's left side. We walked with them to the big iron gates that swung open when they approached. Frau Hurtzig twisted slightly and waved, as the gates slowly closed behind her.

"*Frohe Weihnachten*, happy Christmas. I will see you tomorrow morning, Gust," she said. Then with Hanna stumbling beside her, she followed the soldier who carried a lamp in one hand, and two doll's prams in the other.

The Spot The War Forgot

December 1915
HMHS Britannic Departs Liverpool on her Maiden Voyage as Hospital Ship

The Battle of Pooh

Some of the men blamed the captains who ran away for our horrible awful Christmas, but most of us blamed the new Commandant. Apart from feeling a little melancholy that Christmas had come and the war was not yet over, we had no inkling of the hideous time about to befall us. We awoke anticipating a pleasant day. The first sign of trouble was when the gates did not open immediately after rollcall. Instead, the Commandant announced:

"All privileges are revoked and you are confined to the prison until the two runaways return voluntarily or are brought back under guard. If anyone has any information, come and see me. Dismissed."

Immediately a great noise of grumbling and dissatisfaction arose as the mood in the prison changed from happiness to anger. The married men moved towards us and clustered around Captain Hurtzig.

"Perhaps they will return before the banquet," Captain Hurtzig, said, with a sigh.

"Don't count on it," said Captain Jepsen. "They left during the concert last night when the guards weren't looking. They'll have friends or family in Sydney and want to spend Christmas with them."

"They could have spared a thought for us," said Billy. "While they are living it up, our Christmas is cancelled. What a waste of time turning the courtroom into a banqueting hall yesterday."

"What about my family?" said Captain Hurtzig, rubbing his hand across his forehead. "Lulu will have cooked a special breakfast. She is expecting me at 7:30. When I don't show up, she and the girls will wonder what's happened."

"My life will not be worth living if I ruin Christmas day," said Herr Glintz.

"Perhaps they might let us out for a few minutes to explain things to our wives, and children," said Herr Brauns.

"We could promise to return as soon as we told them the news," said Herr Wallner.

The men nodded.

"It's worth trying," said Captain Jepsen. "Let's ask the guard by the gate, the worst he can say is, *nein*."

Unfortunately, no, was exactly what he said.

"Your wives know how to get information."

"Couldn't you bend the rules a little on Christmas day?" said Captain Hurtzig. My wife and children will be so disappointed."

"I am sorry, Captain," said the guard, his face softening, "I

The Spot The War Forgot

have my orders." He lowered his voice. "You could try asking the Commandant, but I warn you, this new commandant is not like Captain Stoddart. I doubt you will have much luck."

He was quite right. The men asked but the answer was, "NO."

"I suppose our wives will come to the gate when we don't show up," said Captain Hurtzig, sighing.

"I do not envy the man who tells my wife I will not be home for the Christmas dinner she has cooked," said Herr Glintz, with grim satisfaction. "I expect we will hear her scolding him from here."

And so we did. Around nine in the morning we heard a commotion on the other side of the wall by the gates.

"All leave has been stopped until the two men who have gone missing return voluntarily or are brought back," said the guard, in an unemotional tone.

"WHAT!" Frau Glintz's voice was unmistakable.

The guard foolishly repeated his words. Then Frau Glintz let rip in a way that was truly masterful. Herr Glintz puffed out his chest and basked in our admiration. The sheer volume and intensity of the rage his wife shot at the guard was soothing to our angry feelings. At last, Frau Glintz ran out of words, and the disappointed women and children drifted home.

Christmas dinner was meagre.

"I don't blame the cooks," I said, looking at the tiny portion of ham and potatoes on my plate, "they didn't expect to have to cater for the married men or those with houses."

"It is not their fault," Billy nodded, "this was sprung on them, just like it was sprung on us. I hope they let us out soon, the turkey I brought from Annie yesterday, will go off quickly in this heat."

"Lots of us with huts were going to eat outdoors too," said Herman. "My steak will go off in this weather if it is not cooked soon. I was going to barbeque it the Australian way."

After the skimpy lunch, the day dragged on. The highlight was when the women were allowed to send parcels of clean clothing and food to their husbands. (Big deal!) Captain Hurtzig shared his cake and turkey with us but it was little consolation, and every irritation was made worse by our disappointed expectations. We had a boring evening and went to bed angry. Our mood worsened on Boxing Day when the commandant confined us for a second day.

"As a special concession," said the Commandant at morning rollcall, "Hurtzig, Jepsen, Glintz, Wallner, and Brauns, are permitted to go out for an hour to chop wood for their wives. Provided they go with a guard. Dismissed."

Monday was no better for us, and scarcely better for the married men; they were allowed out to see their families but had to stay in the house.

"Life stinks," I grumbled, as we milled about the yard after rollcall.

"Life is not the only thing stinking," said Michael, kicking a stone. "I can smell the pit toilets wherever I go."

"*Ja*, they are very full," said Billy, "they are designed for half the number of men here. If they don't let us out soon, I fear they will overflow."

As the day wore on the latrines rose higher, while our morale dropped lower. I don't know who came up with the idea of using the huge pile of empty jam tins to solve both problems, but the idea of pooh-grenades caught on like wildfire.

The Spot The War Forgot

"Make sure you throw it high enough, Wolfgang," said Michael, as I stood beside the prison wall holding my can of 'business' gingerly. "One fellow's pooh-grenade hit the top of the wall and all its contents bounced back at him."

A volley of swearing arose from the other side of the wall, and the men lobbing pooh-grenades over the south side of the prison cheered and yahooed.

"They must have hit a guard or the cabbage patch," Hermann said with satisfaction.

"Perhaps I should throw mine into the guard's place also?"

"We have enough stuff going in there," said Billy. "It will be more effective if we mess up the village."

"I wouldn't like to hit Frauline Ada," I said, hearing a bicycle rattle along the street."

"That would be bad. Wait a few moments until she's gone. I can hear a man coming."

"If we are lucky, it is Henry Allen," I said, smiling. I waited until the sound of the bicycle faded, and the tread of heavy boots was directly over the wall, then I pulled back my arm and let fly. Almost immediately I heard a roar of fury, followed by several more roars, and a shrill scream, as men rushed over and threw their grenades in the direction of the commotion. "Oh dear, that was a frauline."

"Ah well, it can't be helped, said Hermann, matter-of-factly, "we can't see what we are doing so hitting the wrong person is bound to happen sometimes."

"Besides," said Billy. "Women make more fuss, which will work in our favour."

"*Ja*," Michael smiled. "For sure, the Commandant is getting complaints."

All-day we lobbed pooh-grenades over the wall and the next day the disgusting fountain continued spraying into the streets.

"I feel I have finally joined the army and we are at war," I said, drinking an enormous bottle of water. "I just wish I could throw further."

"Don't worry, some of the engineers are working on a giant slingshot," said Billy.

"I don't think we will need to continue for long," said Hermann. "Henry Allen won't put up with this."

And he was right. Even as we spoke a letter of complaint was on its way to Major Sands who was in charge of all the German Concentration Camps.

We won the Battle of Pooh by Wednesday. The Commandant (under increasing pressure) let us out and only the captains remained locked up.

"Why won't they let them out?" said Frau Hurtzig, when we told her the bad news.

"The men who escaped were of the same rank," said Michael.

"It is unjust to punish the innocent with the guilty." She tossed her head. "Besides, the men who ran away were not real captains, they only commanded small boats that shuttled between the islands!"

"Perhaps it's because they didn't stop us throwing pooh," I said, "the commandant knows we won't defy their orders."

"*Nein*, it is because that new Commandant is a bully who just likes to throw his weight around," said Hermann. "He has ruined our Christmas. We were stuck inside while the villagers played on our Grand Slippery Slide, and dived off

The Spot The War Forgot

our springboards."

"He will ruin New Year's Day just for spite," I growled. "Why should the villagers play with our things while we are locked up?"

I was not the only one feeling this way. In the general mood of disappointment and anger, bitterness and paranoia flourished. Even the arrival of Major Sands from Holsworthy did not dispel the mood. Although his address to us was friendly, and he restored privileges to everyone, we still felt hard done by. The idea the Commandant would destroy New Year's Day by now had such a hold on us, the first thing we did after Major Sands left, was chop down our springboards.

"There, that will stop Henry Allen and his friends diving while we can't," said Billy, kicking the last plank off a tall rock.

Captain Hurtzig, shook his head. "I don't think this is the way to go about things. Lulu thinks we should make an official complaint about the Commandant, and she is right. Although he could not admit it, Major Sands is on our side over this whole sorry affair. I shall talk to the Camp Committee about the idea."

The Camp Committee agreed so letters of complaint were sent to the Department of Justice, and the Department of Defence. The result was a conciliator was sent from Sydney who ruled in our favour.

"Did you hear the news?" said Billy, heaving planks up onto a tall rock in the New Year, "the Commandant is being sent to the European Front."

"I am not sad," said Michael, pushing a board out over the water below.

W.E. Hamilton

"We may have no part in the war," I said, as we rebuilt the springboards, "but we won The Battle of Pooh."

The Spot The War Forgot

January 1916
Gallipoli Evacuation is Completed

The Fight

The weather was oppressively hot on the evening of the big fight. Heavy clouds gathered overhead bringing thunder and lightning, but nothing to fill the water tank, or cool the heat. The collective mood as we milled about the yard after rollcall matched the weather; depressed by the slowness of the war, and disappointed over our ruined Christmas, repressed anger rumbled in every heart, and spurts of temper flared at the least provocation. Herman was madder than anyone. He cracked his knuckles and slammed his fist into his hand.

"I'd like to get my hands on the runaway captains. Because of them, I missed seeing Maria. The day after Boxing Day was the only day she could come. We planned to have a picnic in the woods."

"You are not the only one who would like to punch them," I said. "There isn't a man here who wouldn't find relief in taking his frustrations out on them."

W.E. Hamilton

"I heard a rumour they have been caught," said Michael, "but we won't have the pleasure of teaching them a lesson because the guards aren't foolish enough to put them back in here."

But he was wrong. The words were barely out of his mouth when the key rattled in the lock and guards pushed two men inside the prison before pulling the gates shut, and locking them again. The newcomers sidled around the edge of the wall, shooting furtive glances at the brooding crowd. For a few minutes, nothing happened, but when we realized it was the runaways, Hermann and several other hotheaded men rushed at them, their arms flailing with more passion than skill.

Hermann pounded on one man's chest.

Michael was punched in the face.

Then someone gave a right hook to someone else, and that was it. The whole yard exploded into action as we struggled with one another.

One man was kicked in the face.

Two men pulled him to his feet only to punch him down again.

A bench was knocked over, and a lantern smashed.

I punched the man on my right and hit the man on my left. Blood was in my mouth from a blow to my nose and I heard the faint screech of my shirt ripping. I did not care who I was fighting, or why I was fighting because it felt good.

The gunshot brought us to our senses. Nobody was wounded unless of course, you count the bruise on Captain Altneppen's head made by the rubber bullet when it fell from the sky.

"Everyone is confined to the barracks until further notice," shouted the Commandant, holding his smoking gun. He jerked

The Spot The War Forgot

his head towards the runaway captains. "Guards, put these two men into solitary confinement for the night."

We shuffled towards the barracks as a semicircle of armed guards pressed against us.

I heard later from Hanna, they let the runaways out of solitary confinement the next day. She saw them walking in the yard barefooted and hatless when she talked to one of the guards through the iron grill. I suppose they took their hats and shoes to discourage them from escaping again. Whatever the reason, guards came in a car for them at three in the afternoon and took them off to Liverpool. Once they were gone, we were let out.

"I suppose they are banished to Holsworthy," I said.

"Serve them right if they are," said Hermann. "They caused a lot of trouble. I'm glad I gave him a few good punches."

As he spoke, spits of rain splattered on the ground like spots on a Dalmatian dog and a breeze blew the oppressive heat away. My mood lifted and my head cleared as the air-cooled. I knew the spits would not turn into rain. It would be hot again tomorrow, and tempers would rise with the heat, but there was enough time for a long swim before the bugle call, and right now, that was all that mattered.

"Come on," I said, "let's ride the Grand Slippery Slide."

And forgetting the dreadful war, and our awful Christmas, we strode off to the river, whistling as we went."

W.E. Hamilton

January 1916
Cettinje Falls

Blackberries and a Good Idea

Rumours of raging bushfires had reached us, but although the days were scorching and the vegetation tinder-dry, there was no sign of fire in Berrima. The sky was blue and magpies warbled as Heinrich Bartel, Hugo Bahl, and I walked towards the school. Like the courthouse and the jail, the school was built of sandstone. Although it was merely one room, it was a large substantial room. So large it dwarfed the schoolmaster's wooden cottage, which stuck out from the school's side as if it were an odd afterthought. We could hear the children chanting their history lesson in sing-song voices as we wandered past.

Charles the second born in
sixteen-hundred-and-thirty,
died in sixteen-hundred-and eighty-five.

The Spot The War Forgot

Here lies our sovereign lord and king,
Whose word no man relies on:
Who never said a foolish thing,
And never did a wise one.

"If Germany had such a king, I would rather keep it quiet, than teach such silly rhymes to children," said Hugo.

"Germany could never have a foolish king!" I was shocked by the idea.

Heinrich said nothing, for his mind was on more important things. "I hope the school kids haven't picked all the blackberries," he said, swinging his bucket as he squinted into the distance.

"They will have only picked the ones around the sides of the bramble bush," said Hugo, taking a firmer grip on the plank he carried in his other hand. "Once we get on top, they will be thick."

Heinrich's shoulders slumped and the end of his board dragged in the dirt behind him. "Unless the birds have got them first."

I swapped the ladder in my left hand to my shoulder and jerked my bucket towards the school's corral. "Shall we cut through the horse paddock or go the long way around?"

Heinrich eyed a huge gelding dubiously. "Go around, the ponies look aright, but I don't trust that big brute. He's got piggy eyes."

"Those children have a tough life," said Hugo looking back at the school, "some of them live more than ten miles away. That is a long distance for a young child to ride." He sighed. "And then when they get there, what are they learning? That sour old prune, Packer, is not much of a teacher."

"You seem very informed, how do you know all this?"

"Annie, of course."

"Of course," we laughed. "She is a mine of information."

"Do you know, students have to stay in school until they are eighteen, unless they pass the Qualifying Certificate examination, and the test is very rigorous?"

"Isn't that a good thing? Education is important," I said, as we skirted the horse corral.

"*Ja*, of course, it is. It's designed to equip the poor for the city workforce, but some of those big strapping boys are eager for farm work. They have no interest in algebra or nouns, and what's more, they don't need it. Do cattle care about poetry or trigonometry?"

"I guess not. Why the sudden interest in schooling?"

Hugo puffed out his chest. "Wolfgang, when you become a father you see the world differently. I'm interested in all sorts of things I once considered boring."

I knew he wanted me to ask about his family so I said: "How is your son getting on?"

Hugo beamed and his face lit up. "I got a picture of him yesterday." Without halting, he swapped his bucket into his left hand and hitched the plank into the crook of his arm. "Look at him, isn't he a fine boy?" he said, fishing a photograph from his pocket and holding it out. "Only a year old and already walking."

"Remarkable," I said politely.

"Much more handsome than Lieutenant Dibb's son," said Heinrich, glancing at the photo. He climbed over a stile into a neglected field. "That child is a horror."

The Spot The War Forgot

"He is dreadful," I agreed, shuddering.

"Not everyone can be good looking," said Hugo generously. "The poor child doesn't have the advantage of German bloodlines." Suddenly the proud look disappeared from his face and his mouth settled into grim lines as he tucked the photo away. "But he does have the advantage of being with his father. My first child," he shook his head slowly, "and my only contact is a photograph. How long will this war go on? Will his whole childhood slip away before I get back?"

"And when it is over, will there still be work for us?" said Heinrich.

My eyes flew open as I swung my leg over the fence. "No work!"

"Well, think about it. No matter who wins the war there will be a great deal fewer ships, Hugo will be alright, for he captained the Pontoporros…"

"Only for a short time and it was a field promotion," broke in Hugo.

"That's long enough, but juniors like you and me, Wolfgang, won't be able to compete with more experienced sailors. I think we ought to consider an alternative line of work."

"What kind of work?"

"I don't know yet."

By now we had reached the blackberry patch. The impenetrable thicket of thorny vines stood ten to twelve feet high and spread over a large area.

"There could be a house hidden in the middle of this bush and you would never know," I said, putting my bucket down and leaning my ladder against the wall of brambles.

Hugo put his bucket and plank on the ground, and taking

two lengths of twine from his pocket, tied the loose ends of his trousers close to his ankles. "I could do with my good boots but, instead, they are rotting on the bottom of the sea."

I popped a fat berry into my mouth, "Never mind, the blackberries are perfect and there are plenty of them." I started filling my bucket with the easy-to-reach berries while Hugo climbed the ladder. When he got to the top Heinrich passed both boards up to him.

"How do they look up there, Hugo?"

"Excellent, we should have brought two buckets each."

"We can always come back," I said, "although, there is a limit to how many blackberries we can eat."

"They would make nice pies," said Heinrich. "I saw a book in the library on the art of pastry cooking. It had a recipe for apple streusel. I bet it has a recipe for blackberry pie."

"Apple streusel!" I shut my eyes to visualize it better. "Mmm, I would give anything for a bite of apple streusel."

"Really?" A gleam entered Heinrich's eyes. "Would you buy one if you could?"

"Of course. I would pay three times its normal price. If only I could get my hands on one."

"That's it!" cried Heinrich, "I shall become a pastry cook." His face suddenly fell. "Well, I could if I had an oven."

"That is not a problem," said Hugo, dropping a board onto the crown of the bush. "Have you seen inside my log cabin?

"No."

"Then you must come one day."

"It's like a cosy little house," I said. "It has bright cretonne curtains, a table and chairs, and a bookcase. There are even a laundry and an outhouse behind it."

The Spot The War Forgot

"That's all very nice, but how does that help with my problem?"

"I have a brick oven that works well," said Hugo, picking up the second board before mincing gingerly along the plank. "Some of the engineers helped me build it and they would help you build one too if you asked them."

"Hmm, that could work," said Heinrich, climbing up the ladder. He stepped on the first board as Hugo dropped the second plank down.

"Easy does it," Hugo muttered, inching across the thicket. "I wouldn't like to fall into the middle of this thing."

"No," said Heinrich, vaguely. "He also trod carefully, but it was obvious that his mind was elsewhere, for there was a faraway look in his eyes, and he said nothing as he methodically picked berries.

After about an hour our buckets were full.

"That will do," said Hugo, calling a halt, "any more and we will leave a trail of blackberries from here to the jail." He passed his bucket to Heinrich, and (swearing under his breath) picked up the boards before following hm down the ladder. "That's a vicious bush," he said, leaning the planks against it and sucking blood from long scratches on his hands.

"What about kaffee-kutchen?" said Heinrich suddenly. "Would you buy it?"

"For sure, I love coffee cake."

"I'd buy custard tarts," said Hugo, taking his bucket from Heinrich and picking up a plank.

"This has got potential," said Heinrich, grabbing the other plank. "Regardless of who wins the war people will still eat."

"Especially pastries," I said, pulling the ladder away from

the bush before hoisting it onto my shoulder.

We discussed our favourite foods as we wandered down the hill, over the stile, and skirted the horse corral. We were just passing the school when the jingle-jangle of a bell rang out and looking over the low fence, we saw a barefooted girl leisurely hauling on the rope of a large bell suspended on a waist-high frame.

"Such poverty is pitiful," said Hugo. "Look at that poor girl. No shoes or socks and dressed in a horse-feed sack. It must be very itchy against her skin."

"Perhaps she is one of the foster children some of the villagers take in," I said. "Annie reckons quite a few of the poorer families take in children because they come with a government allowance."

"If so, the government needs to take a closer look at the people they hand orphans over to."

"She doesn't look much different to many of the other children," I said, as a swarm of ragged urchins poured from the schoolroom and flooded the playground.

"I'm not sure if that makes it better or worse," said Hugo, with a sigh of compassion.

"Everyone likes chocolate," said Heinrich, (his mind still on cakes and pastries.)

"You have to make Black Forest cake," said Hugo, forgetting the girl as she was swallowed by the throng.

"And chocolate gateau."

"Definitely chocolate gateau. I wonder if I should build more than one oven?"

We discussed the matter in-depth, and by the time we reached the jail, Bartel had decided to launch into the pastry

The Spot The War Forgot

business.

"I shall call it the Berrima Bush Bakery."

Both Hugo and I thought this was a marvellous idea and could not wait for him to get started, for our mouths watered at the thought of real German cakes and pastries. But alas, his plans for building an oven were delayed, for that night the wind blew the bush fire towards us.

W.E. Hamilton

February 1916
Russians Enter Erzerum

Bush Fires

Billy, Michael and I held a bucket in each hand but we were not blackberrying. It was Washing Day and we stood in the queue beside the river looking at the thick brown haze surrounding us.

"I have never seen weather like this before," I said, "the sky has disappeared and the sun looks like a red moon."

"It's eerie," said Michael, letting his washing bag slide to the ground, "even the birds are distressed by it. See how they pant with their beaks open?"

Billy hitched up the coil of rope slung around his shoulder. "It's all the dust particles in the air from the bush fires, you can smell them."

We shuffled forward as I said: "Do you think the fire will get here?"

"Could do if the wind increases, everything is tinder dry and scorching hot. If it keeps blowing this way it will rip through the bush and the only thing that will stop it is heavy rain."

The Spot The War Forgot

I sighed. "That's not likely. We haven't seen a drop of rain since the flood in November. If the water cistern gets much lower, we will have to carry drinking water from Lambie's well."

Michael groaned. "Don't say that, it is bad enough washing our clothes with river water."

By now we had reached the head of the queue, so we filled our buckets and moved to a flat spot under the trees. There, we loosened the drawstrings of our washing bags and tipped the dirty clothes onto the grass.

"I wish the authorities would hurry up and decide to let us construct a second water cistern." I dipped a shirt into the water before rubbing it with soap. "I don't know why they are taking so long to make up their minds, the engineers have come up with a good system for pumping water from the river, and the plans are detailed."

Billy rolled his eyes. "It's not the plans that are the problem, Wolfgang, they have to get approval to spend money on the pump, and piping."

"You forgot about the wood for the big tub," said Michael, scrubbing a pair of white trousers on his washboard. "Not any old wood will do, we can't just take it from the bush like we usually do."

"The engineers say Lieutenant Williams backs the proposal," said Billy, tying his rope between two trees.

"He is a much better commandant than the last one," I said. "I expect he sees the wisdom of the plan."

"For sure," said Billy, slinging wet clothes over his clothesline. "I expect he also likes the idea of installing water closet toilets. He knows about the Battle of Pooh."

Michael and I assembled our clotheslines.

"I suppose the captains will get us to man the pump as if we were at sea," I said.

"It will be worth it," said Michael. "The toilets won't stink and we will have plenty of water for hosing down the buildings and courtyards. Besides, there are so many of us our shift won't come around often."

A sudden wind whooshed up around us sweeping clouds of yellow dust about, and flakes of ash floated past.

"That is a bad sign," said Billy. "If ash can get here cinders could too. The villagers say to watch out for spot fires made by flying cinders."

"William Davis told me he could see the glow of the fire front in the distance last night," said Michael.

"Perhaps the guards will let us up on the observation platform to have a look?"

"You are full of jokes, Wolfgang," said Billy, twisting water from his shirt before rinsing it in his second bucket.

We were almost finished when the sound of the school bell rang out. It was not the leisurely jingle-jangle of the previous day it was fast, furious, and urgent.

I glanced at my watch. "That's strange, it's not lunchtime or morning break. The bell never rings at this time."

The words were scarcely out of my mouth when shouts of, "FIRE, FIRE," came from beyond the jail at the top of the rise.

"The school's on fire," shouted Billy. He dumped his washing out of his bucket, grabbed a wet shirt, and ran down to the river, topping his bucket up with one swift movement. I followed his lead and he, Michael and I, together with a host of other internees, rushed up the hill, soapy water splashing against

The Spot The War Forgot

our legs as we ran. When we got to the part of Oxley street that passed through the main road, we found pandemonium as farmers and villagers and prisoners, converged at the crossroad beneath the school. Together we swarmed up the street, sidestepping ashen-faced mothers hustling small children to safety. In the schoolyard, the older boys rushed about stamping out grass fires, while nearby the horses galloped around and around in their enclosure until the big gelding broke through the fence and they galloped off in a cloud of dust. Thomas Packer, his face red and sweating, battled to save his home. His white shirt was covered in black smuts as he flailed his jacket against the flames leaping up the walls of the schoolhouse. Into this chaos we charged like white knights; over two-hundred men all carrying washing water.

"OVER HERE," someone cried. "SAVE THE SCHOOLHOUSE."

Suddenly urgent activity exploded around me.
Woosh splat and splash,
Water and buckets,
Yells, flying arms and legs.

I leapt over the low fence and hurled water at the flames. Then flinging my bucket away, ripped off my jacket and thwack slap boof stomp stomp, I beat and stamped on the small fires exploding in the dry grass beneath my feet. I did not notice the sweat running down my face, or the ache in my arms. All around me frenzied whacking and stomping continued but I scarcely noticed, my thoughts were fixated on the flames before me, behind me, and to the right and left.

Then, suddenly, it was over. All that remained was blackened ground and wisps of smoke. The schoolhouse had long streaks of soot running up its walls, but that was all.

"That was a close one," I said to Billy, as we picked up our fallen buckets. "If we hadn't been here the house would certainly have been lost."

"For sure. It's a good thing they have a bell."

We hung around for a while to make sure it did not flare up again. While we milled about, Thomas Packer dismissed the remaining children and disappeared into his house. When we were sure the danger was over, we wandered back to the edge of the river and resumed our washing. We had only just pegged clean clothes on the lines when we saw a black plume of smoke rise from the direction of the village.

"I don't like the look of that," Billy said, as he propped long poles under the line and lifted it high.

"It doesn't look good," said Michael.

I was about to agree but my words were cut short by the shouts of "FIRE, FIRE!"

I grabbed a wet shirt from the line and (tying it around my face like a bandana) rushed to my nearby hut. Wrenching the door open, I hauled out a pile of sacks. Billy and Michael grabbed some, and without speaking, we dunked them in the river. Then scooping water into our buckets, we followed the crowd running along the riverbank and up through the gap between the guard's house and the Surveyor General. Rounding the corner, I saw a wall of fire in the distance and adrenaline surged through my body at the hideous sight.

"WOMEN AND CHILDREN TAKE SHELTER IN THE Jail," shouted the commandant, running down the road.

"If the wind blows this way it will wipe out the houses," cried Hugo Bahl, as he jostled alongside us.

The Spot The War Forgot

Billy swore under his breath and Michael's face went white. William Davis rushed into our midst clutching a bunch of axes with sale tickets dangling off their handles.

"Here, take these and pass them out," he said, his breath coming in short gasps as he thrust the axes at Hugo. "I'll go back and get the rest, and all the buckets and gunny sacking I can find."

By now the orange daylight and the cherry-coloured sun was hidden by eerie darkness. Davis and Hugo shot off in opposite directions and were swallowed into the thick air, and soon after, I heard the thud, thud, plink of chopping, and whoosh, boom of falling trees, as men cut a firebreak around the edge of the village.

"PULL THE FOLIAGE AWAY," came the shout. "AND WET THE AREA AS MUCH AS YOU CAN."

Men swarmed like ants over fallen timber and swiftly hauled branches away, while I joined the bucket brigade stretching down to the river. And not a moment too soon, for we had only just finished when the wind picked up. My mouth went dry and my blood ran cold as birds and fleet footed animals fled before the chasing flames. This fire made the school fire seem like a picnic bonfire. A terrifying red and orange wave rushed towards us shrieking and roaring with the sound of steam engines and train whistles. The firebreak kept the flames at bay, but not the cinders that flew over our heads like fireworks, bursting into flames as they hit the ground, or the shingled rooves of the cottages.

For a second time, arms and legs exploded around me.

Woosh, splat, and splash,

Water, yells, rattling buckets,

W.E. Hamilton

Whack, slap, boof, stomp-stomp.

I beat and stamped on the fires exploding above, below and around me. I did not notice my scorched hands or the burn on my arm, they were unimportant. It was war, we were soldiers fighting a raging enemy. We fought not with guns and cannons but a frenzy of whacking stomping and sloshing, that continued on and on and on as day turned into night, and night gave way to dawn again. By mid-morning, the battle still raged. The fire still lobbed its explosive balls at us and we still whacked, slapped stomped, and sloshed. We were far beyond tiredness or exhaustion. This was life or death. We were fighting for the village, we were fighting for our survival.

I don't recall the exact moment we won, only a vague sense of it being over. Like everyone else, my eyes were bloodshot, my face smeared with soot and sweat, and burns pocked my clothing. We slumped on the ground in the village square, too exhausted to move. While we lay sprawled or sat with our heads hanging, Thomas Packer climbed onto a nearby tree stump and cleared his throat to get our attention. Usually, he stood proudly erect, stern lines embedded into his grim face, but today his thin body was stooped, and his mouth quivered with emotion.

"I just want to say a few words to the Germans," he said, haltingly. "Thank you for saving my house and the village. Without your help, everything would have burned down today and I am grateful to you."

With that, he stepped off the stump and slunk away. He never fully accepted us, he was too old and rigid to change, but from that day on, his antagonism was tempered by respect and gratitude.

The Spot The War Forgot

Guards outside the entrance of the Berrima Jail

2.   Narrow yard between the outer prison wall and the Service Building

W.E. Hamilton

Inside the jail

Interior of one of the cells

The Spot The War Forgot

22nd Berrima Guard

German prisoners marching off to a picnic

W.E. Hamilton

Billy Köster, Gerhardt Paradis and Max Adam's rented house in Oxley Street still standing over a hundred years later

Hansa bridge

The Spot The War Forgot

German prisoners and huts by the Great Lake

Boat decorated for carnival

W.E. Hamilton

Bicycle boat

Alsterburg Villa

The Spot The War Forgot

Julius and his Villa Marcella

Relocation of Emden Hut

W.E. Hamilton

Hurtzig family

The Hurtzig's and Glintz's first shared house at Berrima

The Spot The War Forgot

Bergien and Mönkedieck working on posters

German internees (Captain Marsden in front)

W.E. Hamilton

Bandstand

Theatre and DTB members

The Spot The War Forgot

Prince, the horse the prisoners rescued

Edna Machotka and children with Friedrich Reil

W.E. Hamilton

Prisoner's garden Schmeisshoh

A prisoner's garden

The Spot The War Forgot

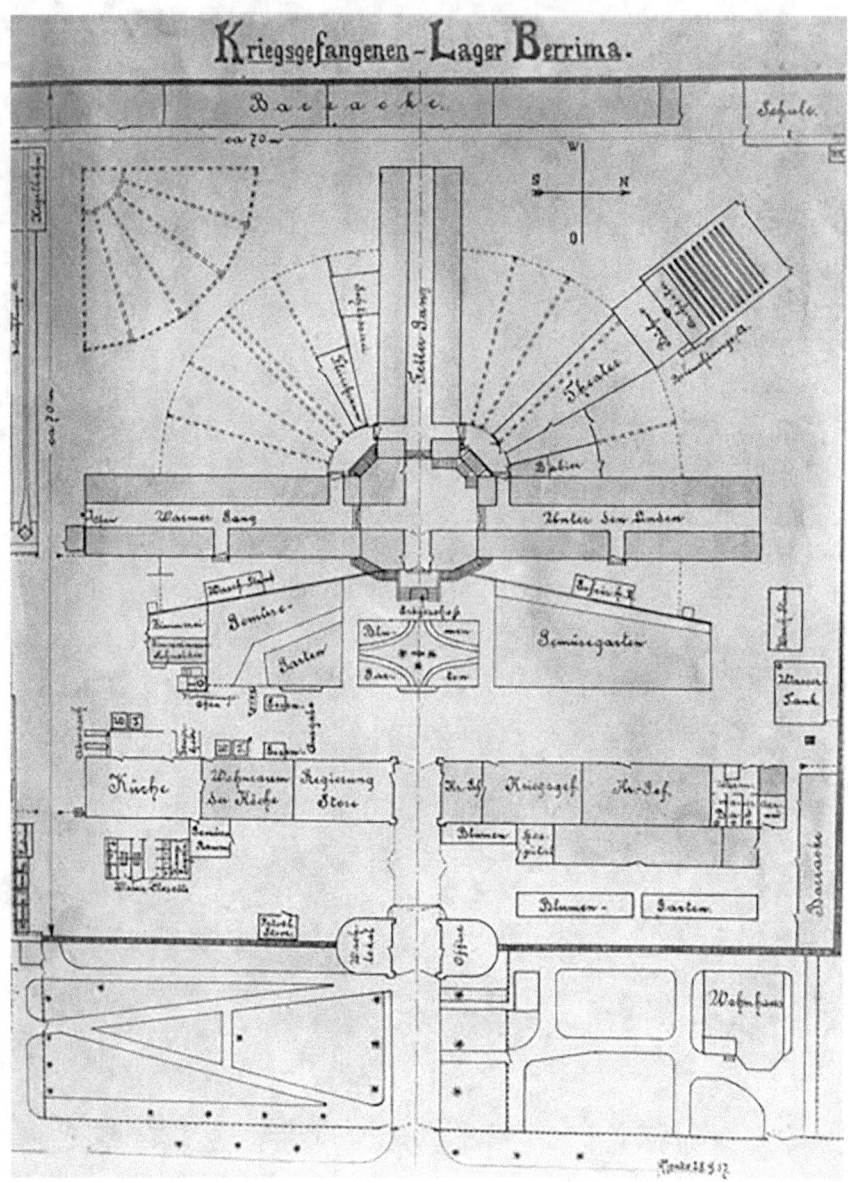

Plan of Berrima POW Camp, Drawn by Menke 28th September 1917. Dubotzki collection, Germany

W.E. Hamilton

February 1916
Germany Launches a Major Offensive against the Fortress of Verdun

Frienemies and a Carnival

Permission to build a water tank and plumbing system was finally granted. Work was well underway when the Department of Defence decided to enclose an area of the left bank for our sole use. Those of us not working on the new water system helped the guards build the fence.

"The villagers should be pleased with the DOD's decision," I said, to Sergeant Major Leonard Hagon as we lifted a tall pole, "the compound is not nearly as extensive as they feared."

Leonard said nothing as we staggered over to the hole we had dug, but after we let go and saw the post drop into place, he answered: "Seventeen and a half acres surrounding the sports area is not excessive, and not much of the riverbank is prohibited. It will make little difference to the villagers."

The Spot The War Forgot

"Henry Allen will still think it is too much," I said, as we backfilled the hole and tamped the dirt around the pole.

"Henry Allen is unreasonable, he should be thankful it is only a bit on the left side of the river, the DOD could have fenced off some of the right bank if they wished to. I expect the men will build their huts within the shelter of the compound from now on."

"I suppose so."

"You're not convinced?"

"It depends on which a man values more, safety or privacy," I said, thinking of the fellow with the pet goanna. "Some of the loners who spend their time in the caves in the ravine might prefer vandals to neighbours."

"It takes all sorts," nodded the guard. "At least you blokes now have a safe place to build huts."

Frau Hurtzig and the children wandered towards us and stopped to watch us work.

"I am so relieved they are not locking us all in a big cage as I feared," she said. "I was so afraid the lovely bush walks would be lost."

"You should get more freedom in the weekends," said the guard. "Now there is a safe area you won't be confined to the jail early."

"That will be a huge advantage," said Frau Hurtzig.

"Not as big as flushing toilets," I said.

"Even I will benefit from that, now it won't matter which way the wind blows," laughed Frau Hurtzig moving off.

Once the fence was finished our thoughts returned to the idea of a Venetian carnival.

"What about holding it on the Kaiser's birthday?" said

Bahl.

"But do you think the commandant will allow us to run it on that day?"

"It's hard to say," said Captain Hurtzig, "permission to celebrate a German festival is unlikely, but not impossible, for the guards are friendly, and now we help them patrol the fence on busy days it feels as if we are on the same team."

"It certainly is difficult to remember we are officially enemies," said Billy.

Michael nodded. "Even Thomas Packer's attitude has softened since the bush fire."

"Who is brave enough to ask?"

"This is a job for the Camp Committee," said Captain Hurtzig.

So the Camp Committee asked the commandant, and to our delight, he agreed.

The morning of the carnival was lovely. The sky was blue above the dark wooded hills and the stretch of water that we called Lake Titicaca. At nine-thirty all the internees, the guards, and a good number of villagers watched as beautiful boats glided on the brown water past Captain Pahran's hut, located at the midpoint of the left bank. After parading our boat several times before the judges, we stood on the riverbank and discussed our chances.

"They are taking a long time to decide on the winner," I said. "Do you think they will make the boats pass them again?"

"The judges take their job very seriously," said, Captain Hurtzig. "Ranking the boats, for the originality of decoration, or witty and striking points takes time and thought."

"They have already seen each boat five times, I would have

The Spot The War Forgot

thought it was obvious that our Venetian gondola is the best."

"For sure your boat is the best," said Frau Hurtzig, loyally.

"I, of course, agree with you," said Billy, leaning on the pole of the gondola, "but, seriously Wolfgang, would you like to choose between our gondola or the model of the Kaiser's yacht. Our mandolin player gives us the edge over the paddle boats, but the Kaiser's yacht, and the fact it is powered by some sort of engine, is strong competition."

"Don't forget the bicycle boat," said Captain Hurtzig. "It's unique."

"It is an ingenious contraption," I admitted. "I'm astonished that anyone could turn the old metal lying about the coal mine into something so marvellous."

"It's like riding a bike on water," said Michael. "Except instead of wheels the peddles drive the paddle at the back."

"What do you think the long floats are made from?"

"Captain Hurtzig put his telescope to his eye. "Some sort of tubing from the look of it. I suppose it came from the coal mine too."

"At least the other gondola is no competition. The candles don't show up in the daylight. If it was night it would look rather pretty."

"Fortunately, it's a sunny day so it's no competition," said Billy. "I'm more worried about the black swan boat. It's striking, and beautifully decorated."

"*Ja*, and the imperial crown mounted on those big arches of oakleaves, are just the sort of thing the judges might like."

"But the white swans make it less original," said Captain Hurtzig. "The other two boats lessen its impact."

We were comforting ourselves with this idea when Hanna,

jiggling with excitement, said:

"Look at the little flag on the pole of the black swan, it's going up and down all by itself."

"How is it doing that, Papa," said Lore?

"It's moved mechanically, *Liebling*."

My shoulders slumped and I sighed. "Perhaps we might come second?"

Captain Hurtzig, ciapped me on the shoulder. "Don't give up before the judges even decide, Wolfgang."

"I don't think we need to concern ourselves with King Neptune," said Michael, "he needs fireworks or fish spraying from his trident to win."

"The Hannover yacht with its funnel and little lifeboats is good," said Hermann.

A horn tooted.

"So is the fireboat," said Billy, "but it takes more than a horn to make a winner. If it was squirting water as well, I would be more troubled."

A movement from the deck of Captain Pahren's hut caught our eye.

"What's happening, Gust?" said Frau Hurtzig, as her husband looked through his telescope.

"I think they are about to announce the winners."

And it was so. The spokesman of the judges lifted his megaphone and shouted:

"First place goes to the Venetian Gondola."

We threw our caps in the air, and were so excited we missed hearing the ranking of the other boats.

Billy went to collect our prize, and when he got back, he said:

The Spot The War Forgot

"You are all invited to share the winnings."

"The prize is not skimpy," said Frau Hurtzig, examining the ham. "This is a huge leg."

"What did the others get?" I asked.

"The standard favourites, cigarettes, tobacco, and cigars," said Billy, handing the ham to Frau Hurtzig for safekeeping."

Now the boat competition was over, we were free to relax and enjoy the rest of the day. There were aquatic entertainments and contests, as well as sporting advents including soccer and faustball. Then there was a special dinner in the courthouse.

"This is what I expected Christmas dinner to be like," I said, looking around the decorated courtroom.

"I am happy we actually get to eat at the tables we laid out," said Hermann.

Michael nodded. "I won't resent cleaning up this time."

"What is the play the theatre is doing tonight, Billy?"

"You have a terrible memory, Wolfgang, I have told you over and over we are performing, *The Honeymoon*."

"Ah, that's right."

"I hear the orchestra and choir have joined forces to help out," said Herman.

"*Ja*."

"Are you playing the bride, Billy?"

"*Nein*, "I only play ugly women or old aunts."

Michael tilted his head to one side and stared at Billy's face. "It's your nose that's the problem."

Billy's eyebrows lowered and he stuck out his chin aggressively. "I'm getting tired of people saying things about my nose. I will bust the nose of the next person who goes on about it."

"I don't know why you are getting angry about it," I said. "You would rather play comedy parts and a large ornamental nose like yours is hilarious."

"It is rather," said Billy calming down, "and I am good at comedy, although I'll never be as good as Valentin Wenk."

I nodded. "He is a natural clown."

"You will be amazed how funny he is while he plays the double bass," said Billy.

"I don't think of a string quartet as a comedy act," said Herman.

"You will after you see the Hackelrieder Quartet tonight," said Billy. "I am wearing the hat and the stripy dress Ada Harper gave me, and Gerald Kruck is wearing a top hat and suit. His impersonation of a musician in distressing circumstances is very funny."

"Who's the other member of the quartet?"

"Erno Molnar, he's the leading violinist, and he makes his eyes sadder than a spaniel puppy." Billy frowned. "I wish I could get a photo of us all."

"I could take it for you. I've watched you work your camera often enough."

"Would you, Wolfie?" said Billy, his face lighting up.

"For sure, just show me how, so I get it right."

"Alright, meet me just before the performance and I'll explain the procedure."

And that is what we did. As the ladies and children took their seats in front of the stage, Billy gave me a crash course on the finer points of photography.

"Do you think you understand," he said, as a cello and a violin started tuning up.

The Spot The War Forgot

"*Ja*," I nodded, "I know what to do."

"Good, I have to go, I will see you after the show."

With that, he was gone, and shortly after, the lights dimmed and the curtains parted.

The play was marvellous and the songs and dances very entertaining, but the *Hackelrieder* Quartet had the audience rolling about holding their sides with laughter.

I nudged Michael. "Look at the commandant and his guests, they are loving this as much as us."

"And so are the guards," said Michael, pointing to a group of them leaning against the gate roaring with laughter.

I took photographs of everything for Billy, but right at the end when we stood to sing, Halt Deutschland Hoch in Ehren, by Ludwig Bauer, I put the camera away, too moved to do anything other than reflect on the words as we sang:

Oh, highly esteemed Germany
Thou art the holy land of loyalty
May the brightness of thy glory
Shine anew forever both in the west and the east.
Thou standest firm like the mountains
Against thy foes' powers and deceptions
Like the Eagle that leaves his nest.

While the sea of voices rose and fell around me, I thought of home and family and the picture of the ship in the eye of the storm, as we sang the chorus:

W.E. Hamilton

Hold firm! Hold firm!
Let the banner flutter!
That we stand together faithfully
That our strength persists
When the battle-cry rages against us!
Hold firm in the roaring storm!
Hold firm in the roaring storm!

And the Australian officers, the commandant, and his guests, all courteously stood with us as we sang our patriotic song.

The Spot The War Forgot

**March 1916
French Airship Mistakenly Sinks British Submarine with Loss of All Hands**

Troubles and Another Carnival

The house swap between the guards and the Hurtzigs and Glintz's worked well for everyone. The smaller brick house enabled each family to have their own apartment, and the bigger stone house gave the guards more space. Frau Hurtzig took pride in her rooms, and spent much time and thought devising ways to make them homely. The guards were also busy adapting their dwelling to their needs. Shortly after moving they acquired a piano, and once a week thereafter, they held a concert in their barracks.

"The officers were really getting into the singing last night," I said, one afternoon as a small group of us gathered at the Hurtzig's house. "They kept me awake last night with their music."

"I didn't hear them after lights out," said Captain Hurtzig.

"That's because your cell is not as close to the wall as mine. I could throw a stone from my window into the barrack's garden if the glass opened."

"Did you hear the bottle music?" said Frau Hurtzig, pouring coffee into china cups.

"What is bottle music? I've never heard of bottle music," said Michael.

"One of the guardsmen hung a row of bottles on a frame and played tunes on them. It was very beautiful."

"I did hear some tinkly music," Billy said. "I wondered what that was, I thought it might have been a xylophone."

"No, it was bottles," said Frau Hurtzig, passing the coffee around. "The officer who thought up the idea and played them, was a real wartime artist."

"Their concerts don't usually go so late," I said.

Frau Hurtzig cut the cake into slices and gave it to Hanna. "Someone must have had a birthday or something. They had the Chinese lanterns hanging off the pine trees in the garden, and they only do that for special occasions."

Hanna offered the cake to her father.

"That must be it," said Captain Hurtzig, taking a piece of chocolate gateau. "If it was anything more important, they would have held a dance in the hall and invited all the villagers."

Hanna stood before me with the mouth-watering treat. "At Holy Trinity Church?" I asked, using the cake knife to scoop a slice onto a plate.

Captain Hurtzig stirred his coffee before putting the spoon on his saucer. "No, the Masonic Hall on the corner of Oxley and Argyle Street."

The Spot The War Forgot

"Ah," I said, suddenly remembering the odd little stone building not far from the Brauns house. "Is it a few doors up from Sovereign Cottage, and looks like a church with a dormer window in the roof?"

"That's right. Annie said it was a Presbyterian church at one time."

Frau Hurtzig was passing the sugar around when there was a knock on the door, and catching sight of Frau Brauns, she called out, "Come in my dear, you are just in time for coffee and cake."

"I see you have visitors," said Frau Brauns, coming in. "I don't want to disturb you."

"You are not a disturbance," said Frau Hurtzig. "It is only Gust and the men."

"Would you have anything for a tummy ache?" said Frau Brauns, taking the cup Frau Hurtzig handed her. "Gertrude has come down with terrible pains in her stomach."

"I've got some slippery elm," said Frau Hurtzig, bustling out to the kitchen. We heard her rummaging about in the cupboard, and shortly after she reappeared with a small jar. "Give the poor girl a teaspoon of this mixed in a little water and see if it helps."

"Thank you, Luise," said Frau Brauns. She drew Frau Hurtzig into a corner of the room and spoke quietly. "There is another matter I want to speak to you about."

Frau Hurtzig gazed into her eyes kindly. "What is troubling you?"

"It's Frau Jepsen, she refuses to have anything to do with Frau Wallner, simply because her husband is a third officer."

"*Ja*, I know." Frau Hurtzig shook her head sorrowfully.

[6] *"Everything is not as it should be among the German families here. It is a pity we do not set a better example for the Australians."*

"Frau Jepsen is very pointed and hurtful in her rejection of Frau Wallner, she refuses to invite her to the afternoon teas at the Ladies Club, and some of the other wives follow her lead."

Frau Hurtzig motioned Hanna to offer cake to Frau Brauns before saying: "I have hinted to her that her behaviour is not the Christian way, and we should band together in these times of trouble, but she says she is keeping the standards up."

Frau Brauns took a slice of cake. "Thank you, Hanna," she said, before turning back to Frau Hurtzig. "I don't know where this will all end. Frau Jepsen's behaviour at the Christmas play was appalling. Poor Frau Wallner is finding her coldness harder than the war."

"How long has Gertrude had the stomach ache?" said Frau Hurtzig, switching subjects as they sat on the couch.

"It started last night and is getting worse by the hour. Eric is at home watching over her at the moment."

"If the slippery elm doesn't work, get Eric to take her to the infirmary in the central tower of the jail. They might have something in their first aid kit that could help."

"I hope it is nothing more than a stomach bug, the Berrima doctor is not that good, and the Bowral one cannot be called after six in the evening."

"Don't get me started on the Berrima doctor! I've consulted him a few times concerning Gust's sloughs of despair, but I won't do it again. The man is useless. 'Madam, he said, your husband is depressed by the war.' I could have diagnosed that

---

6   Taken from Frau Hurtzig's Diary.

The Spot The War Forgot

for free. Everyone is depressed by the war. I thought it would be over by Christmas."

"We all did," said Frau Brauns, with a sigh. She finished her coffee and put the empty cup down. "I best be going, Eric will be wondering where I am. Thank you for the slippery elm and the talk, Luise."

"I wish I could do more about both problems, my dear."

"A sympathetic ear is a great comfort," said Frau Brauns as they walked to the door.

The captain (seeing his wife was preoccupied) slid another piece of cake onto his plate while her back was turned. "The Berrima Guard must be due to host some event," he said, digging his fork into chocolate and cream. "Because they haven't run a dance for some time."

"Did you hear Captain Stoddart is returning?" said Hermann. "The rumour is he will stay three months."

The light of understanding broke over Billy's face. "So that's it. Now I understand! Captain Stoddart was very disappointed when rain cancelled his farewell carnival. He was so looking forward to it. The officers must be planning a welcome-back Venetian carnival."

"What makes you think that?"

"The commandant has asked if the Berrima Guards could borrow our boats on February the 28th."

"What, for the whole day?"

"No only the evening."

"I hope you are right. Captain Stoddart is a good man and liked by all," said Michael. "But I think it is more likely they are on the prowl for men smuggling booze."

We would have tried to find out more about the guard's

mysterious need of our boats, but news that Gertrude had been rushed to Bowral Hospital with a ruptured appendix drove any thoughts other than her health from our heads. For the next two weeks, the volume of mail Rose carted to Moss Vale quadrupled.

"The nurses were very confused," laughed Frau Brauns, when Gertrude returned home safely. "They could not understand how anyone could have so many uncles."

Now the little girl was no longer in danger, our attention shifted back to the commandant's request to borrow our boats. Billy was right; the Berrima Guards were going to welcome back Captain Stoddart with a Venetian Carnival. We were happy to loan our boats but (because we had recently held a carnival) the guards had to come up with something different. For as Michael said:

"Nothing is as exciting the second time around, especially when there is a mere four weeks between both events."

Hosting the second Venetian carnival in the evening, and at the Great Lake waterhole, was clever. The change of venue and time of day made the atmosphere instantly different.

"Just extending our curfew makes this exciting," I said, as we walked down to the river after dinner. "I've not been down here when it's dark."

"You'll have to slip out with me one night, Wolfgang," said Captain Bahl, winking and tapping the side of his nose. "I can show you the river by moonlight and make it worth your while if you know what I mean." He mimed the actions of drinking.

Frau Hurtzig, hitching Lore higher on her hip, frowned. "None of that silly talk here, Hugo Bahl! Don't listen to him, Wolfgang, it is not worth the risk. If you get caught they might

The Spot The War Forgot

banish you from the camp."

"My love, don't fret," said Captain Hurtzig, swinging Hanna's hand as she walked beside him. "They only banish for the very worst crimes, like the man caught in adultery with the wife of a villager."

"Not in front of the children, Gust," said Frau Hurtzig, sucking in her breath sharply and nudging him with her elbow. "Little pitchers have big ears. It is best not to speak of scandals like that."

"Look at all the fairy-lights, Papa," squealed Hanna, as we rounded the corner and the Hansa bridge came in sight.

"The bridge and trees are very pretty, *liebling*. The guards have gone to a lot of trouble stringing up so many lights."

"They have even hung up the Chinese lanterns," said Frau Hurtzig, standing Lore on the ground.

"All those boats on the water look completely different illuminated," I said. "I can hardly believe that's our gondola."

"Their mouth organ doesn't sound as good as our mandolin," said Billy, "and the gondolier should have changed out of his officer's uniform."

"I expect it is the best they can do," said Hermann.

"*Ach komm schom*, they have a piano," Billy said, striking a comical pose.

Hanna giggled. "You're funny Uncle Billy. They couldn't hide a piano under the canopy."

By now we had reached the edge of the water. On the other side of the river, men, women, and children milled about admiring the floating displays.

"Most of the villagers have come," said Frau Hurtzig, waving to Rose Izzard and her husband.

W.E. Hamilton

The young ladies of the town seem very interested in the swan boats," said Captain Hurtzig.

"I think it is the swains in the swans," said Frau Hurtzig. "They're the same girls I see hanging around the younger officers with their autograph books on dance nights."

"They are not opposed to hanging around some of us either," said Billy, as a couple of giggling girls smiled at him from across the water.

Frau Hurtzig pretended to smack his hand. "You keep your eyes off them, Wilhelm, you want a nice German frauline, not an Australian girl. What has happened to Elsa and Maria? I have not seen them for a while."

"The other gondola shows up well in the dark," said Michael, hastily changing the subject. "Perhaps we would not have won if the contest had been at night."

In the round of denials that followed, Elsa and Maria were forgotten. There was much to admire as we wandered along the riverbank, for as dusk darkened into night, the lights, lanterns, and boats, glowed with increasing intensity and beauty. We would have been happy with merely being out of the jail after curfew but the main event was yet to come. Once the vessels were cleared from the lake, two boats sailed into the spotlight. A great howl of pleasure arose as we recognised the SMS Emden and the HMS Sydney. Then the Emden and the Sydney fought a mock battle. I'm not sure what they were lobbing at each other but, be it potatoes or rocks, in the dim light it looked like cannonballs. Like spectators at a football match, we cheered the Emden on, while the villagers shouted for the Sydney, It was tremendously exciting. So exciting, one of the villagers got carried away and fell into the lake. That brought

The Spot The War Forgot

the battle to a sudden halt.

"Hurry up and get out of the water," someone yelled, as the guards fished him out, "we want to see who wins."

We all felt the same and a rousing cheer arose when the battle recommenced. The finale was spectacular and satisfactory to all, for both the Emden and the Sydney went up in flames.

A reporter for the Southern Mail attended the celebration, and a few days later an article appeared in the paper under the heading 'Military Entertainment at Berrima.' Although we were inclined to believe the local paper was biased, we agreed with the villagers, the commandant, the officers, and Captain Stoddart, that the reporter got it right when he wrote:

'The Venetian Carnival held at Berrima was a great occasion.'

W.E. Hamilton

March 1916
Battle of Verdun: Germans Capture Cumieres-Le-Mort-Homme and Chattancourt in France

Focus on Music

Newcomers were constantly trickling into the camp, so much so, we took little interest in them. Occasionally, however, a man arrived whose presence made a huge impact on camp life; Fritz Rittig was a man like that, and his gift to us was music. Hermann was the first to encounter him.

"I want you to meet Fritz Rittig and Ernst Dannemann," said Hermann, as we surged through the gatehouse after rollcall. "These are my friends Wilhelm Köster, Michael Becker, and Wolfgang Schmitt."

"*Guten tag*," said Fritz.

"*Guten tag*," we said, stopping outside the gate. Michael and I shook their hands, but when it came to Billy's turn, he added the word, 'welcome,' to his greeting and said, "My friends call me Billy."

The Spot The War Forgot

"Fritz and Ernst arrived with the group from Hong Kong," said Hermann, "Fritz is a marine engineer and Ernst was a senior sailor on the Herzogin Sophie Charlotte. I thought we could show them around."

I nodded. "*Ja*, good idea, we were on our way to the river, Billy wants to get some photographs."

"Do any of you play an instrument?" said Fritz, as we moved down the path, and past the sentry stationed at the picket fence.

Michael, Hermann and I pointed at Billy and chorused: "He does,"

Fritz beamed. "What do you play?"

"Viola."

"*Wunderbar*, viola players are harder to find than violinists."

We waved to Hanna and Lore playing in the garden in front of their house as Billy answered:

"I play in a quartet with two violinists and a double bass player."

"Good, good. Are there others in the camp who play instruments?"

"I warn you," broke in Ernst, with a chuckle, "once Fritz starts talking about music it's hard to stop him."

We grinned as Billy, ignoring Ernst's warning said:

"*Ja*, Otto Mönkedieck plays the flute, Oskar Bock the guitar, and many men played in ship-bands."

"How many?"

We turned the corner and walked down the street past the north wall of the prison.

"It is hard to say, for there are more musicians than instruments in the camp."

A determined look entered Fritz's eyes. "We will have to

do something about that. What instruments do we have?"

"My viola, two violins, one flute, five zithers," said Billy, ticking them off on his fingers, "a guitar and a mandolin."

"Don't forget the tin cello."

Fritz's eyebrows shot up. "A tin cello?"

"August Lüdeking made it, and it's a real work of art," said Michael. "He made it out of flattened kerosene tins and painted it to look like old wood."

A look of pain crossed Fritz's face.

"I know, the idea is dreadful," said Billy, "but surprisingly, it has a beautiful mellow tone."

"How this is so, I cannot imagine," said Fritz, "but as you are a musician, I must believe you."

"The secret to the cello's success is the wool inside it," said Billy. "I will take you to meet August sometime, and you can hear the wonder yourself."

"Do you play an instrument?" I asked, putting my hands into my pockets as I sauntered along?

"For sure, I play the violin. What about yourself, do you play anything?"

"Not really, I had violin lessons for a few years when I was a child, but that was all. My mother made me and I fought her over it. I wish now I had made more of my opportunity."

"Really?" Fritz turned an intense gaze on me. "It is not too late. In this environment, all you need is a few lessons." He switched his attention to Michael and Hermann. "What about you?"

They shook their heads apologetically. "*Nein.*"

"What do you mean by 'this environment?'" I said, scooping a pebble from the orange dust at my feet.

The Spot The War Forgot

Ernst laughed and pulled a face. "He means all this leisure time, of course, hours and hours to practise until perfect."

"You may laugh my friend, but anything other than striving for musical perfection is a lesser pursuit," said Fritz, seriously.

"We can't practice all the time," Billy said, kicking a stick. "We have some duties."

"*Ja*, we are rostered to chop wood, collect coal, and man the pumps of the water system," I said, throwing the pebble into the air and catching it.

"And once a week we have a 'clean ship' day," said Michael, "plus English lessons are mandatory for the first year."

"That's not even counting sports, hobbies, carnivals, choir practice, or theatre rehearsals," said Hermann, picking up a stick and slashing at a tree overhanging the road.

"No matter how busy you are there is always time to practice music," said Fritz. "It is good for the brain and calms the nerves. I shall start with the musicians and instruments we have."

"Start what?"

Fritz's eyes opened wide, "the orchestra of course. The hardest part will be getting the instruments, especially the piano, but we will find a way."

By now the Hansa bridge was in sight but no one thought to point it out.

"A piano!" I spluttered. "How ever will we get a piano to Berrima?"

"The guards got one last month," said Hermann.

"If the guards can have one, I don't see why we can't," said Billy, with excitement rising in his voice. "There is only twenty-five of them and almost two-hundred and fifty of us.

Just think what it would mean to the theatre if we had an orchestra, we could expand into musicals."

Fritz wagged a finger at Billy. "What I need from you is a list of all the men who can play, and what instrument they need."

"Alright."

"What can I do?" I said, carried away by the growing wave of enthusiasm.

"I'll give you some sheet music when we get back, and you can look over it and familiarize yourself with the notes until we get you a violin."

"I could advertise on the noticeboard for musicians to start an orchestra," said Michael.

Fritz nodded. "Good idea, and spread the word that I will teach anyone interested in learning."

He stopped and looked at the surroundings. "This is a very pleasant spot. When I heard they were sending us to a concentration camp I did not expect it to be such a nice place." He swept his arm around in a semicircle as his eyes scanned the bridge, huts, water-chute, and boats. "To think you have accomplished all this in a year."

While we basked in his praise, the sounds and whistle peeps associated with outdoor sports roared in the background.

"Over there at the top of the slope is the sports grounds," said Billy, pointing to the plateau on the opposite bank.

Ernst glanced at the hill before extracting a packet of cigars from the inside of his jacket and handing them around.

"These are fine cigars," I said, taking one. I looked at the brand label. "Dannemann Cigars?"

"*Ja*, my father is a tobacco merchant in Hamburg," said

The Spot The War Forgot

Ernst, slicing the cap off his cigar and handing his cutter around. "He wanted me to follow in his footsteps but I went to sea instead."

A great roar came from the sports field.

"Someone must have scored a goal," said Hermann. He lit up and sucked gently so the cherry on the cigar's end glowed.

"Or won a tennis match," said Michael, copying Hermann. "If you are into tennis, we have three courts."

"I doubt I will have time to play sport," said Fritz. "I am intending to compose music when I am not teaching and conducting the orchestra."

"That hut just below the sports fields will interest you," Billy said, pointing his camera at it.

Smoke meandered out of Fritz's mouth and nose as he squinted into the distance. "The one with Frieda written over the gable?"

Billy pushed the button on his camera and the shutter clicked. "That's the one. It belongs to Karl Wirthgen. It's made from ten-thousand jam and milk tins filled with clay. He and three other zither players practice their music in there. They say the metal walls reverberate wonderfully."

Fritz's eyes brightened with interest. "Perhaps you can introduce me to Wirthgen, I must visit him sometime."

"You may come across him before that," I said. "If you see someone in a boat called Frieda it will be Karl."

"He seems very fond of the name Frieda," said Ernst, blowing a perfect smoke ring.

"It is the name of his daughter."

"Ah, that explains it."

"These brushwood huts by the water's edge are the first

huts we built," I said, turning right and strolling along the riverbank. I pointed to my hut. "That's mine over there."

"They are not as substantial as the later huts, like that one," said Billy, as we neared the side-creek that fed into the river. "Because we didn't think the war would last long enough to hang the door on them." He pointed his camera at Villa Marcella. "As you can see by this one, they are getting much more elaborate." He balanced his smoking cigar on a rock before twiddling about with the focus of his camera. "In the early days nobody built bridges or heavy arches."

As if by unspoken agreement, we all stood quietly to let Billy concentrate on taking his picture. Into the silence broke an awful sound.

"Oooooh." A loud groan floated from the open window of Villa Marcella.

"What's that noise? said Fritz, his eyebrows shooting up.

"It is only Julius, my cellmate," I said, with a dismissive wave of my hand. He will be reading a letter from his girlfriend."

"Is he alright?"

"For sure, don't worry about him," said Billy, closing his camera and hanging it around his neck. He picked up his cigar. "It is only petty jealousy; the grocer will have delivered a loaf of bread to Marcella or some other trifling matter."

"He is an excitable Hungarian," said Hermann, rolling his eyes. "Tomorrow he will be dancing under his lucky gates because Marcella has written he is a handsome man."

Fritz and Ernst stopped looking anxious and turned their attention back to our surroundings.

"The huts across the water are not spread out like the ones on this side of the river," observed Ernst, as we continued

The Spot The War Forgot

walking. "They are clustered together."

"*Ja*, that is because they were built after we got the Hansa bridge. That is Kittapur village, built by the men who were interned at Kittapur before they came here."

"You and I and our friends from Hong Kong, should build a village, Fritz," said Ernst. "We could call it New Hong Kong."

"You can, Ernst, I shall be too busy with the orchestra."

"If you really want to build a village, stake out your claim soon," I said. "As you can see, new huts are popping up all along the riverbanks."

For the rest of the walk Ernst was on the lookout for a suitable place for New Hong Kong. He was scouting around by the edge of the river when Fritz noticed a log cabin up Nobby's Hill.

"What a handsome hunting lodge!" he called out in wonder. "It would not look out of place in the Black Forest, although placing the logs vertically is a novel idea."

"That is the Alsterburg," said Hermann. "It's a communal hut and a social hub. Even with a team of men working on it, it took six months to build. Its foundation of rocks took weeks to haul up from the river."

"It looks bigger than the others."

"For sure, it is two spacious rooms, and the overhang above the veranda is a storage loft."

"I like that one down there by the edge of the water, also," said Fritz turning his head.

"That's the Alstertal. It's also a communal cabin. It belongs to the men from the steamer the Cannstatt. Captain Madsen is a man you must meet. He is very interested in music."

"Can we visit him?"

"Not at the moment, he's not there. If he was, we'd hear his gramophone."

"It is a pretty cabin."

"It is indeed, Frau Hurtzig reckons it's the prettiest villa of them all; a real home away from home, it even has a laundry and an outhouse."

"Who is Frau Hurtzig?"

"One of the captain's wives. She lives in the brick house by the corner of the prison."

"The house where the little girls were playing in the garden?"

"That's the one. We will introduce you to her and her husband this afternoon if you like. Captain Hurtzig is our great friend, and Frau Hurtzig is a warm and caring woman. She made the long pennant you see flying from the flag pole."

Fritz descended the bank for a closer look at Villa Alstertal. We followed him down to the lawn surrounding the villa.

"It's nice how all the cabins have a mast or flagpole," Ernst said, "gazing at the white flag with red borders flying above him.

I looked around furtively, and when I saw we were alone, I leaned towards him and said in a low voice, "They serve a greater purpose than you realize."

"How so?"

"It is like the old proverb: 'You can't see the wood for the trees," said Michael.

I nodded. "He's right. Tall poles are so common the guards don't notice some of them are antennas."

"Really," Ernst gasped?

"*Ja*," said Michael. "The big villa called White City has a

The Spot The War Forgot

mast eighteen to twenty meters high so it can receive signals from above the trees. We have passed it but I will point it out to you on the way back."

"It's the work of Eric Brauns, Kurt Wittig and a few others," said Billy. "Eric is a wireless engineer from Nauru, and Kurt and the others are wireless operators. It was a simple matter for them to build an efficient receiver. They spend much of their time eavesdropping into Morse code transmissions."

Hermann chuckled. "The guards can't work out how we know things before they hit the newspapers."

"Ingenious," said Ernst. He turned his attention back to the garden. "The terraces and grottos are very nice. If I get around to building a cabin, I would like one close to the water with a landing for my boat like this one. I see why Frau Hurtzig likes it so much." He pointed to a bench under a large branched tree. "It would be very pleasant to sit in the shade and look at the river on a hot day."

"I've been thinking about instruments," said Hermann, as we ambled onward. "The members of the Camp Committee are the ones to approach about getting instruments. The canteen is very successful and they are the ones who decide where the profits are spent. Captain Madsen is on the committee, he would certainly back the idea."

"For sure he would," I said, getting excited, "and I expect Fritz could win the others over for he is exceedingly persuasive."

"If you are going to try for a piano, also ask for a tuber and kettle drums," said Billy, "then anything smaller will seem a simple and reasonable request."

"I wouldn't mind learning how to play some sort of wind

instrument," said Michael, pretending his cigar was a trumpet.

"Are you thinking of having a brass band as well?" said Herman. "I can imagine myself marching with a big drum."

"I can't see why not," said Fritz, airily. "The brass instruments can play in both the orchestra and band."

We discussed the merits of different instruments as we walked. By the time we got to the dam the idea of an orchestra was fixed in our heads. As we leisurely smoked the last of our cigars, we told our new friends about Wallaby rocks further downstream.

"We will pack a picnic and take you there one day," I said, as we turned around and headed back the way we had come. Our timing could not have been better, for passing Villa Alstertal we found Captain Madsen on the veranda rehearsing the zither players, Schönfuss and Pfingst. Behind them, stood August Lüdeking.

"Now you shall meet Captain Madsen and judge for yourself the quality of August's tin cello," Billy cried in excitement.

We introduced Fritz and Ernst to the Captain and the others, and while we chatted, Billy took a photograph of the occasion. When he was done, we left Fritz listening to the tin cello and continued on our way.

"Did I hear you were on the Herzogin Sophie Charlotte, Ernst," Billy said. "Isn't she an NDL windjammer?"

"*Ja*, a many-masted sailing ship. I trained on her as a cadet and remained with her as a senior sailor. The first time I came to Sydney was in 1907, to pick up wool and grain."

"How did you become a POW?"

"When war broke out, I and several of my shipmates tried to get back to Germany as passengers on a Dutch ship.

The Spot The War Forgot

Unfortunately, the ship was stopped by the British and we were sent to Stone Quarry Camp in Hong Kong for eighteen months. What about you?"

"Wolfgang and I have the shameful honour of being captured within the first three hours of Britain declaring war on Germany," said Billy pulling a face.

"*Ja*," I said ruefully. "We were on the freighter the Pfalz, you might have read about us in the news, we were the target of Australia's first cannon shot."

"It is not all bad," said Billy. "This is more like a church summer camp than a prison."

"That's White City Villa, on the opposite bank," I said, cutting in, "see the tall mast."

"Amazing," said Ernst, "I would never have noticed it if you hadn't pointed it out. I was too busy looking at the wharf railings."

"The white crisscrosses are striking," Michael agreed.

We continued walking until we got back to the cluster of bathing huts.

"Welcome to my place," I said, opening the door as we reached it. "It's not as grand as some of the other cabins, but I like it."

Ernst admired my handiwork before asking, "Have you got a cabin, Billy?

"*Ja*, but I don't use it much, as I and two other men rent a cottage in Oxley Street."

Ernst's eyebrows shot up. "You rent a house?"

"Yes, we have to spend the night in the jail but we live there during the day. Would you like to see it?"

Ernst nodded. "Very much."

"Do you want to come, Wolfie?"
"Thank you but *nein*. I want to go for a swim."
"We will see you later then, *Auf Wiedersehen*."
"*Auf Wiedersehen*."

The two men dropped into easy conversation as they moved off. I watched them go, vaguely aware as I waved goodbye, I had just witnessed the start of a close friendship, and the birth of an orchestra.

The Spot The War Forgot

April 1916
France Counterattacks German-held Positions at Meuse and Douaumont France

A New Theatre

The best part of camp life was Deutsches Theatre Berrima or the DTB as we called it. Otto Pahnke, the senior inspector of the NGL was the genius behind the DTB. He was the one who issued invitations to the commandant and guests and ensured everything ran smoothly. The members of the DTB made everything they needed, the costumes, stage furniture, scenery and accessories, and they made them well. The one thing they could not make was the weather. We shivered as we stiffly eased ourselves off the bleachers.

"It's freezing," I said, folding my arms and tucking my hands under my armpits.

"It certainly is," said Billy, "usually I don't want the play to finish, but tonight I'm glad it's over so we can get out of this biting wind."

"It's only March, I shudder to think what it will be like in July," said Michael, rubbing his hands together as we joined the throng pressing their way inside. "We need an indoor theatre."

Unbeknown to us, Otto Pahnke, Fritz, and Karl Mehne, were having a similar conversation, and a few days later a plan for a theatre appeared on the noticeboard.

"An indoor theatre," I said. "I can't wait until this is built for then it won't matter if it rains or is freezing."

Billy pointed at the plan. "Fritz must have been part of the design team, by the look of the size of the orchestra pit, he is hoping to recruit more musicians."

"That sounds like Fritz, now the Camp Committee has agreed to buy instruments, he keeps asking me to take up the violin again."

Michael peered at the blueprint. "Richard Preiss will be happy, I heard him grumbling the other day about how hard it is to make quick changes."

"I don't think the tiny backstage was what he was complaining about," Billy laughed, "he always fusses when he has to put on a woman's corset."

"Then he will be pleased there will be room for someone to help him," I said. "This is a big project for the DTB. I hope it won't stop the plays."

"Only until we get it built. Why don't you help us, Wolfgang, the more helpers the quicker it will get done, and the quicker we will get back to performing."

"Alright," I am not afraid of hard work. What are they building it from?"

Billy squinted at the small writing on the side of the plan. "Bush timber, tarpaper, corrugated iron, and stones from the old army barracks."

"That heap of ruins opposite Holy Trinity Church?"

"*Ja*, for sure. There are thousands of slabs of sandstone lying around there, and if we run out, there is always the bricks from the ruined cottages."

Within days work had started on the new building. Usually, the sports grounds and all along the river hummed with busyness, but suddenly there was a noticeable lessening of activities. Instead, many internees swarmed throughout the village gathering stones and bricks. Ada Harper noticed us lugging materials about as she rode past delivering the mail. Each trip she rode slower and looked longer until one day she stopped her bicycle and dismounted.

"What's going on in the prison?"

"We're building an indoor theatre in the assembly yard," I said between puffs. "We have nearly got the walls built. Once they are done it won't take long to get the roof on."

"Oh, dear," said Ada, wheeling her bike alongside me. "I shall miss the choir. I don't suppose there will be any point sitting on the veranda of the guard's house anymore, the walls will muffle it too much."

I hitched the stone up and strengthened my grip. "I suppose so. It is a pity. The Camp Committee keeps asking the Commandant if the villagers can attend our plays, but he always says no. Maybe the next commandant will say yes."

"Here's hoping. Good luck with your building." She waved, mounted her bike and rode off, as I continued plodding towards the jail.

While we were struggling with the real world of stone and timber others were upgrading the illusionary world. The lathe in the carpentry shop whirled, and men whistled, as they sawed and hammered timber into furniture and doors. They even made a fake fireplace with a handsome mantlepiece. Camp clown, Valentine Wenk, painted the chairs white, while 'actress' Richard Preiss ingeniously cobbled together a wig with long braids. Those two were the stars of the theatre. Another prominent man was Otto Mönkedieck, but he was not a star in the ordinary sense. He was a talented lithographer. He made playbills and posters for the DTB. The posters were beautifully produced with fine calligraphy, and artwork combined with photography. One day I had the privilege of seeing him at work. He sat at a small desk in his cell under the gaze of a large picture of the Kaiser. The two corner shelves jutting out above his head were stacked with books, tobacco tins, and whiskey bottles filled with flowers.

"How did you learn to do this?" I asked as I watched him expertly painting a battleship surging through the sea.

"I was good at art at school. My family are Prussian and not wealthy, so when I was thirteen, I was apprenticed to a lithographic firm in Hannover and learnt the trade."

"How long did you work as a lithographer?"

Otto cleaned his brush with turpentine before dipping it into orange paint. "Until I was almost twenty-one because by then I was liable for compulsory service." He added flames to the ship's guns.

"Of course, I suppose that is when you joined the navy and became the navigator for the famous SMS Emden."

"It was not as straightforward as that," said Otto, blending streaks of red into the orange flares. "But basically that's it."

"Is this the HMS Sydney?"

The Spot The War Forgot

"*Ja,*"

"What happened in the battle between her and the Emden?"

"I don't want to talk about it. I don't even want to paint it, but sometimes I can't help myself."

In the awkward silence, I perused the pictures on the wall.

"That is a nice ship. I would like a copy of that."

"Well, you can have one for a small price. Herr Pahnke wants me to turn my paintings and playbills into postcards to help fund the theatre."

"Trust Pahnke to think of a way to make money. He's rich from a side hustle of bird of paradise feathers, and now he is selling his camp rations at huge prices. Why can't he just give food away to those who are hungry? Not everyone is rich enough to dine out."

"I don't like him much myself, but there is no denying the man has good ideas." Otto cleaned his brush again. "He also suggested we frame the original posters and raffle them for extra funds."

"I wouldn't mind winning this," I said, pointing at a landscape. "I recognize the river and sports fields. Did you paint this from Heinrich's tree hut? I see our Castle and the village in the distance."

"*Ja,*" Otto nodded. "It is a preliminary painting for the huge backdrop Herr Pahnke wants me to paint. We will use it whenever a stage set is not necessary."

"Where will you paint it, there is not enough room here?"

"Oh, I will o it in place once the roof of the theatre is on and enough of the stage is built." He bent over his ship once more, "until then I have this playbill to finish."

I saw he wanted to get on with his work, so I thanked him

for taking the time to talk to me, and left. By now the walls of the theatre were up and there was no further need for stones, so I cast my eye about for another way to make myself useful.

"Come and make music stands," said Billy.

"What if Fritz catches me?" I looked about furtively as I followed my friend to the workshop, "for sure he will enlist me in his orchestra."

"Don't worry you won't see him he is too busy rehearsing the musicians he already has to have time to hunt for more. He wants our first concert in the new theatre to be perfect."

"Alright then, but what about you, why are you here instead of rehearsing?"

"Oh, I'm not staying, Fritz expects me in the dining room with the other musicians, I'm only here to encourage you to get started."

"Thanks a lot! I suppose you want me to make your music stand."

"For sure," laughed Billy. "I am tired of pinning my music on the jacket of the man in front of me."

Despite my initial reluctance, making music stands was fun. It took me a bit to get the knack of it, but once I did, I took pride in my woodwork and felt my stands were nothing to be ashamed of. I was scribing the pattern of a light shade onto a kerosene tin when Billy next saw me.

"You have done a good job, Wolfie," he said, looking at my music stand.

"Once I have finished making the shade for the candle, you can have this one," I said, cutting along the line with tin snips.

Billy stroked the smooth timber. "Thanks, Wolfie."

"Is the theatre finished yet?"

The Spot The War Forgot

"*Ja.* Have you seen the backdrop Mönkedieck painted? It is a work of art."

I folded the tin into shape and fastened it to the stand. "*Nein.* I know about it but I haven't seen it. Has he finished it?"

"*Ja,* but you will have to wait until the concert, for Pahnke has said nobody other than DTB members (and the men installing the gas-pipes under the stage) are allowed in."

It was a clever move to bar us from the theatre. It meant most of us were taken completely by surprise when we filed into the new building. The stone walls were whitewashed and the windows covered with bags to keep the light out. The stage was much bigger than the first rickety stage, and there was an orchestra pit in front of it. There were new curtains, but the bleachers were the same old ones. I noted with pleasure, however, they were now padded with army blankets (a great improvement.) As Michael and I shuffled along a row and took our seats, Captain Hurtzig escorted his wife and children to the front row. I saw Fritz bustling about among the musicians, and soon drones peeps and squeaks sounded as the orchestra tuned up. But the real surprise was when the curtains parted to reveal the new stage setting beautifully illuminated by gaslighting.

"Who would have thought those are the same doors and chairs I helped paint?" gasped Michael. "It looks just like the room of a young man-of-the-world."

"It certainly does, the fireplace is very convincing, and the writing desk and small dresser are a work of art."

"I suppose Captain Jertrum made them," said Michael. "For not the smallest detail is missing.

I did not answer, because the play had started and I was too caught up in it to care who made the furniture. There was a simpler interior for the second act, in which a lady's umbrella flailed about. I glanced at Frau Glintz seated beside the Hurtzigs, for I knew her husband had borrowed it without asking, but like the rest of us, she was roaring with laughter at the ridiculous antics of Wenks as Molonglo von Kong. Apart from, Wenks, there were the eight 'actresses' and three actors, all well-dressed; especially one of the 'ladies' with long hair. Richard's wig had turned out well, and with the dim lighting and distance between us, he looked just like a teenage girl. From beginning to end, it was wonderful.

"A fitting opening for our new theatre," I said, clapping until my hands smarted.

"Marvellous," Michael agreed. "I don't know how the concert tomorrow night can top that!"

But it did, simply because it had the advantage of novelty. For although the choir often sang, and Billy's quartet had performed many times, it was nothing like the musical feast Fritz whipped together. It was a full orchestra complete with trumpets, a drum, flute, clarinets, a violin, mandolin, guitar, zither and Ludiecke's tin cello. There was also Billy's viola, of course, and the guards had kindly lent their piano.

"I liked the items played by the violin and the clarinet the most," said Frau Hurtzig as we chatted after the performance.

"The best part was the star," squeaked Hanna, "when it came down slowly before rising again at the end of Bert's Lullaby."

"Schubert's Lullaby, *Liebling*" corrected her mother. "The way it shone in the dim light was most effective."

"I liked the Chinese lanterns," said Lore, doing a little twirl. "Especially the ones with coloured glass, they looked

The Spot The War Forgot

so pretty. And Herr Glintz and uncle Valentine looked funny dancing around with streamers on their tambourines and castanets," she giggled.

"You played very well," said Captain Hurtzig, as Billy, carrying his viola case came up to us. "What was the lantern song called?"

"O Sole Mio."

"Ah, that was it, I remember now."

"I liked the marching songs at the end and the encore," I said. "The whole evening was wonderful."

"I quite agree," said Michael. "My only disappointment is it did not rain." As if he had wished on the star of Schuberts Lullaby, the staccato pings of rain, suddenly rattled and clattered on the iron roof. "Now it is quite perfect," he said, beaming. "Knowing the weather is powerless to stop the show makes all our hard work worthwhile."

———————

W.E. Hamilton

April 1916
British Capture Biet Asia and Move to Sannaiyat in Last Attempt to Rescue Besieged British Indian Army

Booze Smugglers

The gorge leading to the abandoned mine was a popular place to picnic for those wanting to practice their abseiling skills.

"How was that?" I said, as my feet touched the ground. "That cliff face is as smooth as the prison wall and twice as high."

"Not twice as high," said Hugo Bahl, "you forget the cliff drops steeply from the rear wall."

"Oh," I said, my face falling.

"Cheer up," said Hugo, clapping me on the back. "You'll do."

"Does this mean you will take me smuggling?"

"For sure," said Heinrich Eckerlein. "Once we get the bush cellar dug, we will need men to help haul the cases of whisky."

The Spot The War Forgot

"How soon will that be?" I said, untying the knots that held the rope around me.

"Who can say?" said Hugo "It depends on how often the guards wander around Nobbys Hill. But now Heinrich has built his treehouse, the work will go faster."

"Can you see far from the Crow's Nest," I said, twisting the rope into a neat coil?

"All the way to the jail." Heinrich tried to look modest about his achievement but failed.

"The lookouts warn us in plenty of time to camouflage the pit before the guards arrive," said Hugo.

Heinrich took the rope from me. "Our contact is bringing his wagon through Berrima next week. I think the pit will be ready by then, but if it is not, we can stash the stuff in caves until it's finished.

"We won't need to hide it for long," said Hugo. "Once word leaks out that we have the stuff, sales will be brisk."

"True, but the black market is a trickier business than selling from the canteen. Spread the word over the next few days, 'the Pit Shop will be open at the end of next week. We are selling one bottle per customer, but only if they are wearing a large coat, preferably with a concealed pocket inside the lining.'"

"Does anyone want this last potato?" said Hugo, rolling it from the embers of the fire with a stick. "It seems a pity to waste it."

"I'll eat it if nobody else wants it."

"Go for it."

I picked the black object up gingerly and sat down on a rock. "Climbing has made me hungry again. Do we have time for another cup of tea or do we need to get going?"

W.E. Hamilton

Heinrich looked at his watch. "We've got time, it's only three, it won't take more than a couple of hours to get back if we walk briskly."

"Even if we dawdle, we will get back before the bugle call," said Hugo, rinsing our tin cups in the creek, before hanging a billy of water over the fireplace. He added a few dry sticks and, crouching down, blew a steady stream of air on the embers until the sticks burst into flames.

"How do we get the whisky?" I asked, breaking the potato open and sprinkling it with a little salt.

"One of our friends has a hut on Berrima Common. Our contact will drop twenty cases there," said Heinrich.

"Where is Berrima Common?"

"That strip of riverbank that runs parallel with the Moss Vale road. Although most of the huts are on the western side of the jail, there are some within the two-mile parole radius east; towards Moss Vale."

"Now I know where you are talking about." I dug my spoon into the fluffy white inside of the potato. "Who is our friend?"

"In this business, it is best not to use names."

"Speaking of no-names," said Hugo. "The cobbler is back."

"What! Moonshine Cobbler?" My spoon halted in its path towards my mouth. "I have not heard anything about him since we hid him in the cave, and sent him to a safe-house in the bush."

"He arrived back the other day. It did not go as well for him as we had hoped. It took him several nights to make his way to the safe-house, and when he got there the police were waiting for him."

"Was it a trap? Did the villager double-cross us?" I put the

The Spot The War Forgot

spoonful of potato in my mouth and ate as he answered:

"*Nein*, you know how it is in small towns where everyone knows everyone, it is impossible to keep a secret. The cobbler served a six-month jail sentence, and was released back to Berrima the other day."

"I suppose that has put him off making moonshine in his cottage again."

"*Ja* and he is not interested in our smuggling ring because we go through the bush at night. He said the worst part of running from the law was moving through the trees in the dark."

"Why?"

"Said it was terrifying. He imagined there was a reward on his head and trackers or dogs were pursuing him."

"I hardly think so, he is not Ned Kelly."

"You imagine all sorts of things when you are alone in the bush at night,"

"The smugglers who haul the stuff from the Surveyor General didn't waste any time recruiting him," said Hugo.

"Is he joining them?"

Hugo stirred tea leaves into the boiling billy. "He certainly is. He likes the fact that only fifty paces and a wall stand in the way of quick riches."

"Isn't he afraid of the guards?"

"The risk is small, for the men have meticulously researched the safest way and time to haul the noble stuff in."

"I suppose that means they know which guards can be bribed."

"The cobbler did not elaborate on their methods, but that is undoubtedly true." Hugo handed us each a cup of tea. "So, what is the plan for next week?"

"On Thursday we will (one by one) take a boat up the river to the Berrima Common," said Heinrich, pausing to take a sip of tea. "When you get to the part of the river that comes close to the Moss Vale road, hide your boat and walk back. Seeing as this is your first time, Wolfgang, you can follow me. We will leave at 10 am."

"Then what?"

"That is all you need to know to begin with. When you see me move out, start following, but leave a bit of distance between us so it is not apparent we are together. Oh, and one more thing, Wolfgang, bring the biggest boat you can lay your hands on."

....

"Heinrich said to take the biggest boat," I said to Billy on Thursday morning as we stood looking at our boats. "There are four of us and twenty cases of whiskey to shift."

"Take the Attila then, she is much bigger than the Nelly or the canoe. You can get a couple of cases in the bow and three in the stern easily."

"Good idea," I said, climbing into the boat.

"I see Heinrich coming," said Billy, handing me the oars. "Good luck with your adventure."

"Thanks."

I dipped the oars into the water and with a few strong pulls drew away from the bank. While I waited, I puddled about the lake aimlessly. Heinrich passed without acknowledging me, and when he was a safe distance away, I followed him up the river.

It was a lovely day for paddling about on the water. The

The Spot The War Forgot

sky was blue and the river brown between the dark woods that were thick with yellow wattle flowers. Amidst the tea tree and shrubs rose many eucalyptus trees, whose smooth trunks dripped ribbons of bark, while upon their twisted branches perched cockatoos. I whistled as I pulled at the oars, aware life does not get better than a boat on a river. At length, we came to the stretch of water that ran close to the road. Heinrich moved to the side, and his boat made a soft scraping noise as the bottom rubbed across the sand. I followed his lead and together we pulled our boats onto the riverbank and camouflaged them with branches and leaves.

"This is where everything is supposed to be," said Heinrich, walking towards a lonely hut set halfway between the river and the road. He opened the door and smiled. "I'll just check there are twenty cases here, I don't want to pay for more than I get. Tell me if you see anyone coming."

I nodded and walked a little distance away to a spot where I could see both the road and the river easily. There was no one about.

"So far so good," said Heinrich returning. "The others will be making their way here soon, so we'd best be off. Meet me at midnight, and remember to bring a rope."

Then he slipped into the bush, and I did not see him again until we met by the prison wall under the starry sky. I was proud of how I managed to get up and over the wall that night, for it was no small accomplishment.

"Well done, Wolfgang," whispered Hugo, as my feet touched the ground.

My heart was racing and I shivered. "It felt higher than I expected," I said, looking at the wall rising from the cliff like the battlements of an ancient castle.

The nameless fourth man of our team jumped down beside me. "The first time is the worst," he said, as we untied ourselves. "It gets easier."

We left our ropes dangling and slipped quietly down the steep bank to the well-worn track along the edge of the river. Treading softly and without speaking, we walked single-file under the bridge (that crossed the main road) and through the village. Dogs barked as we passed near houses and small farms, but nobody took any notice. We continued walking and at length, we came to the place where the whiskey and boats were hidden. In the dim moonlight, I saw Heinrich and the others pull their boats into the river. Following their example, I pushed the branches off the Attila and dragged her down to the edge of the water.

"Five cases each," whispered Henrich. "Get them loaded as quick as you can. We don't want to be out here longer than we need to be. Every minute is a minute the guards might find our ropes."

We transferred the cases to our boats swiftly and pushed off. It was quicker rowing downstream. Away we went in real sailor fashion until we came close to the jail, where we shipped our oars and drifted silently past. Once we were a safe distance away the oars came out again, and we rowed with all our strength until we came to Nobbys Hill.

"Will we get all the whisky in the pit?" Hugo asked quietly, as we pulled our boats onto the sand.

"*Ja*, should do," whispered Heinrich, lifting a case from his boat. "We got the pit finished this afternoon. You will see it is much wider and deeper than it was last week. Watch out you

The Spot The War Forgot

don't fall in, it is very dark under the trees."

With the warning ringing in my ears, I swung a crate out of the Attila and picked my way carefully up the black hillside. By day the distance from the river to the bush cellar was about a hundred meters, but that night I swear it stretched into miles. When I got there, the others had removed the camouflage and the planks covering the hole. Henrich slid into the pit.

"Hand them to me and I'll stack them," he said, as Hugo passed him a crate.

One by one we gave him our treasure, before heading back to the river for another load. When all the loot was safely stashed in the pit, Heinrich climbed out and we laid the decking back in place.

"Spread dirt over the wood," said the nameless man, "and then cover it with leaves and grass."

I should have been tired but adrenalin and excitement kept me awake and alert. It wasn't until after we arrived back at the jail and scaled the wall safely, that tiredness hit me. My eyes felt heavy and my hands shook as I coiled my rope.

"How was that, Wolfgang?" said Hugo. "Exciting enough for you?"

"*Wunderbar*" I bluffed, not wishing to appear weak.

"You will like it even better when you get your share of the profit."

The next morning Nobbys Hill was a popular destination. One by one, customers (wearing large coats) scaled the hill to our pit shop. The nameless man took charge of the sales, while Heinrich in the Crow's Nest high above, scanned the landscape with his telescope.

"If you want to join the drinking party, head up the hill,"

said the nameless man, taking money from a customer with one hand as he slipped him a bottle with the other. "There's an overhanging rock not far from the summit, they are sheltering under there. If you hear three whistle blasts, hide your bottles and cups in the bushes, and scatter."

The man nodded as he tucked the bottle inside his jacket.

"One more thing, bury empty bottles under the overhang or leave them in the old solitary confinement cell."

"The one below the cell block?"

"That's the one. It's got double doors and the guards never go there."

"*Jawohl,*."

He moved off, and after a gap of a few minutes, the man at the head of the hidden queue scurried up the bank to our shop in the bush. All day business was brisk and before long we were sold out. My share of the profit was a nice sum, enough to tempt me over the wall at midnight many more times. So often in fact, by the end of our stay, the ground level under the overhanging rock had risen significantly, and the underground cell was two-thirds packed with empty bottles.

The Spot The War Forgot

April 1916
20,000 French Women and Girls Forced to Perform Agricultural Work in Occupied France

The Machotka Family Arrive

The General Store kept a nice selection of pocket knives. I considered the merits of each knife carefully. Nearby Frau Hurtzig and Frau Jepsen chatted as they waited for William Davis to pack their orders.

"What a dreadful Easter," said Frau Hurtzig. "My family would be shocked if they saw the lack of religious fervour in this place."

"I recall that many of your family are clergymen, are they not?"

"*Ja*, it is a disgrace the authorities won't send dear Pastor Treuz down here. When I heard he was interned at the Holsworthy camp, I thought for sure they would listen to my request to transfer him. I even sent my plea through the proper channel of the Camp Committee, along with a list of others who desired his transfer, but nothing!"

"Did you ever get a reply? Perhaps they are still processing it, you know how slow they are."

"They say we can have any pastor except him."

Frau Jepsen's eyebrows shot up. "Why is this?"

"The Government believe him to be an agitator and subversive, because of some view he expressed publicly."

"About what?"

"The relationship between the Prussian State church with either the Australians or Austrians, I'm not sure which, for Tote's dog got the letter before me and the ink had run in parts."

I picked out a bone-handled knife while the women talked and took it to the counter. "Is the sheath included in the price?" I asked Mrs Davis.

"Yes," she said nodding. "That's a good quality knife, made in the U.S.A."

"I'll have it," I said, placing money on the counter.

William Davis finished packing Frau Hurtzig's order as his wife handed me two pennies change.

"A treat for good little girls," said Davis, pulling two lollypops out of a jar. He leant across the counter and handed Hanna and Lore one each.

"What do you say, girls?" prompted their mother.

"Thank you, Herr Davis," they said, smiling.

"I'll carry that home for you Frau Hurtzig," I said, scooping the heavy box off the counter.

"Thank you, Wolfgang."

"I will see you tomorrow, Luise," said Frau Jepsen, picking up a brown paper bag. "*Auf Wiedersehen.*"

The Spot The War Forgot

"*Auf Wiedersehen*," said Frau Hurtzig, before ushering her children out the door.

Davis twisted the OPEN sign on the door to CLOSED as we walked across the road and turned towards Frau Hurtzig's house.

"That is strange," she said, as we passed the sentries standing by the picket fence, "the lamps of the sitting room are alight. I am not expecting Gust to be home, it was his turn to sit with Captain Pharen."

"Poor old Captain Pharen," I said. "He is not the same since the deaths in his family."

Frau Hurtzig, bit her fingernails as she stared at the lights, and answered absently. "*Ja*, it is sad." She clutched my arm suddenly. "I am glad you are with me, Wolfgang."

"I won't leave until we find out what is going on."

"Hanna and Lore, stay out here until Mama calls," said Frau Hurtzig, mounting the steps to the veranda.

I put the groceries down so my hands were free for fighting (should it be necessary) and pushed open the door.

"Hello, Wolfgang," boomed Captain Hurtzig in hearty tones. "Come and meet Paul Machotka and his family. They have just arrived from Bourke."

"How do you do," said Paul, shaking my hand.

His accent sounded like Julius' accent, so while Frau Hurtzig called, "It's alright children, Papa is home." I said, "Are you by any chance Hungarian?"

"Only technically. I come from Bohemia, a province of the Austro-Hungarian Empire, and my wife, Edna, comes from Los Angeles," he said, as Frau Hurtzig and the girls bustled inside.

W.E. Hamilton

Frau Hurtzig greeted him and then we all passed into the front room.

A beautiful woman arose from the couch as we entered, and when I saw her I sucked in my breath sharply. She was trim and delicate of form, with golden-brown hair twisted into a soft pompadour that framed her pretty face. Beside her were three little girls.

"Mrs Machotka. This is my wife, Luise, and our girls Hanna and Lore," said Captain Hurtzig. "And, Luise. This is Edna Machotka and their girls Carmen and Eva." He paused. "I don't recall the baby's name," he added apologetically.

Edna stroked the head of the toddler clinging to her skirts. "This is Manon," she said, with an American twang.

"It is nice to meet you. How wonderful to finally have some children the same age as our girls."

"I am delighted to meet you too, and be here," said Mrs Machotka. "I was desperate to get out of Bourke."

"Was the camp bad?"

"Oh, the hotel was alright, it was the devastating heat, scorching sand storms and flies, that I couldn't stand. The children suffered terribly with the flies. Every child in the camp got eye infections from the stings of those dreadful insects; the babies suffered the most, poor things."

Frau Hurtzig switched her attention to the children. "The girl's eyes do look red and swollen. I'll give you some Golden Ointment for them. We all got terrible eye infections a while ago. The doctor prescribed useless eyewashes that did nothing. We got worse and worse until Rose Izzard told me to get a tube of Golden Ointment from the General Store. It was like a miracle. Cleared our eyes in no time. Since then, I always keep

The Spot The War Forgot

a tube of it in the cupboard."

Who is Rose Izzard?"

"A local woman. She is the district nurse and midwife. When she's not busy delivering babies and dispensing medical advice, she helps her husband run the livery stable."

"Which shipping line did you sail for, Paul?" I asked as we sat down.

"I am not a sailor I am a farmer trained in horticulture. I was sent to Berrima the first time, on account of my cap."

"Your cap?" exclaimed Frau Hurtzig.

"The first time?" I said.

Paul nodded. "Last year, I happened to be wearing a peaked cap and the officer I usually reported to at the barracks in Sydney, was away. The new man assumed I was a seaman because of my hat, and nothing would persuade him differently, so he sent me down here."

"Good heavens, I remember you! You were here on our first night. You're the man with the souvenir hat!

"I was indeed, and as I recall there was no furniture in the jail or hot dinner. We had to sleep on the freezing floor while the wind blew through the open window above us. We called it…"

"Castle Foreboding," I cried. "Worst night of my life. I wondered what we had come to."

"We all did."

"How long did you stay here?" said Captain Hurtzig.

"Only one day, as soon as they discovered the mistake, they moved me to the Holsworthy camp."

"It was awful," said the beautiful woman. "I hoped he would rejoin the girls and I, in Sydney, but they kept him there for months. "I was able to visit him every four weeks for a few hours, and occasionally they let him visit me, but always a guard accompanied him. We were finally reunited early January and sent to the Bourke camp for large families."

"How did you get here?" said Frau Hurtzig.

"Through me," said the beautiful woman. "As a citizen of the United States, I appealed to the American consul for our family to be sent to Berrima."

"And fourteen months after that first night, we are finally here for the second time," finished Paul.

"I am surprised you wished to return after such an awful beginning," said Captain Hurtzig.

"The jail was rough I admit," said Paul, "but during our long walk from the station, I was able to observe the land we passed through, and saw it was good agricultural land. Twenty-four hours was long enough to realize we were going to be given a lot of freedom during the day. That was when I realized I could grow crops here."

"It is my husband's dream to emigrate to Australia so he can work land he actually owns," the beautiful woman explained. "Only the aristocracy may own land in Bohemia. That is a hard thing for a man who comes from a family of beet farmers."

"This area could be turned into the garden of Eden with the right management," said Paul, his face lighting up. "The soil is good and there is enough rainfall, not like the dustbowl of Bourke. There was no hope there. It is not surprising the town has been abandoned."

"You will find Castle Foreboding much more comfortable than you remember it," I said. "It is almost homely."

Captain Hurtzig turned to his wife, "I have invited Mrs

The Spot The War Forgot

Machotka and the children to stay here until they can find a house in the village."

Frau Hurtzig turned pale and stood up. "I'll make another pot of coffee for us all," she said, with brittle brightness. "Come and help me August, the groceries need putting away."

Captain Hurtzig and his wife went into the kitchen and I, picking up the box by the front door, followed.

"I do not wish to be inhospitable, August," hissed his wife, shutting the door behind us, "but where am I going to put an extra woman and three children? This is not a big apartment."

"They can sleep in here."

"It's very awkward working around a guest sleeping in the kitchen." Frau Hurtzig, banged the kettle on the stove. "Especially one I have just met. Besides, the kitchen is shared with Frau Glintz."

I handed Captain Hurtzig a bag of flour and he put it in the cupboard as he answered:

"Don't fret, *liebling*. "I have spoken to Frau Glintz and she is willing to help out. Mrs Machotka seems a nice woman and it will not be for long."

Frau Hurtzig slapped the coffee pot on the kitchen table. "How can you say that, Gust? There is not a house to be had. All the empty ones have been snaffled up by the wealthy men. If we are not careful, we will never get rid of them."

"Would you rather I let them sleep in the street?"

"Of course not, but another family is a lot to squeeze in. It is bad enough Frau Glintz is on the other side of the communicating door."

Captain Hurtzig took a packet of tea from me and poured leaves into the tea caddy. "I am sure something will turn up, my dear."

"I pray it will, although I have little hope. It will take a small miracle for the Machotkas to find a house."

The bugle sounded.

"I must go, Lulu," said Captain Hurtzig, kissing her. "I will see you tomorrow morning."

Then we all said goodbye, and taking Paul with us, we went back to the prison for rollcall and dinner.

The Spot The War Forgot

May 1916
Britain and France Secretly sign the Sykes-Picot Agreement

The Beautiful Woman

Rumours that a beautiful American woman had arrived in town spread like wildfire through the camp. Those who glimpsed her the next morning as she and her husband went house hunting, added more praises to her growing reputation. Even the guard who escorted them around the town was smitten.

"A beautiful woman and a real lady," he said, as we clustered about him that afternoon. "I'm glad she found a house, I was afraid she wouldn't, housing being as scarce as it is."

"Which house is it?"

"The duplex house in Oxley Street that belongs to the Old Maid."

"That will be the house adjoining Dehnicke, Meyer, and Weinreich's place," said Billy, "the one opposite my cottage. I noticed their neighbours shifting out the other day."

"I don't know how she will get on?" said the guard,

frowning. "I saw her luggage. The poor thing has only a couple of trunks, a box of bits and pieces, and feather bedding. At least the bedding will be useful. We set up some army cots for her and the children, but other than that they have nothing, and no money to get anything."

It was obvious the Home Help Squad needed to do something. Billy, Ernst, Michael, Hermann, and I, smiled with pleasure. While we helped out all the families, a poor and beautiful woman inspired an extra measure of chivalry. Along with tools and nails, we gathered packing cases and timber from the bush and went to the beautiful woman's house. I knocked on the door and the beautiful woman opened it.

"Frau Machotka, would you allow us to help you?" I said, bowing and smiling.

The beautiful woman inclined her head like a snow queen and opened the door wide. "You are most kind. My family and I are grateful for any assistance," she said, in a calm moderate tone.

We stepped inside and I looked around. The floorplan of the house was a mirror image to its twin next door. It consisted of four rooms; a living room, kitchen, and two bedrooms. In each of the bedrooms sat a chamber pot, a trunk, army cots, and bedding. In the kitchen were a kettle, three pots, and a few bits of crockery, while on the mantelpiece of the livingroom fireplace, sat a box of delicate Christmas tree ornaments (of Austrian origin.) That was all.

"I am ashamed you should see us like this," said the beautiful woman, with a sigh that pierced our hearts. I had to sell my jewellery and things of value so I and the children wouldn't starve while my husband was in the Holsworthy camp." She

The Spot The War Forgot

turned to him. "Oh Paul, it is so hard that the sale for the Villa in Bohemia fell through. I never would have come if I thought this would happen. We could have stayed on my parent's farm in Los Angeles."

"Don't fret, my darling." Paul put his arm around her shoulders. "Australia is the land of promise. Since my first year of college, I have longed to get here. I am strong, and people in Australia need to eat like everyone else in the world. This is a place where not even war can stop our plans for market gardening." He glanced out the window. "The land is fertile and ours to use. We are better off here than in Bohemia. Once you have had a cup of coffee you will feel better."

"Halloo." A youthful and handsome man strode to the open door.

"Hello, come in," said Machotka."

"I am Captain Meyer," said the man bouncing into the room. He pointed at the two men behind him, "and this is Captain Dehnicke, and Erich Weinriech, we are your neighbours."

Machotka shook hands with the three men. "I am Paul Machotka and this is my wife Edna."

The beautiful woman inclined her head and extended her hand. "I am pleased to make your acquaintance."

"Charmed to meet you," said Captain Meyer, bowing and kissing her lily-white fingers. "We have brooms, buckets, and scrubbing brushes, and are here to clean." He waggled his eyebrows at the children, who were staring at him with owl eyes, and they giggled at his antics.

"So kind." The beautiful woman retrieved her hand and dabbed her eyes with a lace handkerchief. "It is such a comfort to be surrounded with such strong and honourable men."

W.E. Hamilton

At this, we all puffed out our chests and prepared to work. The beautiful woman responded by rescuing the delicate baubles from the mantelpiece. Then she leaned ornamentally against the wall with the box cradled in her hands, watching us. We rolled up our sleeves (so she could see our muscles) and the two captains and Erich, grabbed brooms and started sweeping vigorously, while Ernst, Michael and I, (bending our strong backs and flexing our broad shoulders) sawed and hammered with gusto. We hardly noticed when Machotka took two of the buckets and went to draw water from the well sunk a little distance from the house. While he was gone, Billy fixed the grate in the huge fireplace in the front room and lit the iron stove in the kitchen behind. Ernst started making a table from packing cases, Michael made a cupboard, and Hermann bashed together a bench from bush timber. I, meanwhile, cut saplings into the right lengths to make a chair.

Captain Meyer, unlike the rest of us, did not pick up a hammer or saw, or even a broom. Instead, he flopped on the floor by the children and soon had them squealing with laughter as he pulled silly faces at them, and stacked wood-offcuts into towers. Once Machotka came back with the water, it was not long before scrubbing brushes were scratching away at the walls, and the kettle whistling merrily on the stove. Then Billy made a pot of coffee and while he waited for it to brew, whisked across the road to his cottage and popped back with a Black Forest cake.

"Just as well I bought a cake this morning," he said, slicing it up.

We downed our tools and sat on the floor with our backs leaning against the walls. The beautiful woman perched on

The Spot The War Forgot

my chair and drank genteelly from a china cup, while the rest of us gulped coffee from tumblers or jam jars. Now she had something to sit on, and food and drink, the beautiful woman looked happier. She smiled at the children and Captain Meyer, who had stopped building their castle of blocks and instead, were stuffing their mouths full of chocolate and cream.

"Hello, need any help?" called Richard Priess, as he and Rudolf Carstens, Carl Euringer, and Mahler, crowded into the room. "We heard the clatter of hammers and saws and thought we could lend a hand. What do you need?"

The Machotkas were reluctant to say, but Richard and the others took the situation in at a glance. They scurried off and, by the time we had finished our coffee, were back loaded with pots and pans, dishes, pillows, and blankets. Then Richard, Malher and Eric set to work making beds, while Rudolf fashioned a couch, and the rest of us continued with our carpentry and cleaning. Amid the activity, the beautiful woman cheered us on by her loveliness and words of praise.

"Charming," she said, looking at the packing case beds. "I feel like I am in the old storybook, The Swiss Family Robinson. I keep expecting to see a treehouse somewhere."

"Heinrich Eckerlein has a treehouse and a rope ladder," I said, grinning. "And we are sort of shipwrecked and stranded here, but Heinrich's treehouse is not a family home. It's part of our booze smuggling operation." I turned to the beautiful woman's husband and tapped my nose. "If you want a bottle of whisky, Machotka, just let me know."

Machotka's handsome face under his dark curling hair lit up.

"No, Paul," said the beautiful woman laying a queenly

hand on his arm. "The children need milk."

Machotka's face fell and there was an awkward silence until Rudolf said:

"There, it's finished. Come and try my couch, Mrs Machotka, I made it from the wood and canvass of one of the army cots."

The beautiful woman bit her lip and looked troubled. "Oh dear," she said, "the cots are not ours they were only on loan. The commandant will expect them back."

"Don't worry about it, the commandant won't remember whether he lent you four or five cots, and if he does, just smile at him and say you are sorry for the mistake."

"And if he still fusses, tell him the canteen will pay for it," said Captain Dehnicke. "Compared to all those instruments Fritz Rittig has persuaded them to buy, an army cot is nothing."

The alabaster brow of the beautiful woman smoothed, and we gathered around to watch her sink gracefully into Rudolf's couch.

"Very comfortable," she said. And her smile enslaved us all.

By the end of the week, there was scarcely a man in the camp (starved as we were for female companionship) who was not secretly in love with the beautiful woman.

We of the Home-Help-Squad chopped wood because we loved her.

Billy killed spiders and bugs because he loved her.

Captain Meyer romped with the kids and bounced them on his knees because he loved her.

Men who sailed the far east gave her colourful Japanese wall hangings.

The Spot The War Forgot

And the recluse, Eno Molnar, oozed the despair of unrequited love through his sad eyes as he stared at her like a spaniel gazing at his master.

The beautiful woman's husband was torn between pride in his lovely wife and resentment at the admiration she inspired. But if the beautiful woman was aware of our infatuation, she did not show it by word or deed, or even the slightest look or raise of her eyebrow. Her actions were above reproach, which added to her charm.

By dusk and the bugle call, we were almost done. While Machotka lit two kerosene lanterns, and Billy built up the fire, we stacked the wood offcuts in a basket beside the fireplace and gathered our tools together.

"I can't thank you enough," said the beautiful woman. She looked around. "It feels like a completely different place."

And indeed, it did. In the soft lamplight, the shabby room with its make-do furnishings glowed with warmth and charm. Billy gave one last poke at the fire and the logs flamed bright in the cavernous fireplace, the oily sap in the green logs sizzled out the cut ends with a pungent aroma.

"It is our pleasure, Mrs Machotka," said Captain Meyer, sweeping off his hat and bowing low.

His words were more than a courteous pleasantry. Spending the afternoon in the company of a beautiful woman was a rare and pleasant experience in Berrima in 1916.

W.E. Hamilton

May 1916
In the Biggest Battle yet, Britain's Royal Navy Grand Fleet and Germany's Navy High Seas Fleet fight to a Stalemate

Machotka Begins a Garden

The beautiful woman's house stood well back from the dusty orange road. Twenty-five feet of flat land stretched between the street and the narrow front veranda, while beyond the back veranda, an acre of land dropped in a gradual descent from a rocky barrier, towards the river. The front yard, which was enclosed by a dilapidated paling fence, presented a dismal view of rocks, weeds, old tins, and broken bottles. Scattered between them were pancakes of aged cow dung, baked hard by many summers. Every day as I wandered past their yard, I saw Machotka and his girls diligently working to transform this wasteland into a garden. One morning I heard the high treble of children's voices and drawing alongside the Machotka's yard, I leaned over the fence and spoke to Carmen and Eva

The Spot The War Forgot

who were singing as they picked up rocks.

"What are you doing?"

They stopped singing, and dropped their rocks on the ground, eager for a chat and a rest.

"We are helping Papa. We collect the rocks and junk and take them around the back where he is terracing the steep part," said Carmen. "He's using the rocks for stonewalls, and the bottles and cans as a base for paths and a summerhouse."

"Some friends in Sydney sent Papa seeds, and he is going to plant them beside the long ugly fences and between stone walls and paths. By summer, glorious flowers will border a big veggie garden," said Eva, she sighed and kicked the stone at her feet. "At least that is what Papa says."

"I'm sure it is true because Papa never lies," said Carmen. "But it is hard to imagine."

"I am sure it will be lovely and you girls are a big help to your father."

"I don't mind collecting the rocks and bottles, or even pulling weeds," said Carmen, "but I hate collecting manure. The old hard stuff in our yard is not so bad, but Papa has put wheels on one of our trunks and expects us to go throughout the village and countryside collecting fresh dung." Her face darkened. "It's humiliating, even the poorest village children don't have to collect pooh."

"And we have to pick it up with our hands," said Eva, pulling a face.

"Ah, now, I can help you with that," I said smiling, "I have a shovel you can have if you like."

The girl's faces lit up.

"Ooh, yes, that would be wonderful. If we had a shovel, we

wouldn't have to touch it."

"It will still be humiliating," said Carmen, "but at least our hands will stay clean."

I left them to continue their rock gathering and went to get the shovel from my hut. When I got back the front yard was empty, so I picked my way through the littered ground to the veranda.

Right from the start the Machotkas were hospitable and held an open house. The front door stood ajar most of the time and friends were in and out every day. Frau Hurtzig and her children were there when I arrived, together with Julius. The five children were playing on the back veranda and Julius was showing the women a photograph of Marcella.

"Is she not beautiful?" he said, returning to his photograph after the women had greeted me.

"Indeed," said the beautiful woman, inclining her head.

"Quite lovely," said Frau Hurtzig.

"I have built a Villa in the bush as a token of my love for her."

"How romantic," said Frau Hurtzig. "That is a big thing to do."

Julius puffed out his chest. "I have done more. When war broke out, I was sailing my passenger steamer through the Adriatic Sea, when I saw a mine floating not far from my ship. 'Ah, Julius,' I said to myself. 'Here is your opportunity to impress Marcella by becoming a hero and earning a medal.' So, displaying great bravery, I hitched the mine to the back of my ship on a long rope and towed it into Trieste."

"My goodness!" Frau Hurtzig's eyebrows shot up. "Did you get a medal for bravery?"

The Spot The War Forgot

Julius's face dropped and he slumped in his chair. "No, I was reprimanded harshly, and Marcella heartlessly agreed with my superior."

It seemed the right time to divert the conversation, so I said to the beautiful woman:

"I've brought this shovel for the girls to use on their dung collecting excursions."

"That is most kind, Wolfgang. Are you sure you can spare it?"

"*Ja*, for sure, I have a better one. I found this one abandoned in a derelict shed and the broken handle is too short for me, but it is plenty long enough for your girls."

I had barely finished speaking when Billy breezed through the door.

"The post has come and there is a letter for you Edna."

She glanced at the handwriting and smiled faintly. "From Mother." She slit the envelope with a butter knife and slid out the sad remains of a page. "Surely the censor could have left 'Dear Edna' and 'Love from Mother!' Bitterness warmed her cheeks and tinged her tone as she held up a paper frame.

Frau Hurtzig sighed. "He is excessive with the scissors. He snips out even the slightest hint of war news. At least you know your mother is thinking of you."

"I suppose so," said the beautiful woman, reverting to a gracious snow queen once more.

"I got a lovely letter from Eva yesterday, and a beautiful photograph." Frau Hurtzig took an envelope from her purse. "She looks slim and pretty and is doing very well at school."

I could see she was about to read it aloud and as I had already heard the (letter line by line) and was not anxious to hear it again, I excused myself by saying, "I'll take this to the girls."

"They are out the back," said the beautiful woman, pointing through the kitchen doorway.

I found Carmen and Eva sprawled on the floor of the veranda drawing pictures. After I had given the shovel to them, I walked down the steps and into the backyard. Matchotka was busy fitting rocks on top of a low stone wall. The tall man was the complete opposite in nature to his beautiful wife. Where she was a cool snow queen, he was warm, generous, and inventive. He was also impulsive and explosive. Billy and I agreed that the way he swung between optimism and despair was a lot like Julius.

"Must be the Hungarian blood in him," we said to each other. When he was up, he was wonderful company, but when he was down, we trod carefully, for it was easy to offend his sense of dignity as an officer and a gentleman.

"Hello," growled Machotka, straightening up as I came over to him.

"I have just given your girls a shovel for when they go dung collecting."

Machotka's face flamed into redness. "Are you implying I cannot provide for my family? Because if you are, we can settle this right now with a duel." He lifted his voice and shouted, "Girls bring me my pistols!"

I held up my hands and backed away in alarm. I did not think the guards would let him keep pistols but I did not want to risk it.

"*Nein, nein*, not at all. The shovel is merely a plaything. I do not mean any disrespect."

The Spot The War Forgot

"That is alright then," said Machotka, his face returning to its normal pallor.

I picked up a rock and put it on the top of the wall. "Tell me about the garden, what are you are going to plant?" I could not have chosen a better subject. Machotka was passionate about horticulture. His face changed from gloominess into beaming excitement.

"Dahlias, foxgloves and snapdragons in the terraces and around the borders," he said, pointing to the stone trenches and long fences, "also, Canterbury bells, zinnias and chrysanthemums. Then in the vegetable garden, I will plant root vegetables, melons, horseradish, herbs, and all manner of salad vegetables. Of course, the marigolds will be in with the vegetables, for the best way to keep bugs away from tomatoes is to plant marigolds around them."

"I didn't know that. Where did you learn all this?"

"I come from generations of beet growers and went to horticulture college. Of course, I will be planting beets, and the usual pumpkins and cabbages, but I want to try raising more exotic vegetables like artichokes and celeriac. Asparagus doesn't thrive in this climate and soil," he said, crumbling the orange dirt between his fingers, "but I am convinced if I lightly salt the soil and plant it in mounded rows, I can get it to grow. The trick is to harvest asparagus white."

"White?"

"That is what you call harvesting the spears once they have barely lifted out of the ground."

For the next few hours, I listened to him talk animatedly about plants and the best way to grow them as we continued building the terraces.

W.E. Hamilton

"Machotka's not a bad sort," I said to Billy later that evening. "He is very knowledgeable about plants."

"And hardworking," said Billy. "Every day he and the girls are out there slogging away. It is a large area for a man and two children to dig and water by hand. I suppose that is the reason he has sudden spurts of anger."

"Edna says he used to be high-spirited and fun-loving; adventurous to the point of recklessness. The disappointments and trials of the last few years have worn down his nervous strength."

We were silent for a time as we thought this over. Billy was the first to speak.

"For the kindness the Machotkas show by opening their home to us, I am going to keep their firewood basket full. Chopping wood is one less job Machotka will have to do."

"And I have a spade, I can help dig the garden."

The next day I started digging while Billy chopped wood, and we were not the only friends of the Machotkas who helped them out. The whole time Machotka was at Berrima he was seldom alone in his garden. And as we dug alongside him, weeded, or slopped water on plants from kerosine tins, he imparted horticultural knowledge and inspiration. Paul Machotka was the odd man out, but our respect for him grew as steadily as his garden. He was not a captain, a sailor, or even a German, yet he became the most influential man among us.

The Spot The War Forgot

July 1916
Battle of the Somme. British Suffer 50,000 Casualties on First Day of Fighting

The Orchestra

Fritz Rittig was a marine engineer but he should have been a travelling salesman, for I never met a more persuasive or persistent man. I tried to keep away from him but every so often he caught me. Today was one of those days. I rounded a corner and jumped as I came face to face with him.

"What about it, Wolfgang?" A few lessons and some serious practice will polish your old skills up in no time."

"I haven't a violin," I objected.

"No problem. Thanks to the Camp Committee's generosity I have more violins than players. Just give the word and I can set you up with an instrument and sheet music, the beginner's class is at two pm every second afternoon."

Fritz was hard to resist, his all-consuming passion for music was mesmerizing, and I didn't like to disappoint him.

"I'd be more interested in playing the piano," I stalled, but the bush piano isn't as good as the tin cello, nobody has managed to tune it properly."

"Ah-ha!" Fritz pounced on my words. "My friend you are in luck, I have a piano coming very soon, and Herr Albert has agreed to give music lessons to anyone interested. Until then I will loan you a violin and you can come to my beginner's class to brush up on reading music."

"What could I say?" I said to Billy later, as we sat in his kitchen, "he was so sincere.

"It will do you good," said Billy, unsympathetically. He opened the case of my borrowed instrument and took the violin out carefully. "Playing music is an excellent workout for the brain and soothing for the emotions." He turned the violin over and inspected the seams and the fineness of the scroll before drawing his bow across the strings to test its tone. "You might even decide to stick to the violin once you get started."

I pulled a face. "I should never have complained to a man who loves the viola. I might have guessed you would take his side."

"You will be coming to the concert practice this afternoon in the dining hall, of course."

"But I am only a beginner."

"Makes no difference to Fritz, he will put you in third position and give you something simple to play. The man is a genius at adapting music to everyone's skill level."

I frowned. "I have not heard of third-violin only first and second-violin."

"Fritz invented third-violin, it's part of his adaptions." Billy put my violin back in its case reverently. "We've just enough

The Spot The War Forgot

time for a cup of coffee and then we will go."

We had our coffee and all too soon we were back at the jail and entering the large mess hall. Many men (all carrying instruments) milled about while others rearranged the furniture. Billy and I put our cases down and went to help.

"Why are we rehearsing here instead of the theatre?" I said, pushing tables out of the way. Billy pulled the rough benches into rows fanning out from a central music stand.

"The DTB are using it and don't want us to distract them."

"Fair enough."

Fritz had been busy. There were a lot of newcomers like myself. Those who knew the drill took their seats while the rest of us waited for Fritz to assign us a position in his orchestra. When everyone was seated, Fritz took his conductor's baton and tapping the music stand to focus our attention, proceeded to rehearse us. Then the old prison walls echoed with squeaks and toots, bangs and screeches. Billy was right to call Fritz a genius. I don't know how he managed it, but gradually with growing clarity, a semblance of a melody began to emerge from the pandemonium. By the end of the session it was possible to recognize some of the tunes.

"That will do," said Fritz, calling a halt after a couple of hours. "A few weeks of solid practice and we will be ready for the Whit Sunday concert. You will be pleased to hear the piano is coming tomorrow, so I need plenty of helpers in the morning to lift it off the wagon."

War brings shortages, but the one thing we were never short of in Berrima was manpower. As soon as the horses clattered into the prison yard, a dozen or more men swarmed around and soon had the piano off the wagon.

W.E. Hamilton

"Where do you want it, Rittig?"

"Herr Albert and I have decided the courthouse is the best place for it. Take it there."

So, we carried the piano out the prison gate, past the Hurtzig's house, around the corner, and marched over the road and into the courtroom. There we halted before putting our burden down, not far from a long table where three men sat reading.

"You're not leaving that noisy thing in here, Rittig," said Rittmeister von Klewitz, looking up from his book. He patted the small dog at his feet with the unconcern of one who expects to be obeyed by man and beast. "Move along, this is a reading room."

Herr Albert tipped his hat politely. "I wonder, sir, could you suggest a place for it as the jail is too damp and cold for a piano."

"Oh, is that ancient upright thing a piano?" said von Klewitz, looking down his nose at it.

"Perhaps it could go in the classroom close to the side door," said von Blumenthal.

"No, that is where the language classes are held, and it is seldom empty," said Fritz, "Herr Albert needs somewhere private to teach. What about the other one?"

"Out of the question," said George Mayer, "that is close to von Blumenthal, von Kewitz, and my rooms. We don't want that sort of din coming into our apartments through the wall."

Willy Maiwald, a sailor who acted as a servant to the titled men, cleared his throat before addressing von Blumenthal. "Perhaps I could make a suggestion, sir," he said, with a slight American twang. "The holding cell for prisoners is empty. It

The Spot The War Forgot

is some distance from your rooms and can be shut off from the courtroom. Perhaps the piano could be housed there?"

"Good thinking, Maiwald," said von Blumenthal, nodding approvingly at his servant. "Take the piano in there."

At his command, we marched off to the cell and jiggled the piano through the door. Inside the large room was a small woodstove, and a long table covered with an oilcloth and bench seats. We were about to set the piano down when Herr Albert cried out in alarm:

"Not there! Put it against an inner wall, a piano should never stand against an outside wall, especially a wall of sandstone."

While we did as Herr Albert instructed, both he and Fritz sat down at the table.

"I've got the list of your pupils," said Fritz, pulling a folded sheet of paper from his pocket and handing it to Herr Albert.

Herr Albert opened it and held it up so the light coming from the barred windows high above us fell on it. "This is a long list."

Fritz looked pleased. "It is indeed, eighteen men plus little Carmen Machotka and Gertrude Brauns."

"One piano is not much for twenty pupils. If they each practice half an hour a day that is still ten hours of constant playing; without counting lessons. And what is more, it must all be squeezed in between morning and evening rollcall."

"Only the men, the girls can practice after we go back to the jail."

"That still only lightens it by an hour, and each pupil will need a weekly half-hour music lesson as a bare minimum, which is another ten hours."

"Well, you best get started straight away," said Fritz,

standing up, "for there is no time to lose."

From then on, the courthouse was immersed in the noise of five-finger-exercises, scales and fumbling melodies, as we lugubriously practised. And the courthouse was not the only place of musical industry; trumpets, drums, and clarinets, a flute, viola, mandolin, guitar, several zithers, and many violins, all shrieked or boomed, trilled, thrummed, or screeched throughout the echoing corridors and prison walls. I screeched along with the worst of them for Billy was right, once I got back into the violin, I didn't want to give it up. The difficulty of hitting the right note was so addictive I kept on with it even after the piano lessons started. That the din was not a beautiful sound didn't bother those of us who made the noise, but our comrades were very insulting.

"Get out of here, take that hideous noise away," they said rudely.

They banished us to the cellars of houses or far away in the bush. Finally, after weeks of practice and rehearsals, we were ready. On the day of the concert, we took the piano from the courtroom and carried it over to the theatre, and got ready for the evening's performance.

"I'm glad I continued with the violin," I said to Billy, as we set up, "if I had given up, I would have missed out on performing tonight, or any night for that matter, as there is only room for one pianist and I will never be the best player."

Billy grinned and nodded. "The violin is a better instrument anyway," he said. "Now help me move these benches onto the stage."

We lifted them into place before setting out the customary line of folding chairs.

The Spot The War Forgot

"I can't wait to see Edna's expression when we play the opening number," I said.

"To see her lovely face light up will make all the practising worthwhile," said Billy.

And so it was. She was wearing a flowered tea-gown and her hair shone, when she entered the prison yard with the other five ladies and children. As they moved towards their seats, all three-hundred men stood rigidly at attention. Then Fritz pointed his baton at the orchestra, and in one accord, we struck up the tune of The Star-Spangled Banner. The shocked wonder that crossed the beautiful woman's face as we honoured her country, made my heart swell. That she dabbed her eyes with her handkerchief, made it all the better. When the last notes faded away, our audience took their seats somewhat nervously, for the memory of our earlier attempts still lingered. But they had nothing to fear, Fritz Rittig, through tireless efforts had whipped us into a musical organization that could tackle anything from *'A Hot Time in the Old Town'* to Warger's *'Lohengrin.'* We started with marches to honour Field Marshal von Mackensen's victory over the Serbs, then we performed selections from *The Geisha* and *Lucia di Lammermoor*, concluding the first half of the program with several short duets by a mandolin and guitar. After an interval, there were songs and dances choreographed by Oskar Bock and finally two more marches.

"I confess," said the beautiful woman, as we milled about after the concert, "I looked forward to tonight's concert with some alarm for I have a sensitive ear for music." She laughed. "But I can only say that from the moment of my entrance to the last note, the surprises have never ceased." She scattered her smiles around liberally. "Truly a performance to be proud of, my friends."

I caught one of the smiles as it passed my way, and was glad Fritz Rittig was such a persuasive man.

The Spot The War Forgot

September 1916
In Large Airship Raid 16 German Airships Bomb Southeast England

Rats and Food Cuts

The orchestra gave a concert every two weeks, and once our numbers rose from twenty-three to thirty-five musicians, we formed a brass band. Thereafter, the orchestra and the band alternated their performances, so every week there was a concert of some sort. What with the orchestra, band, choir, upgraded theatre, huts, sports and boats, there was much to occupy our time. It was not all fun and games, however, the war hung over us like a dark cloud. Fears for loved ones on the battlelines and worries over hungry families back home eroded our peace and dominated our conversations.

"Now even Romania has gone to war against us," wheezed Captain Madsen, as (with his arms around our necks) Billy and I half-carried him over to the couch in the Hurtzig's front room. "How can anyone understand that?" We lowered him slowly and lifted his swollen legs onto the cushioned seat, while Frau Hurtzig placed a pillow behind his back.

"It makes no sense," Captain Hurtzig agreed, dropping into a chair beside his friend, "why is another country getting involved in all this bloodletting after seeing the horrendous misery of others?"

Billy put another log on the fire and stirred the flames into fiercer heat. "Once this drizzle stops and you warm up, the pains in your legs will ease a little," he said, encouragingly.

But neither man was ready to cheer up.

"I don't understand why the Romanians have thrown away their good fortune," said Captain Hurtzig, gloomily.

I expected Frau Hurtzig to chip into the conversation with her usual, "I pray to God to help our German brothers," but this morning she said nothing for she had more pressing problems.

"Did you bring the rat trap, Wolfgang?"

"*Ja*," I said, pulling dowel and boards from my pocket.

"That doesn't look like much," she said, frowning.

"Oh, this is only part of it," I reassured her. "I need a bucket."

"Hanna run and get a bucket from the laundry," said Frau Hurtzig.

Hanna sped off and soon returned with a wooden bucket.

"Frau Hurtzig, do you mind if I remove the handle?" I asked as I took the bucket from her daughter.

"Do whatever you need to, just get rid of this plague of rats," she said with a shudder. "They have become so brazen at night they chew books and anything else they fancy."

"Keep the cat inside at night."

"I do, but the cat sleeps while they eat."

The Spot The War Forgot

"Lazy thing," I said, flicking the wire out of the brackets on the bucket's rim.

"Marienchen is outnumbered and expecting kittens any day, so the fight is not fair." She stopped speaking, her attention caught by my actions. "What are you doing?"

"See these nails at the end of this dowel?"

"*Ja.*"

"I poke them through the handle-holes to make a bridge across the bucket."

"How will that help?"

I leant a board against the bucket directly in line with the suspended dowel. "You bait the bucket and the rats climb up and start to cross the bridge but…" I spun the dowel, "voila, the bridge twists around and the rat falls in."

"It doesn't look very effective."

"The best things are often the simplest things."

"So they say." Frau Hurtzig bit her fingernail. "I hope you are right."

"Did you bring any music with you, Captain Masden?" said Lore, sidling up to him.

Hanna following in her wake added: "Remember when Lore and I used to walk over the gangplank to your ship, and you let us listen to your gramophone?"

"I certainly do," and forgetting the war, his face split into a jolly grin. "Wolfgang and Billy, would you run to my cell and bring back my gramophone and some records?"

"For sure."

"Which records do you want?"

"It doesn't matter, just a nice selection the children might enjoy."

Because the prison was close by, it did not take more than a few minutes before we were back with the desired items. Billy (after handing a pile of records to Captain Madsen) pulled a small table close to the couch, and I set the gramophone box on top and slipped the horn into the elbow bracket.

"Can I wind the handle?" said Hanna, as the captain popped a disk on the turntable, "I remember how to do it."

"Alright, make sure you turn smoothly and stop when it gets difficult."

"Where do you think I should put the trap?" said Frau Hurtzig, claiming my attention once more.

"Where are they coming in?"

"Through holes in the floor and skirtings."

"Let's plug them up and leave the trap in the kitchen with the cat."

Frau Hurtzig nodded. So to the melodies of Johann Strauss, we plugged rat holes with small rocks.

"There!" said Frau Hurtzig, brushing her hands together when we had finished. "That will stop the brutes under the house from getting in tonight. And the ones already inside, the trap will take care of, God willing."

"I am sure God is willing," said her husband, brushing off her words. "Is there anything to eat, Lulu?"

"What has got into you lately, Gust? I can't fill you up!"

"They have cut down our rations, instead of one and a half pounds of meat a week, each man only gets ten ounces, and the potatoes and vegetables have been reduced too."

"The dried peas and beans (that were supposed to make up for the lack of meat) have not yet arrived," said Captain Madsen.

The Spot The War Forgot

"And only one tin of jam per week," I added.

"Oh, dear," said Frau Hurtzig, worry lines creasing her forehead, "I noticed my rations were short, but I thought it was a mistake."

"If you have any jam in the cupboard, hide it," said Captain Hurtzig, "for if you save it, they will confiscate it."

"I suppose that is to stop the men using it for moonshine," said Billy.

"Maybe," I said, "or maybe it is just stinginess. I'm surprised they haven't cut our condensed milk ration, it's still one tin every twenty days."

"And that is not lavish," said Frau Hurtzig, sighing. "I'm thankful we have money for food." She snorted. "The commandant had the audacity to ask if I still needed our weekly ten-shilling allowance."

"That is because the Australian government want to introduce compulsory military service but the people are against it," said Captain Masden. "I read in the paper that a shortage of money is the objection."

"What do they imagine we will live on if they take our men's livelihood away?" said Frau Hurtzig. "It is not as if you can go back to sea."

"At least they asked if you needed it, rather than just stopping it," I said.

"That's true. We have much to thank God for. How about a big bowl of porridge? I brought a sack of oats yesterday."

That sounded good to us, so the little woman bustled out to the kitchen and came back shortly with a large pot which she set on the improvised stove in the fireplace.

"Why don't you use the stove in the kitchen?" I asked as

she started stirring the mixture.

"I prefer to cook in here rather than share with Frau Glintz. She is much improved since the baby arrived but she's still not easy to live with. Besides, the kitchen is dirty and the rats swarm over the bench at night. I have to keep food in tins with tight lids."

"I'm pleased to hear the rats have not got into the oatmeal," said Captain Hurtzig, as his wife dished big dollops of thick porridge into plates and handed them around, "but even if they had, I would still eat it I am so hungry."

"Any vermin found in the oatmeal need to watch out," said Billy, taking a plate from Frau Hurtzig, "because I'm hungry enough to eat a rat."

At this, we all laughed because things would have to get a lot worse for that to be true.

"I was hoping the garden would produce vegetables by now," said Captain Hurtzig, looking out the window at a dismal patch of dirt by the cupid fountain, "but nothing has come up yet, apart from a few lettuce seedlings."

"The wet and cold weather is the problem, it is the same with all the other gardens, everything has perished, except Machotka's garden of course," I said. "His is bursting with spinach and silverbeet, kale, broccoli, carrots, and celery."

"Have you seen the size of his cabbages?" said Billy

Captain Masden nodded. "They are huge."

"I brought garlic and spring onions from Edna the other day," said Frau Hurtzig. She pointed to a vase of flowers sitting on the cabinet of her treadle sewing machine, "and she gave me those lovely tulips and daffodils."

Everyone fell silent. The only sound as we ate our food was

The Spot The War Forgot

scratchy music.

Captain Hurtzig was the first to break the bubble of thought. "How does he do it?"

"I don't know," said Captain Madsen slowly. "I thought gardening was similar to fishing. Dig the ground into waves throw in a bit of bait (that's the seeds) then wait, before pulling out something big and tasty."

"That is what we all thought," I said, "but there is obviously more to it than fishing."

Billy tapped his teeth gently with the back of his empty spoon. "Vegetables must need more than dirt and seeds."

"And water."

"*Ja*, for sure, but we have had plenty of that these last few weeks."

"Too much," cut in Frau Hurtzig bitterly,"trying to get the washing dry is a nightmare."

"That is true," I said. "Some of the huts closest to the river have water up to their windows."

Billy's eyes narrowed and he sat up straight. "It's the pooh," he said, his face brightening. "Machotka sends his girls to collect dung every day."

"You're right," I said. "The girls hate it but he insists they do it. There has to be a good reason for that."

"I think there is more to it than that," said Captain Madsen. "The month you plant things makes a difference too. As soon as my legs get better, I'm going to find out what he is doing."

He did not have long to wait. By morning the swelling in his legs had gone down and he was feeling much better. In addition, the rain had stopped and the sun was out. He, Captain Hurtzig, and several others set off to discover the secret of green fingers. They asked me to go with them but I preferred to see how well my trap had performed. When I got to the Hurtzig's house Hanna was cutting newspaper into paper dolls while Lore sat on the couch, the tip of her tongue protruding as she poked knitting needles through a jumbled mass of wool and holes.

"It's no good," said Frau Hurtzig, in answer to my inquiry. "The rats ate the bait and jumped out. They became so cheeky they even attacked the cat and I had to take her into my room."

"It is a sorry thing when a cat must be rescued from rats."

"It is indeed. Perhaps God is not willing we should have relief from this plague."

But it seems he was after all, for the gloomy words had scarcely left Frau Hurtzig's mouth than there was a knock on the door and there stood Rose Izzard holding a big strong rat trap.

"Frau Hurtzig, I hear you are having trouble with rats."

"For sure, trouble is putting it mildly, I and the cat are overwhelmed by the rats."

"Try this," Rose handed her a trap made of wood and wire, "I find this very effective for keeping vermin out of the bags of horse feed."

"How does it work?"

"Put a bit of cheese on the prongs, pull back the spring and clip the long hook over. Be careful, though, it's sensitive, and keep it away from the children, for it can break fingers."

Frau Hurtzig thanked Rose, and after the good woman left, we experimented with setting the trap. I had just sprung it with a stick and we were exclaiming in wonder at the distance it shot across the room, when the children shrieked with excitement.

The Spot The War Forgot

The cat has had kittens," said Lore, throwing her knitting into the air. Frau Hurtzig instantly lost interest in the trap.

"Where? Not on my bed, I hope!"

"Yes, of course, Mama," said Hanna, leaving a trail of paper dolls behind her as she skipped across the room. "It's the softest place."

"I should have shut her in the kitchen," groaned Frau Hurtzig, picking up a cardboard box and dumping a wad of newspapers in the bottom. "Washing always brings on a terrible headache. Blankets will give me a migraine for sure." She sighed as she put the cat and her kittens in the box. "You can look at the kittens, girls, but don't pick them up, leave the cat alone so she can feed them. But before you do that, help me tidy this room, and then we will strip the bed."

She picked up a newspaper and was about to put it away when a headline caught her eye. She scanned the article rapidly with growing agitation.

"Praise God!" she shouted, tucking the paper under her arm. "England and Germany are exchanging prisoners over forty-five!" She grabbed her hat off the hook by the door. "I must find Gust and the older men to tell them the good news." Then ramming her hat on her head, she ran from the house without giving the washing a thought.

W.E. Hamilton

October 1916
France Uses Massive Railway Guns in an Effort to recapture Fort Douaumont from Germans

Disappointments and Surprises

The prisoners had increased from eighty-nine to over three-hundred, which was at least a hundred more than the Camp Committee and the sergeant in charge of vitals, could cope with. They bungled along as best they could but meals got more and more skimpy. At the peak of the famine, Machotka's garden bloomed into luscious vegetables. When the authorities realized there was a problem they sent a new commandant to sort out the muddle. In the hungry time before the problem was solved, gardening became very popular. Every day new gardens were popping up in patches along the river. In October, Machotka extended his garden. We watched him dig and plant his back yard, and copying, we dug and planted the ground around our huts.

The Spot The War Forgot

"What is Machotka doing today?" we asked each other as our stomach rumbled.

If the answer was, "planting lettuce," we planted lettuce. If it was, "thinning carrots," we thinned carrots. We watered when he watered, hoed when he hoed, and weeded when he weeded. We planted by Machotka's 'rules of the art,' and like his children, we were always on the lookout for manure.

Of all my friends Captain Hurtzig was the only one not gardening. His wife was in her front yard sweeping the path when I called with a tray of seedlings.

"Thank you for the offer of cabbages and peas, Wolfgang, but there is no point us planting anything," said Frau Hurtzig, pausing in her task. "For we are going home soon. The Captain is busy putting bracing points on our trunks, and I have travelling clothes to sew for the children."

"I am very happy for you Frau Hurtzig, it is wonderful news."

"Isn't it." She leant on her broom and her eyes shone as she said: "To think we will see our loved ones again. So many things have changed. All three children have grown and Hanna is a schoolgirl now."

"We will miss you very much."

At this Frau Hurtzig's eyes dimmed and her shoulders slumped. "And we will miss all of you. As internees, we have experienced the war together, analysed the news, shared daily tasks, and taken part in everything, even starving. It's a strange thing, Wolfgang, here I am on the brink of going home and while of course, I want to see my loved ones, I am not altogether happy about it. The good side is my husband will have an active life again, but it will be the start of difficulties for me. I shall have to live in the city for our house is rented out." She sighed and said in a small voice: "Except for concern about our homeland, we have no worries here."

I patted her shoulder sympathetically. "Living in the city will not be bad, you might even enjoy it."

The little woman drooped lower.

"The saddest thing of all," she wiped her eyes, "is no written account is allowed to leave the country." Her voice rose to a wail. "I have to surrender my diary! Will I ever see it again?"

I was at a loss for something to say, but happily, the clatter of horse's hooves broke her morbid train of thought as the commandant and his daughter rode past.

"Major Baxter is a good man," she said, her face brightening into a smile. "It's nice to see a father riding around with his seventeen-year-old daughter."

"The camp has been much better since he took over," I said, as we waved. "He understands us better than any of the other commandants. He's reducing the guards by eight for he says we don't need so many."

"More importantly the food rations have gone up," said Frau Hurtzig, whisking a snail off the path. "The captain was almost living on porridge before Major Baxter straightened everything out.

"Did you hear he sent the sergeant responsible for the shortages back to Holsworthy, and an internee is in charge of victuals now?"

"*Nein*, but it is a good idea. A man who eats with us will take care there is enough to go around."

I nodded. "*Ja*, for sure. And a horse and cart go to the Moss Vale station each day to collect provisions. And not only camp provisions. We can order anything we want from Sydney now."

"I'm pleased for you, but there is no point me buying anything, I will only have to pack it up or give it away when we leave."

"When are you going?"

"We don't have an exact date yet, but it is sure to be soon."

"Perhaps I should plant these seedlings for you, just in case it takes longer than you expect. You know how slowly the Government moves."

"I am sure we won't need them, but you could plant some for the Glintz's to use after we are gone. She is a difficult woman but I feel sorry for her. It will be hard for her seeing us leave while she has to stay. Cabbages and peas are always useful."

"Shall I plant them around the fountain?" I asked, pointing to the derelict garden.

"*Ja*, I just hope these plants will do better than the last ones we tried to grow."

"I'm sure they will, now we know gardening is not like fishing, we have much better results."

Frau Hurtzig nodded and started sweeping the path once more, while I wandered over to the dirt patch around the fountain. Cupid was still pointing in the direction I had put him the day the Hurtzigs moved in. It was pointless to wait any longer for his arrow to hit Annie's daughter. The shop was always swarming with men, and no matter how many lollies I bought, she merely smiled professionally. I twisted cupid towards the jail. Perhaps love might blossom if he pointed my direction instead. But both Frau Hurtzig and I were doomed to disappointment, by the end of November the cabbages and peas were flourishing while our hopes withered. There was no sign of romance and the Hurtzigs were still here.

"Our home-going fever has abated somewhat," said Captain Hurtzig, as I helped him weed the patch around the useless cupid. "Until the coalminers break their strike there is no way we can leave."

"I would not have thought coalminers could shut things down like they have," I said, shaking my head as I pulled out a tuft of grass.

"Sixty ships stranded in the harbour, trains not running to schedule, and gas and electricity about to fail," said the Captain, "this strike could go on for a long time." He glanced towards the house swiftly and lowering his voice said, "Don't mention that last bit to the wife, Wolfie, it would upset her if she knew what I really thought. She still believes we are going soon."

We continued weeding in silence until the sound of a woman's voice cut across our thoughts, and looking up, we saw Maria Becker.

"*Guten morgen*, Captain Hurtzig and Wolfgang."

"Maria, what are you doing here?"

"Yesterday I received permission to come."

"How wonderful."

"Yes, isn't it. Hermann doesn't even know yet for there was no time to write. I got the first train coming this way and here I am."

"Maria!" cried Frau Hurtzig, running out of the house. "I thought I recognized your voice. How lovely to see you! How long are you staying?"

"I have permission to stay a week and I can visit Michael

The Spot The War Forgot

and Herman daily. The commandant has even invited me to attend the theatre with you on Saturday evening."

Frau Hurtzig clapped her hands together with joy. "Major Baxter is a thoughtful man, none of the other commandants would have let you attend the theatre."

"He is probably allowing you to come because he loves it himself," I said with a smile. "Nobody laughs louder at Molonglo von Kongo's silly antics than the Major."

"That is true," said Frau Hurtzig. "His wife even sends for Wenk when the commandant is in a punishing mood. Wenk as Molonglo von Kongo has saved us much grief, for Major Baxter forgets his anger once he starts laughing. You, and Hermann, and Michael, must come for coffee on Sunday afternoon and I shall make a Biscotten-Torte and hot scones."

"That sounds marvellous," said Maria. "I would like to stay and talk longer but I am anxious to see Hermann and Michael. Do you know where I could find them?"

"They are probably at the Machotka's place." I washed my hands in a kerosine tin of water before tipping it over the plants. "I will take you there if you like?"

Maria smiled and nodded. It did not take long to get to the Machotka's house, where, as I suspected, we found Billy and Michael. They, along with a crowd of others, were gathered around a teepee shaped bean frame in the garden.

"Pick your beans every day when they are this size," said Machotka, handing beans around. "That will encourage more to grow."

"My brother learning about gardening! Now I have seen everything," said Maria, coming up behind him.

Michael spun around and hugged his sister. "Fancy seeing

you here!"

"I've got permission to stay a week. Where is Hermann?"

"Down by the river, I'll take you to him," said Michael, breaking away from the gardening lesson and moving towards the gate. "Are you coming, Wolfgang?"

"*Nein*. I have a piano lesson with Herr Albert in ten minutes."

We parted company at the gate. Michael and Maria turned left and continued down to the river while I turned right and wandered back to the courthouse. When I got there, I almost tripped over several suitcases by the side door.

"Wolfgang, this is a day of surprises," said Frau Hurtzig bustling up. "This is my good friend Pastor Treuz. I have been praying for a Pastor to take Divine Service and finally, they have let dear Pastor Treuz come. It is a miracle, for they have denied my requests for his transferal many times."

I shook the Pastor's hand and said: "It is a pleasure to meet you, sir, for I have heard good things about you."

As he returned my greeting, the thumping sounds of a piano stopped. The silence was a great improvement, nevertheless, it was my duty to destroy the oasis of peace.

"I must go," I said. "I want to squeeze in a little practice before Herr Albert gets here."

"Where is the empty room in this building?" said Frau Hurtzig, laying a detaining hand on my arm. "The commandant said Pastor Treuz may move into it."

"Over there," I said pointing the way. "It will be very uncomfortable, however, for truly there is nothing in there."

"It is alright, he can sleep on a camp cot in our kitchen for a few days until he gets a few bits of furniture."

The Spot The War Forgot

I nodded and left them. To my surprise, the cell that housed the piano was not empty. A pudgy little girl with nice eyes and buck teeth was pulling out something from behind the stove's metal heat shield.

"Hello Carmen, what have you got there?"

Carmen, jumping at the sound of my voice, spun around and a letter tied with a pink ribbon flew from her fingers and dropped to the floor.

"Don't tell on me, Uncle Wolfgang!" she said looking at me with imploring eyes.

I picked up the letter. "What are you up to, Missy? I'd better have a look at this, for I know a guilty face when I see one." I untied the ribbon, opened the letter and perused it with growing alarm. It seemed cupid's arrows had hit someone after all. "Did Herr Albert send this to you?"

"Of course not." Carmen tossed her head. "I wouldn't be bothered with all that silly lovey-dovey mush. I am a postie like Miss Ada," Her brusque tone faltered. "Well, almost like Miss Ada, I don't have a nice bike as she does."

"Who is the letter for?"

"Miss Baxter."

"The commandant's daughter?"

"Yes. I take their letters back and forth. Herr Albert is good at the piano but bad at English, so sometimes I translate for Miss Baxter."

"Does your mother know about this?"

"No, I promised I wouldn't tell. Can I have the letter now?"

I folded it up and put it in my pocket. "I think not. I will see that the right thing happens to it. Go now or your mother will wonder where you are."

W.E. Hamilton

She skipped off. I said nothing to Herr Albert as I laboured through scales and arpeggios, and by mutual agreement, we finished early. He slunk over to the woodstove while I scurried off. Just before I left the courthouse, I noticed something odd. Willy Maiwald and Richard Mahn (the two servants who lived in the back rooms) were carrying Pastor Treuz bags into the bushes. If I was less preoccupied I might have investigated this strange action but the letter drove all sense of curiosity from my mind. Instead, I rushed across the road and knocked on Frau Hurtzig's door.

"I don't know what to do about this!" I said, handing her the letter as soon as I got inside.

"It is a mystery what he sees in her," said Frau Hurtzig, scanning the page. "Thelma is a lively enough girl but she has neither brains nor beauty. She is not even German."

"I hate to think what will happen if Major Baxter finds out about this, the commandant's daughter is like Caesar's wife, she should be beyond suspicion. The authorities will not turn a blind eye at fraternization of this nature."

"Leave it to me." Frau Hurtzig popped the letter into her handbag and pulled her hat off a hook by the door. "I know what to do."

And it seemed she did, for the intense little affair came to an abrupt halt, and there were no more letters hidden in the stove of the piano's cell. Nevertheless, I took cupid off the top of the fountain and hid him in the bushes just to make sure.

The Spot The War Forgot

December 1916
Turkish Infantry Division Mobilized to Aid Surrounded Germans in Battle of Arges

An Escape

Since Hermann and Maria's engagement was a secret, Michael, not Hermann escorted his sister to the theatre. I expected the talk of the camp the next morning to be about the new lady, and so it was, right up to the moment we heard of the escape.

"It is a rerun of last year," I said bitterly. "I suppose we will be locked up over Christmas while Richard and Willy roam about in freedom."

"Maybe not," said Billy, as the gates opened after rollcall. "Captain Baxter trusts us. If he planned to lock us up until Richard and Willy are captured, he would not have let us go free now."

We merged into the crowd and inched slowly forward until we passed out the arched entrance. "That is true," said

Hermann, "I hope he doesn't change his mind, for Maria and I have waited a long time for this visit."

"Perhaps my wife saw something," said Captain Hurtzig. "Richard and Willy were last seen with her."

Frau Hurtzig stood in her front yard. As the crowd thinned, we glimpsed her by the gate dressed in her Sunday clothes. When she saw her husband, she rushed over to him.

"Oh Gust, something awful has happened. The cook and the steward who live at the courthouse with the titled men have run away. The Commandant was here this morning asking questions. Oh, Gust, if he thinks I helped them he will send us away and I could not bear it."

The Captain put his arm around his trembling wife. "Nobody would suspect you, *liebling*."

"Oh, but he might, for I was the last one to see the men. They lighted our way back to the house as usual and waited with the lantern until our lamps were lit before going out the backdoor. They have done it many times, only this time, they didn't go back to the courthouse. Von Klewitz discovered they had fled this morning when his breakfast did not appear. The runaway's beds were not slept in and their luggage was gone, so they must have left last night directly after seeing me and the children home. So, you see Gust, the Commandant might suspect I helped them."

"Nobody would suspect you of aiding an escape for everyone knows you are honest to a fault."

"That's true," I said, looking at her meaningfully. "Major Baxter knows you don't cover up secret escapades. He would trust you with his daughter."

Frau Hurtzig's face relaxed and the lines on her forehead

The Spot The War Forgot

smoothed out.

"*Ja*, he did seem to believe me when I said I knew nothing about it."

"Besides," said Michael, they didn't need anyone's help. The titled men in the courthouse are never locked up and neither are their servants. It would be simple for them to walk out."

"I am glad dear Pastor Treuz has spent the nights in our kitchen, otherwise he might have fallen under suspicion," said Frau Hurtzig.

"Is he still here?"

"*Nein*, he had breakfast, then he took his bible and went over to the courthouse to get ready for church." The little woman's face broke into a wide smile. "It will be so nice to hear a proper Lutheran sermon in German at long last. The communion goblet and several hymn books are in his bags. I said you would take his luggage over before church, Gust."

When I heard this, the image of the two men carrying bags into the bushes leapt into my mind.

"I thought his luggage was already at the courthouse?"

"Oh, no, most of it came yesterday on the wagon."

"Then those bags by the side door of the courthouse were not Pastor Treuz?"

"Of course not."

"Then they must have been Richard and Willy's bags. I saw them hiding luggage in the bushes a few days ago but thought nothing of it because my mind was on other things."

I had barely finished speaking when Rose Izzard bustled up.

"I have been speaking to the Commandant," she said.

W.E. Hamilton

"About the runaways?" said Frau Hurtzig.

Rose looked surprised. "Yes, do you know about them?"

"The whole camp knows about them," said Michael. "At least, we know they left last night. We don't know where they are going."

"I do," said Rose. "I was at the station collecting the mail when I saw two internees at the ticket office. They were going to Sydney, and not third class, for I saw them get in a first-class carriage."

"I suppose Willy is hoping to pass himself off as an American and get away on a U.S ship," said Billy, "for he speaks English flawlessly with an American accent."

"The fools," said Captain Hurtzig, "as Captain Meyer says, 'their roaming will stop as soon as their money runs out.' Then they will be sent to the Holsworthy camp where conditions are horrible."

"They should have taken note of the tales Tote Schmitt tells."

"Hello, why are you looking so serious?" said Maria, swinging across the road with a light springy step.

"There has been an escape."

"Really?" said Maria, her eyes going round.

We told her all we knew and would have lingered to talk more, but the sound of a tolling bell reminded us it was Sunday, so we scattered, each to his chosen church or activity. We didn't give the runaways much thought after that, for Herman was enamoured with Maria, and the rest of us were caught up in the pre-Christmas rush. We made toys, sent letters and small parcels, and harvested peas, new potatoes, cauliflowers, and beans. Members of the choir, theatre, and orchestra, rehearsed for the

The Spot The War Forgot

Christmas concerts, while Frau Hurtzig baked gingerbread and spice cookies, and the beautiful woman hung wonderful glass birds and little hot-air balloons on her Christmas tree. Finally, Christmas Eve was upon us and we assembled in the theatre as was the camp's custom. Once again there was a tall Christmas tree lit with candles, and Hanna (wearing a white dress and holding a posey of roses) recited the poem *'Lovely Again all Over the World.'* Nobody minded that the clattering of rain on the roof drowned her out, and some even thought our inability to hear Herr Pahnke's speech, was a blessing. All that mattered was she looked innocent and pretty, and he distributed gifts to the children and a cake to each lady. Then we watched a play called *'Graces of Christmas.'*

"*Wunderbar*, simply marvellous," we said, clapping until our hands smarted. "Paul Knoop should have been a playwright, not a marine engineer, he is every bit as good as Oscar Wilde."

"Pinafores," said the beautiful woman, as the children ripped the wrapping off their presents. "How lovely."

"Expensive and good quality silk," said Frau Hurtzig, rubbing the fabric between her fingers. "These pinnies will last the girls their whole childhood."

"I hope I will see you tomorrow morning, Lulu," said Captain Hurtzig, as he escorted his family to the gate. In case I don't, Merry Christmas *liebling's*," he said, kissing them goodbye.

But he had nothing to fear, Christmas Day was far better than last year's dismal fiasco. There was a feast of ham, new potatoes, and fresh peas, followed by stewed plums, and in the evening a wonderful concert, in which I thought the third-violins played particularly well, but Frau Hurtzig liked best the items with the two violins and the piano. And then it was Boxing Day and a raffle was drawn under the candlelit tree. Carmen and Hanna drew the winning tickets from a box and announced the numbers clearly. Frau Hurtzig won a jar of mustard and a packet of Maggi soup cubes, Herr Rittig won a bunch of radishes, and Captain Jepsen won the booby prize of a subscription to a standing place in the theatre. As if that was not enough, there was a Tyrolean concert on the beach of the Great Lake, where we were treated to Austrian folk dancing. The men wore lederhosen and the 'ladies' wore dirndls, and they danced to foot-tapping-music, yodelling and cowbells.

So all in all, we were much too busy to give the runaways another thought. Despite this, news of their capture eventually leaked out through Machotka's friends in the Holsworthy camp. As usual, the front room of the beautiful woman's house was bursting with friends when Machotka (with little Manon sitting on his knee) read parts of his letter aloud.

"Once Richard and Willy got to Sydney, they changed trains and journeyed up the Blue Mountains to the town of Orange where they expected to find friends," he read, before turning the page. "But, instead, they fell in with a couple of confidence men who by the 'three-card-trick,' took most of their money." Machotka looked up. "This next bit is almost funny," he said, suppressing a smile. "They went to the police station in Orange to complain about being robbed, but the police had received a description of them and they were recognized and captured." He sighed as he folded the letter and put it into his pocket. "They were fools to leave."

"Almost the same privileges as von Klewitz and his companions and they threw it away," I said, shaking my head.

The Spot The War Forgot

"Perhaps those titled men are hard to work for."

"Even if they are very difficult to serve, I expect Richard and Willy will find working in Holsworthy's quarry much harder," said Machotka, with the conviction of a man who knows what he is talking about.

"Poor things," said the beautiful woman, taking birds and balloons off the wilted Christmas tree.

"Poor things," we echoed.

And because our Christmas was not ruined by their antics, nobody hungered to punch the runaways on the nose.

———

W.E. Hamilton

> *Feb 1917*
> Germany Resumes Unrestricted Submarine Warfare. In Response U.S.A. Severs Diplomatic Relations with Germany

The Kaiser's Birthday is Overshadowed

The tentative peace between Frau Hurtzig and Frau Glintz exploded into war. Every morning the first thing we heard as we left the jail after rollcall was Frau Glintz screaming insults.

"How does your wife put up with it?" I said, to Captain Hurtzig, as another burst of yelling floated out the window of the brick house.

"She does not have a choice." He sighed and ran a hand over his face. "We agreed to share the house because it halves the cost of rent, and running water plus an inside toilet are rare amenities in this village. We should have foreseen that woman would turn on us one day, for she is unbalanced and loves a fight."

We had almost reached the Hurtzig's gate when the front

The Spot The War Forgot

door slammed and Frau Hurtzig stomped up the path, her hands clutching her head.

"Urgh! She is crazy, that is what she is. As crazy as the red-haired woman who moons around the walls of the jail."

"*Ach komm schon, liebling*, she is not that bad?"

"Perhaps not as touched in the head," admitted Frau Hurtzig. But ten times as nasty, which is much worse. At least the crazy red-head feels sorry for the prisoners. I'd rather live with her than Frau Glintz. It is not pleasant living close to someone who hates me. Even when she is not screaming, I feel her hatred as I pass her in the hall or see her in the laundry." The little woman stamped her foot. "Oh, drat her! I don't know how much longer I can hold my tongue!"

"You will be leaving soon," said Ernst, in an attempt to cheer her up.

Captain Hurtzig grimaced and his wife stamped her foot again.

"Leaving! What a joke. We have been waiting to go for months and still nothing."

The captain put his arm around his wife's thin shoulders and she slumped against him. "Lord forgive me for losing my temper when I should have been counting my blessings," she said, looking up at the sky. "The children picked a big bowl of blackberries yesterday," she said in a lighter tone. "And Edna gave us some wonderful vegetables and a big bunch of flowers. The Machotkas grow everything to perfection, it is amazing how their flowers bloom in such abundance, even giant dahlias in every colour, and all kinds of asters and snapdragons."

"The Kaiser's birthday is another blessing," I said, following her lead. "Herr Mönkedieck has painted a beautiful souvenir program. There is to be a Divine Service at the Courthouse with the choir participating, and later a concert with recitations, solos and music, then finally another Tyrolean dance."

Frau Hurtzig smiled. "That will certainly be something to look forward to." She looked at the kerosene tins and spades in our hands. "What are you boys up to today?"

"We are on the hunt for manure for our gardens."

"Of course you are, silly of me not to realize. It seems everyone is on the hunt for dung. Rose Izzard says her horse only has to lift his tail and a line of men follow him hoping he will drop treasure. I won't keep you talking for I know it is a race."

We tipped our hats and left, for she was right, it was a race.

"Let's go past Harper's Mansion and through the village, perhaps roaming cows have left their calling cards," Ernst said.

"Alright. We might as well continue over the main bridge and down Sutton Street to the sports grounds. Everybody cuts across the Hansa bridge so we might have more luck if we go the long way around."

The idea seemed good to Ernst so we set off up Argyle Street and wandered towards Harper's Mansion. It was a beautiful day and the magpies warbled in the trees as we passed. A flock of large white cockatoos flew into the plum trees in the garden of the big house.

"Quick, chuck something at them," said Ernst, picking up a stick. "They will strip that tree if we let them settle."

I followed his example and we drove them away.

"It wouldn't be so bad if they weren't so wasteful," Ernst said, as the last one flew off, "but they snip fruit off with their beak and after one bite let it fall to the ground."

The Spot The War Forgot

"They ruin fruit like possums," I said, as we turned into the main street. We continued wandering along the road driving birds away from the villager's fruit trees, all the while keeping a sharp lookout for small brown piles.

Henry Allen's bakery was on the corner of Wingecarribee Street and Great South Road. Beside it grew two very fine pear trees, the branches of which, were bent low with fat fruit. The cockatoos settled on them like huge locusts.

"Look at that," said Ernst, with idle curiosity. "The cockies are eating Henry Allen's pears."

"So they are!" I pulled a packet of cigarettes from my pocket. "Would you like a smoke, Ernst?

"Thanks." We lit up and leaned against a nearby fencepost, watching the birds as we leisurely smoked.

"Very efficient beaks," said Ernst, admiringly. "I wouldn't mind a pair of secateurs like that."

"It looks like the trees are raining pears."

"If Henry Allen doesn't get out here soon," said Ernst, with supreme unconcern, "they will have ruined his crop."

I tapped the ash off the end of my cigarette. "He will have to be quick about it for there are not many pears left."

As if he heard us, the door of the bakery flew open and Henry Allen rushed out. "Get along with you, you huns, I won't have you lingering outside my shop," he shouted. His face was red and he shook his fist at us."

Ernst and I slowly ground the butts of our cigarettes on the top of the post, and without saying anything, ambled past his shop.

"We were almost at Holy Trinity church when we spotted dung.

W.E. Hamilton

"Seeing as we both saw it at the same time, let's share it," said Ernst.

"Alright," I said, scooping up half the horse droppings.

Ernst put the rest in his tin. We were so preoccupied with getting every last horse-apple, neither of us noticed the red-haired woman slip from nearby bushes. We both jumped and dropped our tins when she cried out in an impassioned voice:

"Save yourselves, flee, nobody is watching!"

"It's alright, we are quite happy."

I nodded in agreement. "Don't worry about us, we are treated well and this is a good place."

As if we had not spoken the woman repeated:

"Save yourselves, flee, nobody is watching!"

"It's no good," whispered Ernst, "she is not going to believe us. She says it to all the prisoners. Let's run until we are out of sight and she will think we are running away."

"That will work," I whispered back. "Sutton Street is not far." I lifted my voice and said loudly, "Oh, look, Ernst, there are no guards around, we should run away."

"*Ja*," said Ernst.

With that, we grabbed the wire handles of our tins and sprinted down the road, over the bridge, and into Sutton Street. Once we were out of sight we stopped running and caught our breath. But not for long, because there in the middle of the road was a large cow-pat.

"Race you for it," I said.

We sprinted towards the prize but although I had a head start Ernst bet me to it. I expected to hear cries of triumph, but instead, Ernst's shoulders sagged.

"Someone got here first." He pointed at the small stick

The Spot The War Forgot

standing upright in the centre of the pooh. We stared at it in disappointment. Only a scoundrel would ignore this symbol of prior claim. Ernst shook his head sadly. "I expect we will see someone coming to collect it soon."

And sure enough, we had not gone far when Captain Kühlken came up the road whistling cheerily and swinging a kerosene tin.

"Look deeper in the bush if you want manure, my friends, for I have got everything from the Hansa bridge to the end of Sutton Street. You boys have to start earlier if you want to get the easy stuff."

We did as he suggested and found a few piles of droppings in the bush, but not as many as we wanted. At the Hansa bridge, Ernst and I separated. He followed the river bank down to the cluster of huts called New Hong Kong, while I crossed the Hansa bridge to my hut nearby. Huts were still being constructed by newcomers, but those of us who were established with villa's and boats were now engaged in wharf building and gardening. Subsequently, the riverbank had assumed a cultivated look as vegetable patches popped up around the huts, and flowers spilt down to the water. When I got to my hut, I dumped the dung onto my compost pile and spread a layer of weeds over it before inspecting my vegetables. My cabbages and silverbeet were doing well. Moreover, I had harvested enough potatoes to fill two kerosine tins. They made a wonderful supplement to our prison rations (that even under the new management were always a little on the skimpy side.) After weeding and watering my garden it was almost lunchtime, so I washed my hands in the river and headed up the street towards the jail. As I neared the beautiful woman's house, I saw Miss Dangar the village artist was there as usual. The elderly Englishwoman wore a wide-brimmed straw hat and was painting the scene before her. I stared admiringly at the tumbledown house amid abundant flowers on her easel.

"That looks good," I said, raising my hat.

"Thank you," said the prim woman with a smile.

I chatted to her until I noticed Carmen and Eva crawling amongst the poppies with little packets.

"Hello girls," I said, leaning over the fence. "What are you doing?"

"Hello Uncle Wolfgang, we are collecting seeds for Papa."

Eva picked a poppy seedpod and broke it so the tiny black seeds rained into the packet. "They fall like salt from a saltshaker," she giggled.

"Are you enjoying it?"

"It's so hot I'd rather be inside," said Carmen, but it is better than collecting dung."

"Or planting corn and peas," said Eva. "The magpies are so smart we have to trick them by watering as we go, or they follow us and eat everything we plant."

"They are clever, but you girls are smarter."

The door of the adjoining house opened, and the girl's heads whipped around with the alertness of those who expect a treat. An elderly portly man walked across to the fence with the rolling gait of a sailor. It was Captain Weinreich, one of the four sea captains who lived there during the day. He had a long wispy beard that straggled from chin to chest giving him the appearance of a wise old mandarin. And indeed, he had spent much time in Chinese ports and often entertained us with endless yarns of life in these teeming cities.

The Spot The War Forgot

"I wonder what he has for us today?" said Carmen, scrambling to her feet.

"Perhaps it will be more china teacups," said Eva, following her.

"*Liebe kinder,* I have a little surprise for you," Captain Weinreich called, "I thought you might like this antique mah-jongg set, it's made from real ivory."

There were squeals of joy as the girls rushed over to the fence to look at the latest treasure the dear old man had for them. I waved and continued on my way back to the jail. When I got to the assembly yard, I found a crowd gathered around an announcement on the noticeboard.

"It's official," shouted Captain Hurtzig, "men over forty-five will be leaving on February the 7th. I must tell Luise the good news."

With that, he rushed off. From that moment, regardless of our age the idea of an early release dominated our thoughts, for those of us who were not going, had close friends who were. Naturally, the Kaiser's birthday a few days later was upstaged by such stupendous news. We still had the Divine Service and the planned celebrations, but in addition, Captain von Klewitz gave a heartwarming address in which he asked those who would shortly be returning home to deliver greetings from us all. We were very touched by his words, and after three rousing cheers, we sang '*Hail to thee in thy Victory Laurels.*' We would not have cheered so loudly or sung with such overflowing hearts if we realized that once again the planned exchange would come to nothing.

"I wish I had not sold my sewing machine or given away all our household goods, they made our life here more homely," wailed Frau Hurtzig, when the telegram arrived from Holman announcing the suspension of the exchange. "I am left with bare walls and the prospect of staying here until the end of the war. It is the rising and dashing of hopes and the uncertainty of the future that makes this so difficult. Truly, Wolfgang, I think you young men without hope of an early release are better off."

I nodded and felt very sorry for Frau Hurtzig. But my sorrow was not as deep as the red-haired woman's sympathy for us. That evening she made her way to the jail and clasped the gate post of the picket fence. Then with her lovely red hair streaming about her shoulders she shouted:

"⁷Open wide the gates of Heaven, open wide the gates of Hell, and let these suffering men go free!"

"Poor soul," one of the sentries whispered to us as we filed past on our way to rollcall. "Take no notice, she is not right in the head."

Leonard slung his rifle around to his back and got off his horse to lend a hand. "Come on Love," he said, "don't bother yourself on account of these men, they are having a good life." He tried to loosen her hands but she gripped the fencepost with the strength of a madwoman.

"Let them go free," she groaned, throwing her head back in a gesture of despair.

The sentries treated her gently, but it took more than one man to prize her hands-free. As she was led home, I paused before moving under the arched entrance in the jail wall. Over the noise of footsteps and hundreds of men talking, I heard a volley of abuse roll out of the windows of the brick house. It was Frau Glinz letting rip. Frau Hurtzig was right, the red-

---

7   Taken from Hugo Bahl's diary.

The Spot The War Forgot

headed woman was mad in the head, but she was ten times better than Frau Glintz.

W.E. Hamilton

> *March 1917*
> Germany Secretly Proposes Alliance with Mexico should the U.S.A. Enter War

A Picnic and a Plan

Frau Hurtzig was not her normal cheerful self and it was hardly surprising. Even though her possessions were returned, she was bitterly disappointed she was not going home. Also, she had received a letter informing her that her cousin Konni was dead.

"He died a hero," she said, wiping her eyes, "and won an iron cross, but what good is that to his wife and unborn child. It is barely two months since they got married." Her mouth drooped even lower as she added, "And to top it off, someone left my gate open and a wandering cow has eaten the cabbages and torn out the peas."

Captain Hurtzig patted his wife's shoulder. "I have come with a message from Karl Mehne that might make you feel a little better," he said, handing her a note.

The Spot The War Forgot

"What is it, Mama?" said the children gathering close to her.

"It is an invitation to attend the choir's picnic in the bush this afternoon. There is to be coffee and cakes. As their guests, we are not required to bring anything other than our cups."

"Can we go, can we go?" squealed the girls jumping up and down.

"I don't know," said Frau Hurtzig, her shoulders slumping. "I feel I might dampen the mood of the picnic."

"Nonsense, Lulu, this is just what you need, it will take your mind off your sorrow."

"Besides, the Jepsens and the Machotkas are invited," I said, "Karl asked me to pass on the message to them."

"The Machotkas will say yes, and Carmen and Eva will be disappointed if we don't go," said Hanna, tugging at her mother's skirt.

"Well then it is settled," said Frau Hurtzig, standing up straight and speaking in a decided tone. "When you see Edna, Wolfgang, tell her we'll have an early lunch and set off at noon if she wants to join us."

I did as she bid, and shortly after midday, a small group of us gathered outside the picket fence. Billy was there with his camera and we felt very honoured to be included in the list of guests. Especially as we expected it to be more than the usual picnic of potato pancakes, applesauce and billy-tea, for the choir had departed an hour earlier to prepare for our arrival. I was glad the Hurtzig's were coming for already Frau Hurtzig looked happier.

"It's a lovely day for a picnic," she said to the beautiful woman as we set off. "Brilliant sunshine but not too hot for walking."

The beautiful woman inclined her head. "Yes, it certainly is."

Frau Jepsen frowned. "How will we find the spot once we leave the road? I hope we won't get lost."

"It is alright," said Captain Hurtzig, "Karl said someone will meet us by the confusing part."

And sure enough, two choristers met us and guided us through the bush to the picnic ground. It took three-quarters of an hour to walk from the jail to the picnic area. We could tell we were nearing the appointed place, for the sound of music grew louder as we got closer. At last, we came upon the choir, and a group of musicians playing, guitars, zithers and mandolins. They were gathered in front of a sheer rockface, next to a brook that tumbled over and between large boulders.

"This is utterly charming," said the beautiful woman, sinking gracefully onto a flat rock. "Fancy finding a natural theatre in the bush!"

Her husband crumbled dirt between his fingers. "Nice soil," he said, "plenty of leaf mould."

"Oh, Paul, stop looking at the dirt," said the beautiful woman, "the choir is about to sing for us."

We sat down, and when we were settled, Karl motioned with his conductor's stick and they began. We enjoyed their items enormously and even joined in with the numbers Karl had selected as singalongs. At the end, we clapped and cheered.

"That was very good," said Frau Hurtzig, "I'm so glad I came."

"I'm pleased you enjoyed it," said Karl, "but the best is yet to come." He turned to Hanna, "would you mind helping pass the cakes around?"

Frau Hurtzig poked her daughter in the back discreetly, and the child instantly bobbed a little curtsy and said, "I would be delighted to, Herr Mehne."

"Such a polite child," said Frau Jepsen, as they walked off. "She is a credit to you, Luise."

Frau Hurtzig smiled and swelled with pride as Hanna passed the plates of food around without any mishaps.

The pies, cakes and pastries looked exceptionally good. When the plate came to me, I chose a pie and bit into it.

"Wow, this is delicious!"

"What wonderful cakes?" said Frau Hurtzig, munching a slice of chocolate gateau. "The last time I tasted anything as good as these was when we were in Brisbane. Do you remember the cakes Frau Eschenhagen sent us when we were under ship-arrest in Brisbane, Gust?"

"What cakes, and who is Frau Eschenhagen?"

"Oh, August Hurtzig, surely you remember! Frau Eschenhagen is the widow who owns the large café and restaurant on the main street of Brisbane. Don't you remember the mud cakes she sent one evening – the small ones with fantastic strawberries on top."

A light of understanding broke over her husband's face. "Oh, those."

"I remember them," said Lore, speaking with her mouth full, "they were in little boxes and we had one each."

"I don't care about the cakes in Brisbane," said Frau Jepsen, impatiently, "what I want to know, Karl, is how did you find such pastries in Berrima?" She gazed in wonder at the apple strudel in her hand. "I haven't been able to find anything like this around here. Henry Allen's cakes are so plain and dry they are little more than bread."

"These are excellent," agreed the beautiful woman, nibbling a tart.

"Heinrich Bartle made everything." Karl lifted his voice and called, "come over here Heinrich, the ladies are impressed with your baking."

"I'm so glad," said Heinrich, coming over.

"So, you've actually done it," I said, remembering our conversation in the blackberry patch.

"I have," laughed Heinrich. "I have finished building my bakery next to the amphitheatre, and I'm opening for business next Sunday afternoon."

"Smart idea," said Captain Jepsen. "All the people at the open-air concerts are sure to buy cakes and pastries. Especially authentic German ones like these."

"You can count on my custom," said Frau Hurtzig. "Your cakes and pastries taste of home."

"Where did you learn to bake like this?" said the beautiful woman.

"When I arrived here, I was nervous about the future of shipping, for we have no idea what might happen, so I decided it would not hurt to consider an alternative calling. One day I was in the library when I came upon a cookbook, and after talking to Wolfgang and a few others, I decided to become a pastry cook."

"You have a talent for it," I said. "It will not take you long to collect regular customers. We shall have to be quick on Sunday, for you will be sold out in no time."

"Where did you get the cherries?" said Machotka, dissecting

his pie. "They are a good size. I should like to see the tree they grew on."

"I bought them from a farm called Robinson on Mandemar Road. They also have apple trees and I bought the entire crop of a tree for six shillings."

Billy, seeing Machotka's intense interest in the subject, added, "There are plenty of untended apple trees growing about the place. Berrima must have been apple country at one time."

"Perhaps Johnnie Appleseed came to this land too," said the beautiful woman with a calm smile.

"Who?"

"He is an old American folk hero who went through the land planting apple orchards."

Machotka looked thoughtful, "I should like to see these trees," he said, slowly. "Perhaps there is a possibility of renting land and orchards."

"We can go back that way," said Billy.

Machotka leapt up and was all for leaving straight away but the beautiful woman put a restraining hand on his arm. "Sit down, Paul, we have not finished afternoon tea. The trees are not going anywhere."

Although Machotka was jiggling with impatience, he did as he was told. And after the coffee was finished and the cakes and pastries were eaten, there was a further delay as Billy wanted to take a photograph so we would have a memento of the day.

"I hope it comes out," said Frau Hurtzig, brushing leaves off her skirt, "for it would be nice to have a picture of the entire group."

W.E. Hamilton

"It should do," Billy shut the camera case and slung the long strap over his head, "and I shall have extra copies made so you can have one."

When everyone was ready to go, Heinrich picked up the empty hamper, and Karl waved his little stick at the band. Then I hoisted Lore onto my shoulders, and we marched through the bush singing *The Millar's Song'* until we came to the neglected orchard. There we halted. Machotka wandered among the trees examining their condition, while the rest of us filled our empty cups with Black Heart cherries from a nearby tree.

"Damson and Queen Anne apples," said Machotka rubbing his chin. "These trees desperately need a good prune and are riddled with coddling moth, but if I could get hold of them before winter, I think I could salvage many of them. I wonder who owns this field?"

I swallowed a cherry. "Ada Harper will know, the Harper family have lived here for generations and, furthermore, she is the postie."

Machotka nodded, "I will ask her about this land and other unused fields. We have the potential of developing a good business."

"For sure," I said. "Produce is expensive and hard to come by in Berrima. I have thought of making extra money by selling my vegetables."

Paul shook his head slowly. "Small individual gardens won't produce enough to feed over three-hundred men, but if some of us band together and developed a community garden, we could boost productivity and easily become the main supplier for the prison."

"I want to be involved, and I think many of the others would

The Spot The War Forgot

be interested; especially those who already have gardens."

Karl seeing Machotka had finished looking at the trees, waved his little stick once more and the musicians struck up another tune.

"Time to move on," said Machotka, pocketing two apples. He and I continued talking as we trailed (at some distance) behind the main group, who were marching to a tune by the American composer Sousa.

"Now every inch of my yard is planted out, I think it is time to expand into the land behind the jail," said Machotka. "If it belongs to the prison as I suspect it does, it should not be difficult to gain permission to cultivate it." He took an apple from his pocket and tossed it into the air. "I shall call it Neu Pommern."

Naming the land made the market garden seem real.

"That's an ideal spot," I said, "it is sunny and close to water."

"And high enough not to flood," said Machotka.

"That is important, we don't want all our cabbages floating down the river at the first heavy rain."

The more we talked about it the more it seemed possible. By the time we got to the Hurtzig's gate and the singing stopped, Machotka and I had rented most of the district and transformed the wilderness into the Garden of Eden; at least we had in theory, the practical outworkings of the plan would take many men and months of hard work before it became a reality.

Frau Hurtzig turned to Karl and the members of the choir as she lifted the latch of her gate. "Thank you. That was wonderful, you have lightened my sorrow and given me something happy to think about."

"You are welcome."

Then because it was almost rollcall, the women and children went to their houses while the rest of us went home to our comfortable jail.

The Spot The War Forgot

July 1917
Allied Troops Launch an Attack to Seize Key Ridges Near Ypres

A School

Changes were happening. The beautiful woman was going to need Rose Izzard's midwifery skills, and a church service took place in the courtroom every Sunday. Pastor Treuz's arrival pleased not only the Hurtzigs but also the Brauns and the Machotkas.

Frau Hurtzig was pleased because he was a Lutheran.

The Brauns were pleased because he could confirm their daughter Gertrude.

The Machotka's were pleased because he undertook to teach religious education to Carmen and Eva.

"To be sure my girls need it, "the beautiful woman said to Frau Hurtzig. "I have set up a 'schoolroom' at an end of the back veranda where I teach them lessons. I am fine with English grammar and arithmetic, but when it comes to religion the girls know nothing beyond 'The Lord's Prayer' and 'Now I lay me down to sleep.'"

Frau Hurtzig was appalled by the Machotka girls lack of scripture knowledge but impressed with them doing schoolwork.

"What a good idea!" She slipped a tape measure around the beautiful woman's swelling waist before jotting the figure down in a notebook. "Hanna and Lore know very little about English grammar and arithmetic." She looked up hopefully. "Would you mind if they joined your classes, Edna?"

"Not at all. It is the least I can do in return for the new dresses. The girls can start tomorrow. We do schoolwork from nine in the morning to ten (because that is all I can cope with) and then Pastor Truez helps with reading and writing, and teaches them scripture lessons until eleven."

Frau Hurtzig was pleased with the arrangement. The girls had an opportunity to learn, while she had uninterrupted hours for sewing.

Personally, I would not have known or cared about the schooling of four little girls if it were not for Billy, who kept a close eye on everything the Machotkas did. His slavish devotion for the beautiful woman motivated him to chivalry beyond cutting firewood, hauling water and pulling weeds.

"This schooling is too much for Edna, especially in her condition," he confided in me one day as we kayaked along the river, "those children need extra instruction. How about it, Wolfgang, do you want to become a teacher?"

I stopped paddling and stared at him in horror. "*Nein*! I have done my time in school and having escaped I am not subjecting myself to it again, even for a woman expecting a

The Spot The War Forgot

baby. Her husband can help out."

"*Ach komm schon*, it's not that bad. You know Machotka is too busy developing the community garden. Is only for an hour a day Monday to Friday. Pastor Truez, Von Klewitz and Captain Hannig are helping out. Von Klewitz is teaching general knowledge, and Captain Hannig, world geography."

I snorted as I resumed paddling. "Geography of the Orient and the Yangtze Kiang River, you mean."

"Also, Penang, Batavia, Nagasaki and Rotorua," Billy corrected me. "Someone with firsthand experience of places makes a great teacher. You teach geography if you can do better."

I shook my head as we skirted around a brush-houseboat in the middle of the river. "I am sure he is a wonderful teacher. Why don't you teach more subjects?"

Billy grinned. "I am already the headmaster, and I am teaching German grammar, reading and writing. Also, arithmetic (when Edna is not feeling well.)"

"Good luck to you teaching anything to Eva Machotka," I said, "she is a true child of nature. I suppose you have to drag her from the bush and lock up her dog and chickens to get her to school. And even then, I bet her mind is on flowers and how many vegetables she can peddle around the neighbourhood rather than her ABCs."

Billy grimaced. "Blast you, Wolfgang, you are horribly accurate. She is a child of the devil. I don't know how an angelic woman like Edna, got such an impish daughter."

"Eva must take after her father," I said, as we headed to the shore.

"That must be it," Billy nodded.

W.E. Hamilton

We got out and pulled our kayaks onto the sandy beach. "I suppose it's time you went to give your German lesson."

"*Ja.*"

"Best of luck." I should have left it at that but, instead, I added maliciously, "I will think of you squashed into that tiny room doing sums while I read a book."

"We need a proper schoolhouse," said Billy, slipping the paddle into the kayak. "The end of the veranda is too cramped."

I slapped Billy on the shoulder. "It might be big enough if Fanny Lyons did not ride in from the bush to flirt with you so often."

"She doesn't come often."

"You can't fool me! I see her scraggy little pony tied to the Machotka's fence. Don't tell me that Australian girl is coming to learn arithmetic. She would not understand a word of your lessons for she does not speak German."

Billy's shoulders slumped and he sighed. "It is awkward and I don't know what to do about it. I don't want to send Fanny away for it is fun to joke with a girl near my age, there are so few of them here, but Carmen has a schoolgirl crush on me and glares at Fanny the whole time."

I didn't know what to say to that, so we trudged up the hill in companionable silence and parted at the Machotka's gate. I was almost at the Hurtzigs house when I heard Frau Hurtzig calling to me from the front porch.

"Wolfgang, could you carry two suitcases to the Machotkas for me?"

"For sure, Frau Hurtzig," I said, lifting the latch of the gate and walking down the path.

"I've just had a most unexpected visitor; an English woman

The Spot The War Forgot

I have never met before," she said. "The good woman heard from Rose Izzard one of the German families had a baby and brought me the presents by mistake."

"But the Machotka's baby is not born yet."

"I know, Mrs S. got the date wrong, but it does not matter. There is no harm in an expectant mother receiving things a little early. I enjoyed a pleasant visit with Mrs S. and promised her that I would see that Edna received her gifts."

"Is the woman still here?" I said, picking up the suitcases.

Frau Hurtzig put on her hat and scooped up a large paper package. "*Nein*, sadly she had to go. But not before we had a nice visit. I even managed to bake her an apple cake before she left." She pulled the door shut and we walked up the street and around the corner to the Machotka's place.

When we arrived, little Manon was sitting in the middle of the floor quietly building a castle with the ivory bricks of Captain Weinreich's mah-jongg set. Nearby, a gnarled old seaman sat on the couch beside the beautiful woman as she wrestled with knitting needles. In the background, we could hear the sing-song chanting of the times-tables.

"Knit two together twice," said Captain Riel, pointing a knobbly finger at the knitting, "you'll see the heel start to form soon."

The beautiful woman looked up at our arrival and sighed with relief.

"Thank goodness for a distraction," she said, laying the black stocking aside. "Knitting is such hard work. I don't think I'll ever get the hang of casting on and off."

"Keep at it, my dear," said Captain Riel, patting her hand in a fatherly way, "you'll get it eventually."

W.E. Hamilton

"Oh Edna, something most exciting happened this morning," said Frau Hurtzig, laying the parcel on a nearby chair. "An English woman arrived on my doorstep under the mistaken idea that I was you. She has sent you gifts."

"Gifts?" The beautiful woman's eyes opened wide. "But I don't know any English women!"

"I will leave you ladies to it," said Captain Reil, his knees creaking as he stood up. "I'll call in tomorrow to see how you are getting on. "He bowed to the women. Good morning, Mrs Machotka, good morning Frau Hurtzig." With that, he picked up his hat, waved and was gone.

Frau Hurtzig motioned for me to place the suitcases on the ground as the beautiful woman repeated: "I don't know any English woman. It can't be for me."

"That is the astonishing thing. Mrs S. is a complete stranger. Such a kind woman. We got on so well I find it impossible to view her as an enemy. I wish she could have stayed longer." Frau Hurtzig flipped the catches of the first suitcase open. "Let's see what she sent."

The beautiful woman leant forward with an expression of calm interest on her face, while little Frau Hurtzig unpacked the goodies enthusiastically.

"Fruit and eggs," she said, handling them carefully. "Chocolates and a woollen blanket." She flicked open the next case and lifted out knitted garments. "Very nice, a shawl and baby clothes."

"How kind," said the beautiful woman, "so different to Henry Allen's attitude towards us."

"Indeed," said Frau Hurtzig. "If only the rest of the world was like Mrs S." She sighed and fingered the shawl gently.

The Spot The War Forgot

After a few moments of silence, she put the shawl back into the suitcase and snapped the catches down. "I finished your dresses, Edna," she said brightening. She leaned forward and I pretended not to listen as she whispered, "They are laced at the back so they expand."

She opened the parcel and the two women peered at the mysterious laces while I looked the other way. They were still poking about in the parcel, and Manon was putting another row of ivory bricks on her castle when the sound of shouting and fighting broke out.

Frau Hurtzig's head shot up. "I hope that is not my children causing all that rumpus," she said, looking stricken.

The beautiful woman sighed. "No matter who is fighting, Eva will be at the bottom of the trouble." She hoisted herself out of the couch. "The size of the classroom does not help the situation. We really need a schoolhouse."

"We certainly do," said Billy, overhearing her words as he stomped out. His face was red and he was in a towering rage. "This is not working."

"You're on the Camp Committee this year, Billy," I said, "why don't you get the Committee involved. Surely it can't be hard to get their backing, there are only seven of you. You could win Captain Madsen over easily, and Max Adam won't want to fall out with you as you share a house."

"That is a *wunderbar* idea, I don't know why I didn't think of it before. I will call an emergency meeting to see what we can do about it."

Once Billy put the problem before them the Camp Committee was swift to act.

"They have agreed to provide basic school supplies," said

W.E. Hamilton

Billy, "but we need men to help build a classroom."

Although I did not want to teach, I did not mind building, and neither did the rest of the Home Help team. We built the school on the right bank halfway between the Hansa bridge and Lambies Well. It was a single room made of bark and situated not far from the girl's homes. The camp Committee equipped it with a blackboard, tables and chairs, books, charts and writing materials, and Otto Monkedeik painted a sign that said '*Tochterschule* Berrima 1917.' It was a great improvement on the veranda-classroom, and for a time the German Girl's school at Berrima ran smoothly.

The Spot The War Forgot

September 1917
German Troops Overrun Riga, Latvia

A New Baby

Generally, the war had little impact on our day to day lives. The children trotted off to school while the rest of us occupied ourselves with various pursuits. We devoured news headlines and grieved when loved ones died, but neither of these things altered a picnic trip or boating on the river. School soon settled into a predictable routine, enlivened by Eva's antics with frogs, pet chickens, and attempts at winemaking. Every so often, however, something happened to highlight our sense of being blown around by forces beyond our control. One of those moments was when Pastor Treuz was suddenly sent back to Holsworthy. I was filling the firewood basket in the beautiful woman's house when Frau Hurtzig burst through the front door.

"Oh Edna, they are taking Pastor Treuz from us." She wrung her hands in despair. "Hanna came home from school at lunchtime and told me the news. They have given us no reason or warning whatsoever. Our Pastor will be gone before rollcall this evening."

The beautiful woman's head tilted to the side in a way that pulled at my heart. "I know, I was at the school when the commandant told him. It is hard to be so powerless."

"I've met the Pastor they have sent to replace our dear Pastor Treuz." Frau Hurtzig was trembling with indignation. "He is elderly with a grizzled moustache and a goatee, and has lived in Australia so long he has forgotten how to speak German! He told me he won't help out at the school, and even worse, has no intention of conducting divine service!"

"Oh dear, that is bad news."

"It is not all bad, however," said Frau Hurtzig calming down. "Do you know Dierke Voss?"

"Yes, the young man they brought from the Holsworthy camp, the star of the theatre company?"

"*Ja*, he is the one. Before he was interned, he was about to sit his final exams as a teacher."

"Really? I did not know that."

Frau Hurtzig nodded. "Yes, really. The Camp Committee has called an emergency meeting and appointed him as the *Tochterschule* schoolmaster.

"I won't be sorry to hand the responsibility over to a proper school teacher," said the beautiful woman, sighing with relief, "especially with my confinement so close. I was wondering what I would do once the baby was born."

Dierke Voss started the next day. He was a temperamental young man, big on literature but short on patience. Eva quickly discovered how to annoy him to the point of apoplexy. Although it was forbidden, more than once Voss laid the naughty girl over his knee and gave her a well-deserved spanking. But even then, Eva eventually got the better of him. I saw him fleeing from the schoolroom one day, his face flaming with anger, shortly after Eva bested him.

"What happened," I said, as she danced outside and began digging in the sandbank.

"Oh, Herr Voss was about to spank me so I wet my pants before he could." She pulled a sauce-bottle out of the sand and washed it in the river. "I think I need a drink after all that rumpus," she added, pulling out the cork and swigging squashed raspberries.

"You are a child of the devil," I said, laughing as I rumpled her hair. "I hope you won't lead your new little brother or sister into mischief when he or she gets older."

"It won't be a girl, I'm getting a brother," said Eva, reeling about pretending she was tipsy. "Mother and father haven't even bothered to pick out a girl's name, for they say after three girls it has to be a boy."

But they were wrong. Rose Izzard came to the Machotka's house on September the thirtieth, but a baby boy did not.

"Such a perfect little girl," said Frau Hurtzig, holding the baby for a full minute soon after her birth. She reminds me of someone but I can't think who."

"We would like you to be the baby's Godmother," said Paul Machotka, holding his wife's hand as she sat propped up in bed.

"I would be delighted," said Frau Hurtzig, sticking her finger out so the baby could wrap her little hand around it. "I love babies."

"What are you going to call her?" said Rose, shutting her

medical bag with a click.

"There was an awkward pause. "We don't know."

When the news got out that the Machotka's new baby did not have a name the whole camp came up with suggestions. The choir wanted her named after opera singers or heroines of songs, while the members of the theatre opted for famous actresses. I was in favour of them calling her Gretchen; for that was my mother's name.

"You should name her Carmen Sylva," said Ernst Molnar, looking at the beautiful woman with the sad eyes of a spaniel. "It is the Queen of Romania's pen name. She is my heroine."

"We can't have two children named Carmen," said the beautiful woman gently, "and I'm not keen on the name Sylva, it sounds too much like something for me to polish. But I like the name, Sylvia." She turned to her husband. "What do you think, Paul?"

"Sylvia it is," said Machotka, who was keen to get back to his spring planting.

"Now we need a second name," said the beautiful woman.

"We don't have to decide that today," said Machotka, we have two weeks before her christening."

"Two weeks is not long," said the beautiful woman.

"It's long enough," said Machotka.

They were both right.

The christening took place on a wonderfully sunny day. Frau Hurtzig had made fluffy white dresses for Carmen, Eva, and Manon, and the Machotka's rewarded her kindness by choosing Liselotte (Louise for short) as the baby's second name. Never did a new baby have so many 'Uncles.' We went overboard decorating the courthouse for the occasion.

The Spot The War Forgot

Men scoured through the bush for yellow wattle blooms, fur boughs, and native flowers until the make-do-church was a bower of loveliness. Someone from the theatre group made two enormous American and Austrian flags from bits of leftover silk, which they draped behind the baptismal font. Everyone came to the ceremony of the prison's baby, and a few of the older men (when they thought nobody was looking) even shed quiet tears for their children far away. The beautiful woman looked beautiful as usual, and even the devil child, Eva, looked like a little angel. Frau Hurtzig and Frau Jepsen stood with the family and took turns at holding the baby while Pastor Millat officiated. This kindly old man after initially refusing to teach school and take divine service had given way on both issues. He still did less than the younger and more energetic Pastor Treuz, but armed with a beautifully illustrated children's bible, he regularly taught bible class at school during the week and stumbled and stuttered his way through services on Sundays. At the christening service, he managed the naming part of the ceremony alright, but when he started on the sermon, we realized there was a good reason why Pastor Millat was a reluctant preacher.

"That homily was so poor," said Frau Hurtzig, as everyone shuffled towards the door, "it is little wonder church attendance is dwindling."

"Oh, but the fine singing of all those strong deep voices was so moving," said the beautiful woman, stepping onto the portico. "I nearly broke down when I looked at all those hundreds of noble men dressed in spotless white." She dabbed her eyes. "And as for the flags, I was deeply touched by such an unexpected tribute."

W.E. Hamilton

Now the ceremony was over, most of the men disbursed. But those of us closely connected with the Machotka family lingered in a group beside the tall ionic columns at the front of the courthouse. Frau Jepsen (whose turn it was to hold the baby) looked searchingly into little Sylvia Liselotte's face. "She reminds me of someone, I just can't think who."

Frau Hurtzig peered over Frau Jepsen's shoulder. "I thought the same thing."

Suddenly Dierke Voss let out a dreadful moan and struck the theatrical pose of a dying man. "She looks like Eva," he said, in a hollow voice. He rubbed his hand over his eyes before adding in broken tones:

"I hope the war is over before Sylvia gets to school age, for two of them is more than I can bear."

The Spot The War Forgot

November 1917
Britain Issues a Statement of Support for the Establishment of a Jewish Nation in Palestine in the Balfour Declaration

Christmas and Swimming Lessons

Dierke Voss did not need to fear the new baby for two reasons; the first was Little Sylvia was nothing like Eva. She was so sweet-natured her father called her his 'little mouse.' She could amuse herself by the hour. The only thing to cause screams of distress, was a large framed picture of Kaiser Franz Joseph which hung over her crib. Unfortunately, the beautiful woman did not diagnose the problem immediately, which made visiting most unpleasant for a spell, but once she turned the bewhiskered gentleman's face to the wall peace descended, to the relief of us all. The second reason Dierke Voss had nothing to fear was that he was inexplicably recalled to Holsworthy camp. On the day he left an emergency meeting was called in the Machotka's house. The children were playing in the garden, and I was in the kitchen filling a pitcher with well-water while those effected by Voss's departure talked the problem over.

"I suppose this means we are back to teaching the children ourselves," said Billy, as I put the pitcher and tumblers on a small table between the two women in the room.

"It seems that way," said the beautiful woman. She sat with the box of Christmas decorations on her lap, fingering the feathered tail on a glass bird. "At least we had a teacher during my confinement time."

"I could teach German Grammar," said Frau Hurtzig, pouring herself a drink, "and August has agreed to help out where he can."

"And I am happy to be the geography teacher again," said Captain Hannig.

"That reminds me," said Frau Hurtzig, putting down her cup and clapping her hands with excitement, "Yesterday I received a parcel from Germany and in it were children's books and an atlas."

"New books and an atlas, good. We managed alright before Voss so we will manage alright again," said Billy, conveniently forgetting the towering rage Eva reduced him to by the end of each lesson.

Pastor Millat spoke up. "I shall do my bit by teaching the children Christmas carols and a narration of the nativity story."

"That will be a wonderful addition to the Christmas festivities." The beautiful woman put down the bird and picked up a glass reindeer, "I can't decide whether to decorate the tree with animals or stars and iridescent balls."

Ernst picked up an apple and a soldier. "These are the most appropriate for a Berrima Christmas, guards and gardens."

The Spot The War Forgot

"How can you even think of Christmas," said Frau Hurtzig, with vim? "I cannot raise the slightest feeling of Christmas with the sun shining and chickens being killed outside. The dark evenings, twinkling lights, sleigh bells, and snow, are entirely missing in this country."

"Fritz has said we can borrow a harmonium to practice our carol singing," said Pastor Millat, "could we keep it at your house, Frau Hurtzig?"

"*Ja*, I would like that, at least we can have carolling."

Machotka, who was sitting quietly in the corner suddenly blurted out, "As my contribution to the school, I shall teach the children and Edna to swim."

We all stared at him and the beautiful woman lost her usual cool and calm expression.

"You can teach the children, but I refuse to enter the water, Paul. It is impossible for me to swim!"

"*Ach komm schon*, Honey, anybody can learn to swim."

"Not me. You can say 'oh come on' all you like, Paul, I cannot swim."

"I am surprised you don't swim," I said, "I thought everyone from Southern California could swim."

"My parents never allowed my sisters and me to swim in the ocean, we were permitted to wade in waves but not swim."

"It's high time you became a water sprite," said Machotka, fired with enthusiasm, "we shall start tomorrow."

"No, Paul!" The beautiful woman had an edge to her voice and her eyes were cold, "I am not going swimming."

Machotka's eyebrows plunged and he scowled at his wife.

"Teach the children, Paul, we will discuss the other idea in private."

W.E. Hamilton

There was an awkward silence before Machotka said, "Oh, all right, but once they can swim it will be your turn to learn."

Nobody knew what to say for the atmosphere was frosty, but Billy saved the day by coughing and changing the subject. "The people at Bourke asked for help in making Christmas bright for their children."

"It's too hot to rake up much enthusiasm for making Christmas gifts," I said, "Frau Hurtzig is right, it does not seem like Christmas."

"A lot of the men are feeling that way, so the Camp Committee is organizing an entertainment evening to get us into the spirit of gift-giving. There is to be music and song and Gertrude Brauns will recite poetry. I hope you will all come."

Of course, we went. Despite the sweltering heat the music and song helped remind us we were nearing Christmas. Yet it was not the music or song or even the poetry that motivated me to sign up for toymaking. It was Gertrude's white dress and the ribboned wreaths she distributed amongst us on behalf of the theatre, that did the trick. For the next two weeks, the prison once again became Santa's workshop. Machotka was not one of Santa's elves, for his garden had spread far beyond his yard, and he was very busy supervising an army of gardeners. In between picking beans and turning the compost, he coached the children in swimming.

"Although, coaching is stretching the truth somewhat," I said to Billy as we watched the children floundering about in the shallows. "Will those kids ever float?"

"I see why Edna is not keen on being taught to swim by Machotka," said Billy, "there's not much teaching going on."

"More learning by trial and error."

The Spot The War Forgot

And yet to our amazement, Eva and Hanna were floating by the time we put the wheels on the last train and stitched the mouth on the last rag-doll. And a few days after the Commandant sent vast quantities of gifts to Bourke, even Carmen and Lore were waterborne. Although most of our gifts were destined for the children of other camps, we had not forgotten our own children. The theatre group set a tall pine in the centre of the stage and decorated it. Meanwhile, the beautiful woman hung glass fruit and soldiers on a real tree in a 'forbidden' room in her house, and Frau Hurtzig tied spice cookies onto the artificial tree by her bay-window. Then on Christmas Eve, we all assembled in the theatre for the great gift-giving ceremony. The children's eyes grew wide as they looked at the tree and the table near it, loaded with parcels.

"So many presents for eight children," said Frau Hurtzig, as Herr Panke invited the girls, and the mothers with babies to come forward.

"I made the sailor dolls and their strollers, Lulu," murmured Captain Hurtzig under the cover of movement and footsteps. "I can't wait for Lore and Hanna to see them."

"The tree looks magical now the candles are all lit," I whispered to Billy, "Those chaff bags over the windows are keeping the light out better than I expected."

"I told you it was worth the hassle, if I wasn't here to boss you out of your lazy ways you would miss out on so much, Wolfgang."

I pulled a face. "Maybe so, but in my defence, the ravine we got the tree from was a long way away, and it takes ages to make so many tree ornaments by hand."

While we were whispering, Father Christmas himself

arrived on stage.

"Have you been good this year?" he asked, as the children gathered around him.

There was a great deal of head-nodding, while the babies smiled from within the circle of their mother's arms. Eva went as far as to say she had been extra good, which made us all roar with laugher. Father Christmas (smothering a smile) wisely overlooked this outrageous lie, and with equal wisdom treated fourteen-year-old Gertrude with grave dignity (because she was too old for the Santa business.) She was not above following him and the younger ones over to the loaded table, however, where they all received so many presents they could not carry them off the stage in one go. Then Hanna, Lore, Eva, and Carmen, told the story of the birth of Christ. Each of them reciting their well-rehearsed piece without stumbling (thanks to Pastor Millat's diligent efforts.) Then we sang carols and finally, there was an excellent monologue written and performed by one of the prisoners, in a North German accent.

"That was a wonderful evening," said Frau Hurtzig, as Leonard (carrying a candle) came to light the way home for her. "I shall see you tomorrow morning, leiblings," said Captain Hurtzig, kissing his family goodnight, "provided no one ruins it by escaping."

Nobody bothered running away, so Christmas day passed smoothly with the usual banquet in the courthouse, followed by items from the orchestra, choir and finally a play. Then there were sports, and picnics, and open-air concerts in the days between Christmas and New Year. It was a festive time and Bartels bakehouse did a roaring trade in cakes and pastries.

Machotka waited until the Christmas decorations were

The Spot The War Forgot

back in their box, and the tree was in the compost bin before he tackled his wife over swimming lessons once more. I don't know what he said to make her change her mind, but whatever it was, it got the job done. I was about to ride the slippery slope when I saw the Machotka family walking to the river one morning. It was not unusual to see them down by the river, what caught my attention was the outfit the beautiful woman had on. She was wearing knee-length bloomers of blue cotton print, topped with a flounced matching bodice. Her legs were encased in black stockings that ended in yellow canvas shoes, and her long hair was confined in a ruffled mob cap. Even more surprising, was the tightly stitched burlap belt that encircled her upper torso and was attached to a long rope that Machotka held.

"What on earth is Edna wearing?" I said to Billy, who was next in line.

"It looks like a homemade replica of the 'Gibson Girl' bathing costume."

"I can see that, I'm talking about the leash wrapped around her. It looks like Machotka is walking his dog."

"Judging from the bathing costume, it is some sort of swimming apparatus."

"Are you going to get on the slide or not?" said Tote impatiently.

"Not. You can take my place, I have spotted better entertainment.

"I think I will come with you," said Billy, "this is too good to miss."

We made our way down to the sandy beach opposite the tall rocks where the diving boards jutted out. The beautiful woman stood gingerly at the edge of the water while Machotka (still holding the end of the rope) climbed up to the diving board above. When he was securely seated on the end of the plank, he called down to his wife:

"Jump in Edna."

"Oh, Paul," there was a whiny tone to the beautiful woman's voice, "I don't think this is a good idea."

"Nonsense, Edna, you'll be swimming in no time."

"Can't I start in the shallow water as the children did?"

"That will take too long, I want you swimming before the water carnival, then you can come boating with me."

"But it looks awfully deep, Paul."

"You'll be fine, if you start to sink, I will pull you up again."

"You'll be alright Mama," chorused the girls, "swimming is easy."

"No," said the beautiful woman, stalling. "It is not fair to leave Luise to look after Sylvia and Manon for so long."

"Oh, Mother, Frau Hurtzig loves babies."

But the beautiful woman was not convinced by Carmen's words. Eva was much more persuasive.

"In you go," she said, giving her mother a hard shove in the back.

The beautiful woman wobbled and slipped and fell with a shriek into the water.

"That's the way, Edna," shouted Machotka, as his wife flailed about in the water, "just keep moving like that and you will find yourself swimming."

But she did not. Despite much activity, the beautiful woman sank from sight.

I leapt to my feet in horror. "Oh no, she is going to drown,"

The Spot The War Forgot

I said, "pulling off my shoes and shirt. I was about to dive in when Billy said:

"Relax, there is no need to play the white knight, Machotka has got it all in hand."

And to my amazement, I saw Billy was right, for Machotka yanked on the rope and hauled his wife to the surface.

"Now, try to move more smoothly this time," he yelled, "push the water aside with your arms and move your legs like a frog."

"I'm drowning," shouted the beautiful woman.

"No, you are not, but you will get your mouth full of water if you keep talking."

He let out the rope and the beautiful woman sank like livebait on the end of a fishing rod. The next time he hauled her up she shrieked at him:

"I told you I couldn't swim."

"You won't with that sort of attitude, now concentrate on making the proper movements."

He let the rope slip through his fingers and once more his wife sank like a stone. This performance was repeated until it became clear that the beautiful woman would never swim.

"I think perhaps your parents knew what they were doing when they only allowed you to wade in the ocean," said Machotka, as he and the girls pulled her up the bank.

The beautiful woman's mob cap sat plastered to her head like frilly seaweed, her bloomers sagged with water, and the rope hung like a rat's tail. Her yellow shoes squelched as she stamped her foot, and turning a red glowering face on her husband, she hissed, "I told you so."

W.E. Hamilton

December 1917
British Capture Jerusalem from the Ottomans

The Boating Carnival

Henry Allen's cow died, and even though we had nothing to do with his cow's death, it was all our fault.

"Everything is always 'the German's fault,' according to Henry Allen," I said bitterly, as I leaned on the railing of the Hansa bridge. "Anything unusual, from a stranger in the paddock to a missing cat, he always blames us."

"Don't get wound up, Wolfgang," said Hermann, "some people are like that."

I threw a stick in the water and watched it float away. "You are only saying that because you are happy about the letter you found in the salami Maria sent you."

"Maybe. And also, because the commandant and Lieutenant Samuels have agreed to let us celebrate the Kaiser's birthday.

"That is wonderful," I said, forgetting hateful Henry Allen. "Can we hold it on January the twenty-eighth?"

"Sort of, the first day can't be on his actual birthday, and

The Spot The War Forgot

we are not allowed to display national emblems or flags, but if we start on the day before, it is alright for the celebrations to continue onto his birthday."

"Nice." I threw another stick into the water.

"It certainly is. This is going to be our biggest water carnival yet. We are inviting the commandant, and the members of the guard and the villagers to attend the first day's celebrations this year.

"Will Captain Foulkes allow that?"

"Not only has the commandant allowed it, but he has also accepted the invitation on behalf of the guard."

"How come you know all this?"

Hermann tapped his nose. "I have my sources of information."

"I suppose you have been talking to Billy and Max."

Hermann grinned. "They had just got back from a Camp Committee meeting."

"So, what else do you know?"

"The first day is a water carnival and aquatic sports and the next day is given over to a tennis tournament, sporting contests, and gymnastic displays, followed by dinner in the evening and a grand concert (for which the curfew has been extended to 11 pm.)"

I rubbed my chin thoughtfully. "I wonder how we should decorate the Attilla this year?"

Hermann was about to answer, but our conversation was interrupted by Henry Allen stomping onto the bridge.

"You Huns stay away from my new cow," he yelled, shaking his fist at us. If I see you giving her the evil eye, I will take my shotgun to you!"

W.E. Hamilton

"I hope Henry Allen will not come to the carnival," I said, watching him march away.

"He will come for sure, and he'll spend the whole time snooping around for things to make a fuss about."

"I hope you are wrong."

But Hermann was horribly right. And what's more, Henry Allen found exactly what he was looking for, but not at the beginning of the day.

By 1918 the fame of our water carnivals had spread way beyond Berrima. Curious people came from Sydney in great numbers. Henry Allen mingled among them, but other than scowling at us, he made no trouble. I forgot him as the day progressed and the carnival atmosphere swept me along in its wake of festivities. The swimming sports went off without a hitch, and the high diving contest wowed the spectators lined thickly along the shore. There was a very beautiful and unusual pageant in which our entire fleet of vessels was pressed into service, and of course, there was a competition for the best-decorated boat. This year there was a Chinese junk, several perfectly rigged sailing ships and a weird dragon ship in glorious colours. Carmen, Eva, Hanna, and Lore, (dressed in sailor suits) sailed about on the floral encrusted Emil, while the Attila (renamed Vierlanden and bedecked in flowers and vegetables) followed. Many of the boats were easy to identify and despite their disguises, we recognized them. A few of them, however, had us guessing.

"I think the dragon-boat is the Aradne," I said, squinting at it speculatively.

"Probably," said Billy, as he sized up the competition. "I don't think we will win first prize this year."

The Spot The War Forgot

"No, our boat is pretty but not unique enough."

"Still, it was worth it, look at those kids' faces. They are loving it."

I nodded. "The submarine might win. It is a clever idea to equip one of the large kayaks with a cardboard conning tower and a cannon."

"Possibly, but the zeppelin is good too. I think it stands an equal chance of winning."

But in the end, it was not the zeppelin or the sub that won, it was Captain Hannig's odd bicycle boat disguised as a floatplane that took first prize.

After that twenty pretty canoes entertained us by forming all sorts of patterns, and even 'danced' a Polonaise! Then there were boat races. By the time they were finished and propeller-driven model boats had steamed about the lake for some time, I was hungry. And I was not alone in thinking about food.

"Billy and Wolfgang, come and join us for afternoon tea," Frau Hurtzig, called from the midst of a group moving towards the Bush Bakehouse.

The idea seemed good to us, so without hesitation, we fell in step with the crowd.

"I have inside information that Heinrich has just taken a new batch of strudel out of the oven," said Captain Hurtzig, "if we are quick, we can get some before he sells out."

We got there in time to purchase apple strudels, but we had to sit on the bank, for all the narrow semi-circular tables and benches were already taken by Australian girls and young internees.

"It is disgusting how those girls flirt so openly with the men," said lieutenant Samuels, sitting down nearby. "I can't understand why they do it."

I strained my ears to hear the commandant's answer, but his reply was drowned out as the band on the stage of the small rock amphitheatre started a rousing march. While we ate, William Davis wandered over to us.

"Can I join you?"

"For sure," we said, making room for him.

"How is the garden doing on the land I rented you, Machotka?"

"Very good. I've planted tomatoes and cucumbers on the patch behind the Surveyor General Hotel and they are coming up well."

"Do you think they will be ready by the beginning of March?"

"I should think they will be at their peak by then."

Davis smiled. "Good, very good."

"Why do you ask?"

"No particular reason, just interested. Do you think I could have a few tomatoes and cucumbers when they are ready?"

"Of course, you can have what you want for your family. It is nice of you to ask permission, most of the villagers just steal from our gardens like the crows and rabbits."

"Oh, I wouldn't do that," said Davis, clapping Machotka on the shoulder before getting up. "All the best with your garden. Be seeing you."

He left and we followed him shortly after because we saw on the program that Valentin Wenk was about to perform at the Great Lake.

"And I certainly would not want to miss that," said the beautiful woman. "I don't have a clue what he will do but it

The Spot The War Forgot

will be hilarious."

And so it was. He threw us into paroxysms of laughter, as dressed in a ruffled red silk gown and many fluffy petticoats, he climbed a greasy pole leaning out over the river. Henry Allen was the only one not amused. He stood watching with a sour expression on his face. I nudged Billy.

"I suppose Allen is angry because he hasn't found anything to complain about."

"He hasn't yet, but there is still time. He might find what he is looking for in the next item."

"What do you mean, what is the next item?"

Billy whispered so those around us could not hear. "It's a mock battle between an English fishing boat and a zep and a plane. The zep and the plane will attack the fishing boat and set it on fire so it will sink in a blaze of flames."

"So, what is the problem with that? The Berrima Guard staged one like that a couple of years ago and the villagers loved it. Remember the man who got so carried away he fell in the water and they had to fish him out in the middle of the battle?"

"I know, but Henry Allen is the sort of man to make a big fuss about it."

"We shall soon see if you are right," I said, clapping as Wenk bowed and departed, "for here comes the 'English fishing boat.'"

"Whatever happens, it will make an exciting end to the day."

And even more exciting than anyone expected, for things went awry when the wind suddenly freshened and the zep (unable to hold its position) knocked into the plane and all three collided and went up in flames. The spectators were greatly shocked, not by the battle itself, but by the crews of the ill-fated vessels diving overboard to escape the flames. Nobody was burnt and nobody drowned, but some of the Australian girls were so overcome by the spectacle, they needed to lean on the strong arms of the young internees beside them.

Henry Allen watched it gleefully, but he did not say or do anything - at least, he didn't say or do anything right away. When it was all over, we dispersed; some to the village, some to cars and wagons, but most to the jail.

"I am glad tomorrow's celebrations are not open to the public," I said to Billy, as we entered the prison, "because Henry Allen cannot come."

"He doesn't need to," said Billy, "he has enough ammunition already."

The Spot The War Forgot

January 1918
U.S. President Woodrow Outlines Fourteen Points for Peace

The Kaiser's Birthday

I stared into the small mirror on my cell wall and stuck a blue cornflower in my buttonhole.

"We might not be allowed German flags or insignias, Julius, but at least I can wear the national flower of my country."

"I would wear the national flower of my country but tulips are not in season,"

"You could wear a blue flower in honour of the Kaiser even though you are Hungarian."

"I might if I feel in the mood, it all depends on the post. I fear my Marcella is not faithful to me. If she writes me a good letter, I will wear a flower but if it is bad, I will not."

"You are not going to waste the whole morning moping in your cell waiting for the post, are you? The tennis tournament is about to start, come with me."

"Alright." Julius swung his legs over the side of his bunk and jumped down. "I would not like to deprive the lovely Mrs

Machotka of my company."

"She is sure to be there," I said, fiddling with the flower so it sat straight.

Julius brushed his hair hastily and twirled his moustache. "Let us be off then," he said.

The three tennis courts were draped with colourful bunting and the first matches had started when we arrived. A large crowd stood around watching the games. Like me, almost everyone was wearing a blue flower in their buttonhole. Julius and I made our way over to the Hurtzigs and the Machotkas. Frau Hurtzig was wearing a sensible cotton dress, but the beautiful woman was draped in white and held a frilly parasol above her golden head. I greeted my friends in the usual way, but Julius swept off his hat with a flourish and bowing, kissed the beautiful woman's hand.

"Dear lady, you are more lovely than all the flowers in the buttonholes here."

The beautiful woman acknowledged his greeting by inclining her dainty head like a queen.

"That's enough of that, Poszipisch," growled Machotka, "watch the game, not my wife."

"The prize for the winner is very generous," said Frau Hurtzig, hastily, "a silver cigarette case."

"Solid silver and good quality," said Billy, overhearing the conversation as he came up to us, "for I saw what the Camp Committee paid for it."

"I expect Captain Niemann will win," said Captain Hurtzig.

"He's the favourite," Billy pointed to a group of men huddled in the corner, "you can place a bet on him over there if you want."

The Spot The War Forgot

The sudden gleam that entered Captain Hurtzig's eye died when his wife said primly:

"Captain Hurtzig is a church-going man, Billy, he does not gamble and neither should any of you. Gambling is the devil's game."

What other prizes are there?" said the beautiful woman, skillfully sliding off the subject.

"Mainly edible," said Billy, "sausages, bags of assorted vegetables, a live duck and a live pig. Then there are cigarettes and cigars of course.

We watched the tennis for some time, and when we tired of that there were plenty of other sporting events to see. As the sun rose higher the heat rose with it, until it was so scorching only the most dedicated sportsmen and their supporters were left sweltering on the land. The rest of us were riding the grand slippery slope, diving, or swimming in the river. By mid-afternoon, the sports were over. As expected, Captain Niemann won the cigarette case. I did not see the other prizes awarded but I assumed Richard Peytsch excelled in some sport, for I saw him wandering about carrying a little pig.

"Congratulations on your win," I said, "that is a tasty treat you have in your arms. Are you going to slaughter it yourself or pay Annie to do it?"

Richard hugged the pig closer to his chest and glared at me.

"I'm not going to let that big fat woman kill Anton," he said, in horrified tones. He looked down at the dog trotting at his heels. "A small faithful dog and a little pig are better friends than most of this lot." With that, he spun around and stalked off.

"What has made Richard so morose," I asked Michael, as

he sauntered past me on his way to the Bush Bakehouse.

"He's a loner, probably can't handle so many people near his hut."

"I've offended him by suggesting he would eat the pig. Apparently, the pig's name is Anton and he is one of Richard's few friends."

Michael gave a snort of laughter. "He probably likes the pig because it doesn't say more than a grunt now and then." He clapped me on the shoulder, "do not look so troubled, Wolfgang, forget Richard and come and have some afternoon tea. The brass band is about to perform and the Camp Committee has provided a sumptuous feast."

I took his advice and forgot Richard as I ate Black Forest gateau and Chocolate Mud cake. I had also forgotten Julius who I had not seen since the post arrived. He was thrust back into my mind, however, when loud cries of "FIRE" interrupted the brass band's performance. A little distance downstream, a hut was going up in flames.

"It's Villa Marcella, Julius's hut!" I shouted, running across the rough ground.

When I got there, men were trying to put the fire out. I scooped water from the river with my tin mug and threw it on the flames. It was pitiful and without buckets close at hand there was no way we could stop the destruction. Villa Marcella blazed like a funeral pyre, and as it burnt Julius stood clutching a letter in his upraised hand shouting:

"You unfaithful, backstabbing woman! You prefer another man to me, do you! You have broken my heart with your callus rejection, so I will destroy my token of love to you!"

"Come away, Julius," I said pulling at him. "There are

The Spot The War Forgot

plenty of other women in the world."

But Julius was not having a bit of it.

"That spiteful cruel woman has broken my heart forever. I will never get over her." He clutched his hair. "I might as well end it all now for my life is no longer worth living."

He made a rush at the fire as if he was going to throw himself into the flames, but we grabbed him and held him back.

It was customary to keep a bucket of water behind the door of each hut in case of fire. Men were not long in arriving with the buckets and once they formed a chain gang to the river, things improved. They were not able to save Villa Marcella, but more importantly, they prevented a bush fire, for another inferno like the one last year was a terrifying thought. At last, the flames were quenched, but sadly, the inferno inside Julius still raged. Three of us held onto him but none of us could calm him, he was like a mad man.

The Machotka's stood a little distance away. I saw Machotka say something to his wife and the beautiful woman nodded. Then she came over and laid a slim white hand on Julius's arm.

"My dear gallant Julius, you have had a shock."

At the touch of her hand, Julius instantly calmed down.

"Yes," he said, "Marcella is a backstabbing woman."

The beautiful woman nodded. "She doesn't deserve you." She slipped her arm around his elbow. "Come and have afternoon tea at my house. You will feel much better after something to eat and drink."

With that, she drew him away from the sad ruins of his 'token of love'. Machotka took his other arm and together they walked quietly along the riverbank. Once they had disappeared the band struck up a rousing tune and Heinrich brought out another load of cakes. I did not see Julius again until the evening banquet, and by then he was much recovered for the Machotkas had done a marvellous job of restoring his sense of wellbeing.

"Edna says I am a handsome man and I could do better than Marcella," he said, stabbing his fork into a slice of ham, "and it is true. I never liked Marcella's nose, anyway." He switched subjects suddenly. "I am looking forward to the grand concert tonight."

I swallowed a mouthful of potato. "I hope you enjoy it," I said, "for Fritz has been driving us so hard you would think we were Germany's Symphony Orchestra about to perform before the King."

"And the choir have been slaving away too," said Ernst, pushing peas around his plate, "Karl expects a very high standard. There are so many of us I don't know how he can spot who is singing off-key, but he can."

But nobody sang off-key that night and the orchestra played well. At the end of the concert there was a huge round of applause and then a respectful silence before we finished off with our customary song. We did not know this was the Kaiser's last official birthday, but even if we had, we could not have sung, *Halt Deutschland Hoch in Ehren,* with more heartfelt fervour. And the commandant and the members of the guard (not one bit hoodwinked) stood respectfully as we honoured the Kaiser with the patriotic song and blue flowers in our buttonholes. It was a good thing Henry Allen was not there to witness it.

The Spot The War Forgot

**March 1918
Deadly Spanish Influenza Spreads Rapidly**

Henry Allen Strikes Out

It was almost a month before Henry Allen struck at us. And when he did, it was through a Red Cross meeting. I was perusing the Southern Mail at breakfast one morning, when the headline. 'Moss Vale Indignant,' caught my eye.

"I say, listen to this," I said, banging my empty cup on the table. "At a public meeting for the Red Cross, there was a complaint about us. Henry Allen and E.E. Row (the Moss Vale bank manager) are incensed by us celebrating the Kaiser's birthday, and allege two-hundred of us goosestepped about the country accompanied by a military band."

"We knew Allen was angry about the mock battle," said Billy, "but when did two-hundred of us ever goosestep to a military band?"

"Let me look at that," said Captain Hurtzig.

"I passed the paper across the table to him and he scanned the article swiftly.

W.E. Hamilton

"As I thought!" he stabbed his finger on a line. "This is the date of the choir picnic. There were not two-hundred of us. How many went on the picnic, Karl?"

Karl sucked in his lower lip and stared into the air absently as he calculated. "I doubt there were more than sixty-eight of us, including the women and children."

"And we didn't goosestep! We are sailors, I don't even know how to goosestep," I said indignantly. "We march so the older ones don't straggle behind."

"Henry Allen knows nothing about music, said Fritz, "for if he did, he would know the tune we marched to was written by, Sousa, an American composer."

Captain Hurtzig looked at the paper once more.

"*Ach komm schon*," he blurted out, slapping the paper down in disgust, "they unanimously moved a motion to restrict us to the compound because they claim…" he grabbed the paper again, and read, "'it is unreasonable to allow them free use of the river.'" He slung the paper across to me.

"Allen is behind that motion," said Machotka, picking it up. "Remember when, as a trustee of the Berrima common, he challenged Captain Foulkes for prohibiting civilians taking boats on the stretch of river running past our compound."

"The whole thing was ridiculous, as the common is quite a distance upstream from the disputed area," said Fritz. "That was Allen trying to get back at Captain Foulkes because the commandant complained about the quality of his bread."

"It says here," said Machotka, "they forwarded the resolutions to the Minister of Defence." (We all looked shocked at that.) "But Senator Pearce responded that, *'he was not going to accept the statement of an infuriated municipal councillor until he had proved it to be true.'"*

"Good for him," I said.

"The Department of Defence has instructed Captain Wallace of Army Intelligence to go to Berrima," continued Machotka, "to investigate, report and make recommendations."

There was a silence. Captain Hurtzig was the first to speak.

"I hope Captain Wallace is a reasonable man. Could we keep this information to ourselves? I'd rather my wife didn't know about it, for the last time they were talking about restricting us to a compound she got very upset."

"Of course."

"My wife shouldn't hear of it either," said Machotka.

"Won't they read about it anyway?"

"Luise doesn't bother with Australian papers," said Captain Hurtzig, "she says they are hopelessly biased."

"Edna doesn't read them either," said Machotka, "she prefers the American ones the villagers smuggle to us."

"Speaking of the ladies," said Captain Hurtzig, picking up his dirty plates, "we'd best wash up for it is nearly rollcall, and my wife will expect to see me directly the gates open."

I folded the paper and stuck it under my arm before picking up my plates. Then we moved towards the basins of hot soapy water.

"Henry Allen probably complained to the Moss Vale Red Cross because he couldn't whip up enough anti-German feeling in Berrima," said Billy, as we scrubbed our plates.

Machotka nodded. "The villagers are much more interested in Moss Vale's upcoming Agricultural and Pastoral show than Allen's petty allegations."

We laughed because it was so true. While the members of

W.E. Hamilton

the Red Cross raged over goose-stepping that never happened, the Berrima farmers measured the circumference of their pigs and weighed the milk in their pails each morning. Women arranged and rearranged bouquets, preserved produce, and baked pies, Miss Dangar dithered over her paintings of the beautiful woman's cottage, trying to decide which was the best, and Fanny Lyons hopped her small pony, Rangy, over low jumps and braided his hair. Even the children and members of the Guard had things to exhibit. Captain Kühlken's little friends Mollie and Nola were entering the colouring-in competition, and their father, Sergeant Major Hagon, was hoping to win Best Tomato. He was riding back and forth in front of the picket fence as I passed out the gate.

"How are the tomatoes getting on, Leonard?"

The mounted guard drew in his reins, and his bored horse stopped plodding, flopped her ears sideways, and tilted one of her back hooves onto its tip. Leonard leaned forward with his elbow on the pommel of the saddle.

"Very good, thanks for asking, Wolfgang. "The rate they are growing one of them is sure to be the biggest in the show. I know all the growers around here and nobody's tomatoes are as good as mine. It's those seeds Machotka gave me."

"It's a pity he can't enter something in the show."

"I'm glad of it, for I wouldn't stand a chance against him. Or any of you blokes for that matter. How many acres have you turned into gardens now?"

"Including the orchards and small farms we rent, it's about ten acres."

The guard whistled admiringly. "Ten acres, that is a lot of fruit and vegetables."

The Spot The War Forgot

"We couldn't do it without Machotka's advice."

"That's true. That man is a genius with plants. He has even helped me out with gardening tips. Pop your head over the fence," said Leonard, jerking his head towards the front yard of the guard's quarters, "and take a *dekko* at my tomatoes."

"Alright," I said.

The guard turned his horse around and we walked to the end of the picket fence. There we stopped and peered at the plants on the other side of the palings. They were neatly tied to wooden stakes and covered with netting to keep the birds off.

"They are fine specimens," I said. "I would love to go to the Moss Vale Show and see them win."

Leonard shook his head. "You don't want to do that." "The commandant is right to refuse to let you go. You're not safe anywhere other than Berrima, anti-German hysteria is sweeping the nation. It's all the fault of the Melbourne newspapers. Keith Murdoch writes savage editorials. He's the one calling for stricter controls and complete internment of enemy aliens."

"The Moss Vale Council rejected his proposals."

"Yes, thank goodness, but the Manly Municipal Council are still recommending his schemes, and Moss Vale's civilized attitude is getting rather tattered as the war drags on."

"Who else is entering the gardening competition?" I said, turning back to the tomatoes.

"The butcher, the schoolmaster, the girls from the Post Office and James Harper from the Hotel."

"Somehow I can't imagine Annie as a gardener."

"Not her," Leonard dismissed the idea with a wave of his hand. "Her husband. My tomatoes are better than his and

W.E. Hamilton

Thomas Packer's tomatoes, and the Post Office girls are only growing flowers."

"Is Henry Allen entering anything?"

"No, the cockies ruined his pears."

I tried not to smile. "What about William Davis?"

"No, he never enters. It's a good thing you blokes are renting his land behind the hotel because he never did anything with it."

While we were talking Captain Kühlken wandered past.

"Hello, Leonard, is it alright if I take the girls down to the river to build sandcastles this morning?"

"That would be bonza, my wife would be grateful if you took them off her hands, for it is washday."

"I'll go and get them now," said Captain Kühlken, waving goodbye.

"He's a kind man," said Leonard, "he, Henry Reineke, and Raymond Stuparich, take such a fatherly interest in my girls."

"They miss their own children," I said. "Did you see the cartoon Henry drew of the three of them and Mollie and Nola?"

"Yes, it was marvellous." He looked at the sentry standing guard at the gate and sighed. "I'd rather stay here talking to you about tomatoes, Wolfgang, but I'd better get back to my duties."

"I'll be thinking of you on Friday," I said, as we parted company. "You are sure to win."

But he didn't. To everyone's surprise, William Davis won.

"I could not believe my eyes," said the Sergeant Major, as I kept in step with his horse the morning after his shock. "I got nothing, but William Davis won a blue ribbon for his tomatoes and cucumbers in the section for first-time-exhibitors. There

The Spot The War Forgot

is something fishy about this for he has no garden and doesn't even grow chives on his windowsill."

"Tomatoes and cucumbers, that's funny," I said slowly, as a memory flashed into my mind.

"You're dead right it's funny," said Leonard sourly, "and not the ha-ha kind of funny."

"I remember at the boating carnival," I said, casting my mind back to afternoon tea on the riverbank, "Davis asked Machotka if he could take some of his tomatoes and cucumbers when they were ready."

"Really?" Leonard sat up so suddenly his horse threw her head up in surprise. "As soon as I have finished my shift, I am going back to the Show to investigate."

Investigations, be they army investigations or investigations into competition frauds, take time. Captain Wallace on behalf of the Department of Defence, and Leonard on behalf of his tomatoes, both had questions to be answered. Captain Wallace took evidence from Captain Foulkes and interviewed several villagers (including Allen and E.E. Row.) Meanwhile, Leonard took evidence from Machotka's garden and interviewed villagers (including William Davis.) By the time Wallace concluded the alleged military formation was merely a picnic, the Southern Mail had exposed William's deception, and the shopkeeper's triumph had turned to shame.

"Machotka should have got the ribbon," said Leonard as we discussed the sorry affair over the picket fence. "He deserved it, and he is a local even if he is a prisoner."

"He had the honour of a scathing article in the Southern Mail entitled, 'Made in Germany,'" I said sarcastically.

"Huh, the reporter was a smart-Alek," said Leonard. He

W.E. Hamilton

leaned forward in his saddle and looked me in the eye. "War or no war, it wasn't fair, it doesn't matter which side you are on, a prize-winning tomato deserves a prize."

The Spot The War Forgot

July 1918
Major Turning Point On Western Front a Black Day for German Army

Reshuffles and Upheavals

Apart from much of 1917, the guards changed every month. If this was to stop them and us getting friendly, it was a failure. Particularly, as many guards and commandants kept reappearing. Already Captain Stoddart had received several farewells and goodbye mementoes; including a War Chart from the SMS Emden, and two carved shields. We were discussing this issue in the prison workshop as we worked.

"Two shields are enough for anyone," said Captain Jertrum, slapping the workbench. "Next time he can give a shield back to me and I'll add the new dates and names of the guard."

"That's tough. He deserves another memento," I said, as I painted a cabinet white. "Captain Stoddart is a good man and liked by all."

Anton Gallwitzer took a finished chair spindle off the lathe.

W.E. Hamilton

"I'll make the next farewell shield if you like?"

"Don't forget it is your turn to make one for Major Baxter at the end of this month," said Captain Jertrum, pulling a piece of wood out of the timber rack. He's another one who keeps turning up."

Gallwitzer sawed the excess timber off the ends of his spindle. "You say that as if it were a bad thing."

"Of course it's not a bad thing," said Captain Jertrum, inspecting the grain of the wood carefully, "he understands us and sorted out the dreadful food shortages. I don't begrudge him a hundred shields. It's inserting his photograph behind the glass I can't face; especially as the glass follows the shape of the shield."

"I don't mind carving the fiddly bits," said Gallwitzer, "I'll do all the shields if you like, but first I must finish the stage props for the new theatre."

"What's happening with the theatre?" I said, dipping my brush in the paint.

"They've pulled the old one down and the new one is going to be much bigger, with thick stone walls, a proper roof, and slow combustion stoves, it will be much more comfortable, especially in the winter months," said Gallwitzer.

"The stage will be wider, deeper and higher," added Captain Jertrum, "and the orchestra pit is larger."

"I know all that, I'm talking about the lighting. Has Major Baxter had success with the Department of Defence?"

Gallwitzer put the spindle on a pile of matching spindles. "Oh, you mean the generator and the motor to drive it?"

"Ja."

"Not yet. They say, no, but the Major won't accept their

decision. He's told the theatre members to build the generator shed while he keeps arguing with the DOD."

"He will win, eventually," said Captain Jertrum, clamping his timber in a vice grip and picking up a hand-plane, "for he loves the theatre and says he will keep badgering the Defence Department until they are so sick of him, they will give us what we want."

"The DOD is not going to spend money on electricity for a POW theatre."

"Oh, the Major knows that, his argument is that his office and the cell blocks need electricity. Once he gets the generator and motor, it is a small matter to run additional wires across to the theatre."

"But until then, we have to continue with the carbide lamps," said Captain Jertrum, shaving a curl of wood off the lumber.

I pulled a face and opened my mouth to complain about the poor lighting, but before I could speak, Billy rushed in. He was in such a state of agitation I shut my mouth and looked at him expectantly.

"What's up, Köster?" said Captain Jertrum.

"An order has just been posted on the noticeboard. The adjutant general has decreed all huts upstream of the Hansa bridge must be removed at once. Anyone with a hut or villa in that area needs to move it into the compound immediately."

"Whew," I said, in relief, "my hut is downstream from the bridge."

"But Schoene Aussicht is not. The Emden men need help to move their castle by the sea."

"I can help," I said, dumping my paintbrush in water, and

cleaning my hands on a rag.

I followed Billy outside and we hurried down to the river. When we got there, we found many men scurrying about the left bank salvaging what they could of their huts. The smaller bathing huts were easy enough to pull apart and reconstruct within the compound, but Schoene Aussicht (the Emden hut) was not. The villa was the first building upstream of the bridge and was the most imposing of all the summerhouses. It sat in a prime position with a commanding view across the Great Lake swimming pool. The Emden men had completed it in the spring of 1916, and since then beautified it with a flag pole, stonewall terraces, and steps that led down to the water. It was made of brush woven through upright poles, and lined with termite mud for warmth, and had a charming veranda and a bark roof with a small turret. Nobody wanted to see it destroyed. A knot of engineers stood in a group calculating long numbers, while several ship's carpenters crawled around the base of Schoene Aussicht, poking at the foundations with wrecking bars. At last (after a heated discussion) all the engineers and carpenters agreed. Then Karl Muller called for quiet and addressed us.

"What we propose to do, is dig under the foundations and slide saplings underneath so the building is supported by a series of poles. There is a team of men selecting trees for this purpose even as I speak. Once we have the poles in place and the dirt cleared away from the large corner posts, we will need about eight men on each side to carry her down the river."

"Where are we taking her?" called Michael.

"Keep walking until you come to the spot where the men are flattening the ground, you can't miss it."

"Let's get to it," shouted Eric Brauns, waving his spade.

The Spot The War Forgot

We cheered and rushed towards the building. Then those with spades and shovels dug the dirt from under the walls while the rest of us rolled the stone foundations away. Once the poles arrived it did not take long to get them under the hut. What was trickier, was lifting it. I stationed myself at one of the corners and gripped the thick upright supporting post, while men (two deep) clutched the ends of the long poles bearing the hut.

"Lift SLOWLY," shouted Karl, "on the count of three."

"*Eins zwei drei*, LIFT."

We heaved and strained and bit by bit the villa rose. Once we got it clear of the ground, and the men got the poles on their shoulders, things got a little easier. The worst part was keeping everything roughly level as the ground rose and fell beneath our feet. We shuffled along until at last, we came to the new resting ground for Schoene Aussicht. The men in charge of flattening the ground had also dug the holes for the supporting poles. I positioned myself over a corner hole and on Karl's command, lowered my burden into the ground. Then the carpenters rushed around with levels as we lifted and dropped and generally jiggled things about while others dribbled dirt into the holes. We kept doing this until the carpenters smiled and twisted their thumbs up. Then we let go and shovelled the dirt around the foundation posts before tamping it down firmly. When we finished, Karl tried to shake the wall, and finding it impossible, shouted:

"Alright, you can pull the poles out from underneath."

Slowly and carefully, we did as he said, and as the last pole slipped out from under, we cheered.

"I'm very glad to have saved the villa," said Karl, "but I am sad to lose our prime position. The view was beautiful and we put a lot of work into landscaping the garden."

"I nearly broke my back making those steps down to the boat landing," said Otto.

"Don't worry," said Eric Brauns, "it will not take you long to get established again. By spring you will have gardens once more."

"Surely the war will be over by then," said Karl, responding automatically with the well-worn phrase.

But it wasn't, furthermore, the war had been going for so long we had settled into a comfortable routine. Apart from the ever-present worry about loved ones overseas, life ticked along pleasantly. The bugle sounded morning and evening, and the mail arrived once a day. We 'cleaned the ship' once a week, and enjoyed an open-air concert and a German afternoon tea every Sunday. The orchestra played alternate weeks with the brass band, and the theatre performed every two weeks. Our paychecks kept rolling in regularly and bank accounts grew healthy. Before Easter, we painted elaborate patterns on eggs, which we hid among the cabbages and chrysanthemums for the children to find. After Easter, we painted stage backdrops for comedies and dramas. Rifles and cannons tore through Europe while we boated and picnicked, acted, sang, and made music. As the future became increasingly unpredictable, the jail felt more and more like a safe haven.

Then unexpectedly our camp received a severe shock. Suddenly without warning, the Hurtzigs, Glintz's, Jepsens, and Brauns were gone. To those of us who had daily contact with them, it felt like we'd lost family members. When we saw the empty houses, we rushed to the Machotka's expecting to see their house also empty. But to our surprise, the front door stood

The Spot The War Forgot

open as usual. What was odd was the children were crying in the garden. Inside, we found Machotka sitting beside his wife with his arm around her.

"It's a dreadful blow," said the beautiful woman, twisting her handkerchief. "Luise was my dear friend. I shall miss her and the other women terribly. And the children have not stopped grieving since they saw Hanna and Lore leave. It is a sad loss."

"Why did they go, and where are they taking them?" I said in bewilderment.

"The internee's wives and children suffered such hardship in the Bourke camp the Government is transferring all families to Molonglo. They should have done it earlier, for the flies and heat in that dreadful place are terrible," said the beautiful woman with a shudder, "but there is no need to shift anyone from here for the climate is cool and there are few flies."

"Why are you still here?"

"The Government always gets confused by us," said Machotka, bitterly. "I suppose it is because I am not a German or a mariner."

"I only hope they will let us remain here," said the beautiful woman, dabbing her eyes.

"I don't mind where they send us," said Machotka, "so long as they don't split us up or send me back to the Holsworthy camp."

But that is exactly what happened. For a while it looked like the little family could stay put, but one day, within one hour, Paul Machotka was gone. We rallied around the beautiful woman and assured her we would help out more than ever. It was small compensation for the loss of her husband, but it was better than nothing.

"Bad luck usually comes in threes." The beautiful woman shook her head sorrowfully. "I am afraid of what may come next."

I did not share her superstition, nevertheless, I trembled when the Southern Mail announced the death of Captain Stoddart, and wished little Frau Hurtzig was still around to remind us God is in charge of everything (even things we don't understand.)

"He was only thirty-six, poor man," said Gallwitzer, as he inserted a photograph of Major Baxter into a wooden shield. I thought for sure he would be our next commandant."

"Apparently, he died of yellow fever," said Captain Jertrum, leaning against the workshop bench.

I looked up from the paper I held. "Did you know he was an assayer and worked for ten years in the Royal Mint in Sydney?"

"That explains why he took such an interest in the geology club," said Gallwitzer. "He and those fellows were often talking with Arnold and Annie about their limestone quarry in Marulan and the possibility of manufacturing cement."

"I wonder if Captain Stoddart identified any minerals in Berrima suitable for Portland cement? I must ask Annie."

"I wish I hadn't complained about making farewell shields for the poor old commandant," said Captain Jertrum, returning to the subject. "I would happily make him a hundred shields if it would bring him back to life."

"Thirty-six!" Hugo Bahl banged the workbench with his fist. "He was younger than me. Life is passing us by. Here we are stuck on the other side of the world playing games

The Spot The War Forgot

while our loved ones are struggling to survive. My son is four years old and I have not set eyes on him." He sighed and his shoulders dropped. "When will this dreadful war end?"

I was about to say, 'It feels like it will go on forever and ever,' when Billy rushed in, hot and puffing. He was in such a state of agitation I shut my mouth and looked at him expectantly.

"Have you heard the news?" he shouted.

"What news?"

"The news we have all been waiting for."

"Is the fighting over?" we shouted in unison.

Billy nodded. "THE FIGHTING IS OVER!"

———————————

W.E. Hamilton

September 1918
Germany Forced to Sign the Treaty of Versailles

Armistice

Nobody threw their hats in the air or danced in the streets when the Armistice was signed. Even the Southern Mail had nothing to say about the great event. I guess the villagers felt the same as us; our initial euphoria was fleeting for we were weary of riding the undulating waves of hope and despair.

"Perhaps it is just another rumour like the false armistice in October, or will end up like the fiasco of prisoner swapping," said Hugo Bahl, dumping a pile of firewood by the beautiful woman's stove. "How many times did Frau Hurtzig think she was going home?"

"I can't remember," I said, raking ashes from the firebox. "Remember the time she gave away all her household goods because she thought they were going the next day?"

"That was cruel." Billy tipped his bucket of spring water into the barrel next to the sink-bench. "We who had no hope of going were in a much better position."

The Spot The War Forgot

"Speaking of Luise," said the beautiful woman coming into the kitchen and catching the tail end of our conversation, "I received a letter from her yesterday. It is addressed to you too. Shall I read it aloud?"

We nodded and called the others to gather around as she pulled a chair out from the table and sat down.

"My dear Edna and home-help friends," she read.

"*[8]Something remarkable happened today! The Captain announced, "fighting has ceased on all fronts and negotiations are proceeding. There is an armistice and peace talks are underway." We have waited and hoped for these exact words for such a long time! And now, when we hear them, we can hardly believe them. At least I myself cannot properly realize it. How can it happen that I find it so overwhelming, I am unable to stop crying? Is it because we have been let down so often that it is impossible to feel real happiness? There will be endless time from now until our journey home, but the big thing is the fighting and murdering is to end.*

Generous people are preparing almost endless Christmas joy for the seventy-five children who live here in Molonglo under these very unusual circumstances. We, adults, share in the children's joy, but at the same time, we feel the pain and worries that distress our homeland and our future. It is true there is an armistice, but under what terms? And what is happening to our beloved country? The Kaiser is gone. What kind of Government will come to power? Will we be able to live in our home, and will there be enough money, food and bread for everyone? There has to be a God, and it will be the same old God in the coming year. The papers are utterly

---

[8]   Taken from Frau Hurtzig's diary

confusing, and while we feel everything for everybody, we are unable to form a clear picture of what is happening at home. When will we be reassured? We have no idea and so will have to be patient, hoping that when we get home there will be work for the men?"

The beautiful Woman stopped reading and the room was very quiet, for little Frau Hurtzig had expressed the fears and uncertainty we all felt. The collective mood was spiralling into gloominess when the devil child bounced in scattering angel dust of rambunctious joy.

"Can we eat Papa's present?" she shouted, flourishing a box of chocolates.

"Please, Mama," said Carmen, as she and Manon followed their irrepressible sister.

"Oh yes," said the beautiful woman, putting the letter to one side. She looked at us as she motioned Eva to pass the box around, "I won't bore you with the rest of Luise's letter for it is mainly about mending and cooking."

This thoughtfulness combined with the chocolates lifted our spirits wonderfully, and suddenly we felt jolly; for even the smell of dark chocolate is cheerful.

"Eat them carefully," said the beautiful woman, taking one topped with nuts, "the address was heavily underscored so I know Paul has hidden a message in one of them."

We raised our eyebrows, but Hermann merely chuckled.

"You took my advice?"

"Yes, and the courier system is working a treat. Paul sent a letter in a sausage the other day, and I replied by baking my answer in a cake."

"What would we do without wax paper? Maria sent me a

The Spot The War Forgot

note in a jar of jam."

"I must try that one. I sewed the last letter into the lapel of Paul's coat. I get sick of ripping clothes apart and restitching them, but stealth is the only way of communicating without our letters passing under half a dozen pairs of eyes."

"I'm glad Machotka sent his letter via chocolates not ripped trousers," I said. I bit into my chocolate in happy anticipation, but it tasted like a crayon, and spitting the wax out, I pulled a hard blob from my mouth. "I think I have found your message, Edna." I dunked it in a cup of water and removed the thread wound around the thin paper before giving it to the beautiful woman.

She smiled as she took it and opened it carefully, but as she scanned the contents her smile faded and her hand flew to her mouth in fear.

"Listen to this," she cried. "My Darling I don't want to alarm you but there has been a terrible outbreak of the Spanish Influenza in the camp. When it began the Australian officer in charge panicked and left the camp for several days, by the time he returned to assemble some sort of order, hundreds were dead or beyond help. Unfortunately, crowded together in open tents as we are, we are easy prey to the deadly scourge, and those who get it are not separated from the healthy. Neither is there an adequate hospital and only the simplest remedies in the camp."

"We haven't heard anything about Spanish Influenza in the Holsworthy camp," I broke in.

"I don't know why you sound so surprised, Wolfgang," said Hugo, "the censors will keep it very hushed up."

"Let Edna continue," said Billy frowning at us.

W.E. Hamilton

"Don't be afraid, I am fine. My biggest ailment is lack of sleep, as those of us who are well, spend the night building coffins for those who have died during the day. As soon as darkness falls the camp resounds with hammers and saws. At dawn, the dead are piled on a huge truck (ten or twelve coffins a load) and hauled away to be buried somewhere."

"Is Papa going to die?" said Carmen, creeping up to her mother with terror in her eyes.

"Oh dear, I forgot you children were in the room." She stood up and drew the girls to her side. "No of course not. He is young and healthy and he is fine."

"I wish Papa would come home," said Eva, bursting into tears.

The beautiful woman pulled her closer. "We all do honey. Now the fighting has stopped the war will be over very soon and he will be set free."

"That's right," said Anton Gallwitzer, crouching down and chucking Eva under her chin, "we will all be home by Christmas."

"Home by Christmas," we echoed, joy welling up in our hearts, for we were convinced he spoke the truth.

But nobody was home by the twenty-fifth of December. Christmas was a non-event and after New Year there was no birthday for our fallen Kaiser. The special days came and went with little celebration for life had entered into perpetual waiting. Hut building ceased, and plants went to seed in the untended gardens. Even boating on the river waned as the guards relaxed regulations. They still called the roll, morning and evening, but they did not lock us in at night, with the result, Billy and the others with rented cottages shifted into them permanently, and those with substantial huts often stayed the night in them. The rest of us continued to use the jail as a dormitory for it was much less crowded. It was never locked nowadays and the two-mile parole was increasingly ignored. As guards turned a blind eye to crossing the boundaries, wider exploration became a popular pastime and there were frequent trips to Moss Vale and expeditions to the large mountains ten miles away. The camp commandant, Major Evans, even organized overnight fox-hunting parties.

"Do you want to come hunting, Wolfgang and Gallwitzer?" shouted Billy, coming into the workshop one morning in February. "We will be away for three days."

I stopped gouging the middle out of a wooden bowl and switched off the lathe. "What is the point of going hunting if I don't have a gun?"

"The Major is supplying guns for everyone."

"Even prisoners?"

"*Ja*, even prisoners.

Gallwitzer laid down his fretsaw and looked at Billy intently. "Who is going?"

"The commandant, several soldiers, a couple of civilians, Fokken, Mahler, Preiss, Reinecke, Siebenkittel, and me. What about it, do you want to come?"

"I'd better not," I said, sighing. "Fritz has urged the members of the orchestra not to let rehearsals fall apart because of Armistice. "I promised him I would start practising again even though it seems pointless when we could be gone tomorrow."

"Well, I for one am not willing to continue living in limbo like this," said Gallwitzer. "I won't be coming hunting, but thank you, Billy, for letting me know the commandant is going away. That is the opportunity I have been waiting for."

"What are you up to, Anton?"

"I'm not telling you, Köster, you're on the Camp Committee," said Gallwitzer, packing his carpentry tools in a canvass bag hastily, "you'll know soon enough."

With that, he hoisted his bag onto his shoulder and strode out the door.

"I don't like the sound of that," said Billy, "keep an eye on him while I'm gone will you, Wolfgang? I fear he is going to do something foolish. I hope he is not thinking of running away."

But that is exactly what Anton had in mind, for shortly after the foxhunting party departed, he went missing. He had taken his tools and clothes and the walls of his cell were stripped bare of photographs. The only thing left was a note that said:

'Farewell, my friends. *I'm off to Sydney to have a good time.*'

His good time can't have been much fun for we heard shortly after (through a bottle of jam) he had given himself up at Holsworthy.

"He should have stayed here," said Billy, stretching a fox pelt onto a fleshing board. "Until we are actually on our way home, it is pointless looking for fun or happiness." He sighed. "I know it is a strange thing to say, but I miss the settled life of war."

I nodded. "I know exactly what you mean. How ironic Armistice has ruined our peace."

The Spot The War Forgot

August 1919
Weimar Republic Begins in Germany

Packing

Once shipping became available and a few people got permission to go home, explorations and hunting expeditions gave way to an endless round of packing and repacking. The camp canteen allowed its stock to dwindle away as we were more interested in buying trunks and suitcases than shirts and sweets.

"I have no idea what to take or leave," I said to Michael, as he lounged on Julius's empty bunk. "I have acquired far more than the eighty-four pounds of luggage I can ship for free."

"Just pay the overweight charge," said Michael, lighting a cigarette, "then you can take it all."

I snorted. "Not at forty-two pounds per ton, and that is only from Moss Vale to Rotterdam, without insurance!" I picked up the carved tray Anton had made for me and put it in the bottom of my steamer trunk.

Michael blew out a plume of smoke. "You're leaving your

packing very late. I was finished weeks ago."

"Oh, this is not my first time. I pack and repack every few days."

"You had better hurry up and make up your mind, we are going tomorrow."

"I know, I know," I said, putting a wooden bowl in my trunk.

"I wonder how Julius and the Glintz's and Hurtzigs are getting on?" said Michael, gazing at the ceiling and swinging his leg idly. "They should be home by now. I envy them getting to go on the SS Kursk in May. Just my luck all the other ships were delayed because of another outbreak of Spanish flu in the Holsworthy and Liverpool camps. It's been one disappointment after another, for after the flue it was a broken rudder, and after that, a shipping strike!"

I stopped packing and twisted to look at him. "You were saved a lot of grief. The Kursk was a filthy old Russian tub."

"How would you know?"

"Didn't you see the letter Frau Hurtzig sent Edna?"

"*Nein.*"

"Then you don't know about poor Julius?"

"What about him?"

"He's dead."

"Dead?" Michael sat bolt upright and turned white.

"*Ja*, sadly it is true. Frau Hurtzig wrote they were in the Indian Ocean when Spanish flu broke out."

"Julius died of the Spanish flu. That is terrible."

"*Nein*, he was not one of the eighteen who died. He was still well when they pulled into Durban where the ship was quarantined and fumigated. He got sick when the passengers of

The Spot The War Forgot

the Kursk were moved to another port. They were transported in open cattle cars under the burning desert sun, and later he died of heat exposure on a ship when they passed through the Suez Canal."

"That's awful. I can hardly believe it."

"Captain Hurtzig also became ill with encephalitis during the journey."

"Oh no, don't tell me he died too?"

"Fortunately, he had recovered by the time he got home."

"That is a relief. I assume the children and the Glintz's are alright for you would have told me if they weren't, but what about the others who went on the Kursk; von Klewitz, von Blumenthal and the men from the Emden? Are they alright?"

"They are well and Captain Hurtzig has received the command of a merchant ship."

"He is one of the lucky ones then. By the time we get back, the few ships Germany has left will already have their captains and crews."

I pulled a face. "Unfortunately, you are right. Twenty-thousand jobs disappeared when we lost those seventy-four warships."

Michael ground his teeth and his face changed to a dull red as he slammed his fist on the wall. "I'm glad von Reuter scuttled fifty-two of them before the handover to the Allies. It is not right they expect Germany to exist with only an army of one-hundred-thousand men and six battleships."

"Not a single aeroplane left," I said, folding a shirt and putting it on top of the tray, "and no submarines. Heinrich Bartle was smart to consider an alternative calling. Germany has little need for sailors, but everyone must eat."

"Everyone must eat but a pastry cook might not be the best career choice," said Michael, "for I fear there is little in Germany for Bartel to cook."

I took the picture my sister had painted off the wall and stared at the serene ship surrounded by the stormy sea. "I miss my family terribly," I said, placing the picture in the trunk, "but sometimes I think I would rather stay here than face an uncertain future back home."

"I know what you mean. It feels safe here. Australians won't starve but an unemployed sailor in Germany might. In the middle of the night, I despair over it."

I gazed at him searchingly. "You are not thinking to do what Albert Engfer did, are you?"

"Suicide! Not likely. I get depressed but not that depressed. Engfer was profoundly depressed. It was more than conditions back home that pushed him over the edge."

"*Ja*, it was the death of his two brothers."

"It's a pity we didn't involve him in the theatre. I wish I had encouraged him to act or paint scenery. He might have pulled through if he had something to keep his mind off his troubles."

I lifted a framed playbill off the wall and put it in my trunk. "Don't blame yourself, Michael, the theatre helped us from spiralling into depression, but once a man falls as low as Engfer painting backdrops and watching Wenks' antics as Molonglo von Kongo is probably not going to help much."

"I suppose so, though it is hard to believe," said Michael, lounging back on Julius's bunk, "Wenks' comedy routine with that dilapidated umbrella was so funny, surely it must have lifted Engfer's spirits at least a little. It is a good thing we enlarged the theatre when we did, and Major Baxter got the

The Spot The War Forgot

DOD to provide electricity, for I don't know how we would have made it through this dismal time without it. I see you have one of Mönkedieck's posters."

"*Ja*, I won it in one of the lotteries."

"You're lucky, I've collected postcards of all his work but it's not the same as owning an original full-sized poster. Mönkedieck is a talented man. If you decide to leave it behind, I'll buy it off you."

I shook my head. "I could never part with it, the theatre and the orchestra have been the brightest spots of my time here."

"True, if you don't count the river, boats and huts."

"I can hardly take them home with me!"

"What are we going to do about the boats and huts?" said Michael, stubbing out his cigarette.

"Billy told me Colonel Holman said that if he were in our place, he would burn them for they will only attract the hooligans of the neighbourhood, but the general feeling in the camp is to leave them as a gesture of goodwill for the locals."

"I like that idea much better. They are a memento of our time here?"

I nodded. "Something like that." I put a stack of books in my trunk. "Captain Kulhken wants to leave his hut and boat for his little friends Molly and Nola to play in, and the village would benefit financially from the tourists continuing to come down from Sydney."

"The tourists will be good for Edna too. Did you hear that she has rented the cottage next door?"

"*Ja*, she is going to turn it into a tearoom until Machotka is released from Holsworthy."

"I know. We took all the theatre chairs over there yesterday and helped her set up."

"The white chairs with the padded blue seats?" I asked, laying a folded coat over the books.

"*Ja*, and the settees, the little tables, and the hemp floor matting. Also, the vases and pictures we used as props in Charley's Aunt."

I smiled. "That's nice. I'm glad she has them."

"While we were there," continued Michael, "Edna told us Machotka is granted the right to stay in Australia and Lebbeus Horden has offered him a position as the head gardener at Hopewood on Centennial Road. It seems his work at Berrima has gained him the reputation of an outstanding agriculturalist and gardener. Edna is delighted because the job comes with a cottage, and the children are thrilled because they can have a pony."

"I am so pleased," I said, easing my violin into its case. "That family deserves some good luck after all the hardship they have been through."

"You're not going to pack that in your trunk, are you?"

"Well, I was, until you said something. Why shouldn't I? I want to take it with me and think this is the safest way."

"Billy is going to carry his viola, and all the others are taking their instruments as hand luggage for they expect to perform on the ship. The brass band is even going to play as we march to Moss Vale."

"Oh, I'll carry it then." I leaned the case against a suitcase and scooped up a pile of clothes. "There I am finished," I said, dumping them in and shutting the lid with a bang. "The only thing that remains to be done is to say farewell to all the friends we are leaving behind."

The Spot The War Forgot

"That will be quite sad," said Michael, swinging his legs over the side of the bunk and jumping down. "Many of us owe a great deal to Rose Izzard, and the Harpers from the Surveyor General Hotel have been very accommodating; if you know what I mean?" He tapped the side of his nose and mimed drinking motions with his hand.

I nodded. "They were very helpful. And so were the guards who turned a blind eye to the booze going over the wall."

"And all the villagers who took subscriptions for American Newspapers and smuggled them to us," said Michael.

"And Ada and the Post Office girls, who never got around to reporting the villagers' sudden change of reading habits."

"Remember the time we rescued the horse that fell into the cistern and saved the school and the village from burning down? Even Packer softened towards us after that."

"What about the battle of pooh?"

Michael burst out laughing. "That made the commandant regret confining us to the barracks."

"And the time the devil child wet her pants when Voss was about to spank her."

"Don't forget Edna's swimming lessons."

"How could I ever forget! She looked like a yo-yo on the end of Machotka's rope."

By now we were both roaring with laughter. When we quietened, Michael said:

"Let's keep in touch once we get home."

"I'd like that. We should have reunions in Hamburg from time to time." I handed him a notebook and a pen. "Here, write down your address."

We had only just finished swapping information when

W.E. Hamilton

Hugo came running down the corridor shouting:

"There is an emergency meeting in the assembly yard."

I poked my head out of the doorway and jerked my thumb towards Hugo's fleeing figure. "What's that all about?" I said to the man coming out of the opposite door.

"There has been an incident at the Trial Bay camp."

"What kind of incident?" said Michael, as we hurried out to the assembly yard. "A monument and four German graves have been desecrated."

"*The Sun* says it was a four-sided obelisk of granite blocks," shouted Billy, addressing the large crowd milling about, "it was five meters tall with a grave on each side." He waved the newspaper he held in his hand. "Some returned Australian soldiers blew it up, and now the graves are covered in a pile of rubble."

On hearing this, the mood of the group instantly changed from curiosity to smouldering rage and shouting broke out. Billy motioned with his hands for us to settle down. When we were quiet, he continued.

"I know it is sad to end on a sour note, but the Camp Committee thinks Colonel Holman's advice to burn the huts is probably the best course of action, for then no alien hand can desecrate the hearths we have called home for so many years. Everyone must decide for himself what he wishes to do, but I will be burning my hut and sinking my boats. Come with me if you want to do the same."

As he moved towards the prison entrance, a great shout rang out and with one accord we followed him down to the river. When we got there, we divided at the bridge and each man scattered to his place. I was one of the first to get my hut

The Spot The War Forgot

ablaze for it was close by, and its flimsy brush cladding soon caught alight.

[9] *"That's for the destruction of the memorial,"* Billy chanted, as it and several other huts flared into great funeral pyres. His words were caught up and all along the river bank as the huts were torched, the words rang out:

"That's for the destruction of the memorial. That's for the destruction of the memorial."

Once my hut was beyond redeeming, I turned my attention to the boats. I hauled the Nelly to the river while Billy dragged Attila to her doom. Then flicking open my pocket knife I lunged at the canvas bottom. I stabbed and ripped and ripped and slashed. All the tension of the last ten months since Armistice was unleashed into a frenzy of destruction.

"That's for the shipping delays," I shouted as I stabbed. "This is for blaming Germany for starting the war." Slash. "That's for taking our army." Rip. "This is for those who were killed." Stab. "And this is for the needless deaths of Engfer and Julius." By now the boat was well underwater but I kept lunging and stabbing at it. It was Major Baxter and the old General who brought me to my senses.

"STOP! WHAT ARE YOU DOING?" they shouted, rushing down the hill.

I stopped and stood still; my pocket knife clenched in my shaking hand.

"I demand an explanation for this," said the General, waving his hand towards the lines of bonfires. "The Department of Defence has long considered Berrima Camp as the 'showplace' of our operation. I am very upset by your actions."

---

9   Taken from Hugo Bahl's diary.

410

W.E. Hamilton

"How could you do this?" said Major Baxter, with betrayal in his eyes, "I thought we were friends. I even gave you a photograph of myself and Thelma for Christmas, Billy."

"We *are* friends," said Billy. "This is not a protest against you or our time here."

"Why did you do it then?"

"We will write you a letter laying out our reasons."

"I am saddened by this, but as it is too late to do anything about it, I will have to accept it," said Major Baxter, sighing. "Come, General, they are honourable men, I am sure they have a good reason."

Shortly after, the Camp Committee wrote this letter.

'We the undersigned Members of the German Committee of Berrima Detention Barracks do certify that on one of his visits to the camp in December 1918, Lt Colonel Holman told us, on being asked what we should do with our huts on the riverbanks, that, of course, he could not give us the advice to burn down the huts, but if he were in our place, he would do so. Colonel Holman further said that if the huts did remain, they would only attract the larrikin-element of the neighbourhood and the Authorities did not like this idea, as the buildings of the jail were intended for certain purposes.

Berrima 11th August 1919

Signed, Carl Haug, E Dannemann, W Köster, J Lange.

"In some ways, I am glad it ended like this," I said to Billy, that evening as we watched the last of the flames reflecting on the water and little sparks lifting into the darkness. "It makes it easier to leave."

"Take a long look and then turn your back," said Billy. "Tomorrow is the beginning of our new life."

The Spot The War Forgot

I stared hard at the little pile of embers that used to be my hut, while Billy gazed at the spot where our boats went down. Then without speaking we turned and trudged up the hill.

W.E. Hamilton

August 1919
Friedrich Ebert Becomes Germany's First President

Goodbye Berrima

We got up before dawn the next day, dressed in civilian clothes and ate a hasty breakfast. Then as the sun rose over a frosted landscape, five large horse-drawn drays clattered up to the courthouse. Billy and Ernst leapt onto the deck of the first dray.

"Load the trunks first," shouted Billy, rubbing his cold hands together, "then the suitcases; bags, baskets and light stuff on top."

"To think we arrived with little more than a change of clothing," I said, to Michael, as we hoisted trunks up to Billy and Ernst. "Now we need five wool-wagons."

Michael heaved a bag to Hermann who clambered up a stack of trunks before swinging it on to a pile of suitcases. "We probably needed six wagons. I hope none of this stuff falls off."

At last, everything was loaded and the horses dragged the

The Spot The War Forgot

towers of luggage away. Then we answered rollcall for the final time. After the last man called "HERE," Major Baxter shut the book and shouted:

"Move to the front of the jail and line up behind the band."

I put on my hat, buttoned my overcoat and picked up my hold-all and violin case.

"This is it, we are on our way home," I said to Michael, who walked beside me. We wandered past the majestic columns of the courthouse and rounded the corner. To our surprise, lined all along the street were the villagers and people from the surrounding countryside.

"Some of these people must have got up in the wee hours of the morning to be here," I said, gazing in amazement at the huge crowd.

"So different to when we first came," said Michael, waving at Annie and the Izzards, "remember how they hid in their houses and peeped at us from behind curtains."

"I sure do." My eyes scanned the crowd for the beautiful woman. I knew she would be there, and sure enough, I spotted her and the girls in the front yard of the Hurtzig's old house standing by the fountain. She was forlornly holding the baby on her hip, Carmen and Manon huddled into her side. The only sign of Eva was a waving bush and the excited yips of her little dog. As I strode through the gate, she emerged from the shrubbery carrying cupid.

"Look what I found, Uncle Wolfgang! I wondered where he'd got to." She went over to the fountain and tried to lift the small statue on top.

"Here, let me help you," I said, and putting my cases down I lifted cupid back into the place where he belonged.

"I shall miss all my three-hundred uncles," Eva said mournfully, as the home-help team gathered around the little family."

"And we will miss you, you little scallywag," said Billy rumpling her hair. "Try to be good for your mother and stop pretending you don't know the times' tables."

Eva's little pixie face lit into an impish grin. "Did you bring me sweets, uncle Billy?"

"Here you go, you child of the devil," said Billy, digging deep into his pocket and pulling out a handful of toffees. "Share these with your sisters."

"I can never thank you enough for your kindness towards us," said the beautiful woman, as Eva doled the treats out evenly. "I don't know how I would have managed without you." She dabbed her eyes with her handkerchief. "I shall miss you terribly. The place will be very empty once you are gone."

I patted her on the shoulder. "It won't be long before Paul is back and then you won't miss us at all, you will be so caught up in your new life."

Leonard hitched his rifle onto his shoulder and leaned over the fence. "Hurry up you lot, we are ready to move out."

We nodded and moved towards the gate.

"Have you heard when he will be released," said Billy, as the beautiful woman walked with us?

"Not yet, but surely it can't be much longer."

"I'm sure it won't be."

"Farewell. Safe journey," cried the beautiful woman, waving as we took our places at the end of the line in front of the rear guards.

"Farewell, God bless you," we called, tipping our hats.

The Spot The War Forgot

Then the band at the front struck up the tune *'Now, now, must I from this little town,'* and with Major Baxter and half the Berrima guard leading the way, we marched forward, followed by a crowd of sightseers and well-wishers. At the Surveyor General Hotel, the procession stopped.

"Three cheers for the hotel's truly accomplished service," came the shout.

"HIP, HIP, HOORAY"

"HIP, HIP, HOORAY"

"HIP, HIP, HOORAY," we bawled and whistled.

And pulling handkerchiefs from our pockets, we waved with all our strength at the Harper family standing outside. Then still waving, we moved past the bakery and the Post Office, past Holy Trinity Church, and over the bridge. At the bridge, the town's folk dropped off, and as the column wheeled around and passed the Catholic church, only the beautiful woman and her children remained. They stood in the road waving. Just before the town disappeared from sight, I twisted my head for one last look at the old jail that had sheltered us from the world's time of turmoil. The sun's rays at that exact moment hit the wall on an angle that made the yellow sandstone glow like gold, and my sister's painting flashed into my mind. Truly we had sailed smoothly in the eye of a raging tempest. God had indeed kept us safe through the storm.

World War 1 was not a good war, no war is ever good, but for three-hundred-and-thirty German mariners, it was a great war.

W.E. Hamilton

Berrima Postscript
A Century Later

More than a century has passed since the Great War. The derelict town steeped in poverty that the POWs encountered is nowadays a boutique village for the wealthy. Gone are the tumbledown hovels, and none of the schoolchildren wear sacks. Nevertheless, many of the fine buildings, such as the jail, courthouse, general store, the Surveyor General Hotel, Harper's Mansion, the churches, Billy Köster's house, the green, and the main street, are easily recognizable. Inarguably, the beginning of Berrima's change in fortune traces back to the POWs.

During the war, many of the prisoners continued to receive wages from their shipping lines while interned. This positively affected the local economy. The butcher and baker benefitted from the sudden population increase, as did the bank, post office, general store, livery stable, and hotels. Curious tourists from Sydney brought in further revenue. Hordes of spectators came during the weekends and holidays to look at the prisoners, their huts, boats, carnivals, bridge, and outdoor musical events. These activities, along with the ship captain's leadership, and the Berrima Guard's humane treatment, combined to make Berrima Jail Australia's showcase POW camp. When the war ended, the villagers were sad to see them leave. But the POWs contribution to the area did not finish with their

The Spot The War Forgot

departure. Legend holds that Arnold Taylor was influenced to start the Berrima cement works by knowledge gained from the internees.

To commemorate this extraordinary eye-of-peace in the storm of World War One, the locals have built a museum and a river walk. The walk has signs erected at seventeen spots along the river, marking out places of interest. The golden sand is gone, and mere hollows in the ground or piles of stones mark the huts. Only ducks swim where the homemade boats once floated, and there is no sign of the bridge or the dam the internees made. But it is possible to still walk the paths among the bush that the prisoners walked, to gaze upon the river and Nobbys Hill, and imagine the place buzzing with the activity and sounds of a hundred years ago.

W.E. Hamilton

Berrima River Walk Map

1. Berrima German School
2. Great Lake and giant slippery slide
3. Schöne Aussicht Villa
4. Hansa Bridge
5. Frieda
6. White City
7. Sentry box and sunbathing enclosure
8. Villa Marcella
9. Alsterburg
10. Alstertal
11. Amphitheatre
12. Crow's Nest Lookout
13. Log cabin
14. Bark hut
15. Lloyd hall I and II
16. Lake Titicaca
17. Scheisshöh Vegetable Garden and Dam Site

Scan for Audio Tour

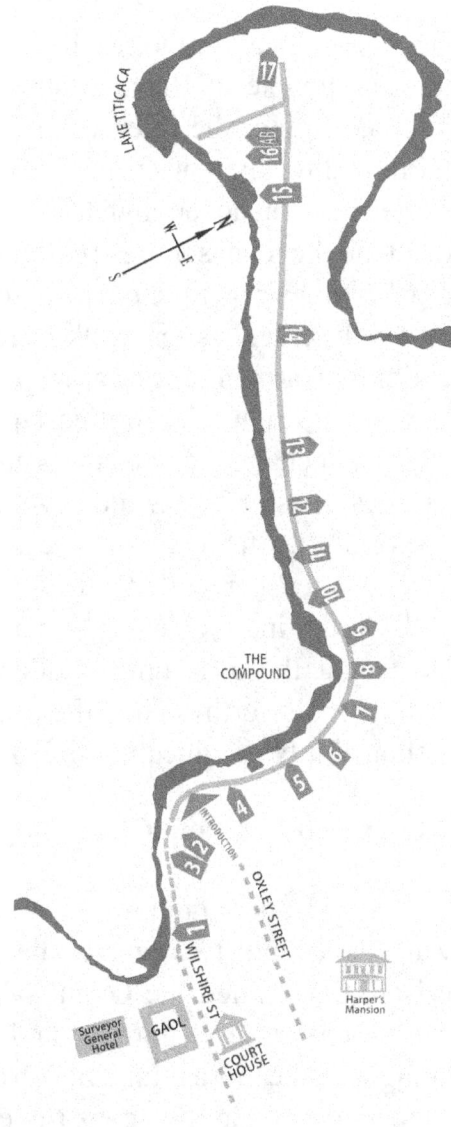

The Spot The War Forgot

Walk Information

1 Töchterschule Berrima (Berrima German Girl's School.)

Berrima's local schoolteacher, Thomas Packer, was one of the few people in Berrima strongly opposed to the German internees. After the internees saved the Berrima school from burning down in a bush fire, his attitude toward them softened somewhat. But not enough to allow the children of the prisoners to attend the local school. To compensate for this, the prisoners organised their own school. The school building was a tiny bark hut by the river, a short walk from the homes of the Machotka children, Carmen and Eva, and the Hurtzig girls, Hanna and Lore. The Camp Committee equipped it with a blackboard, tables and chairs, books, charts and writing materials. Initially, Lutheran Pastor Treuz and several of the prisoners shared the responsibility for teaching the children. This continued until a school teacher called Dierke Voss was brought from the Holsworthy internee camp and appointed as the schoolmaster. He taught the girls until suddenly, the authorities sent him back to Holsworthy. Then the prisoners once again shared the responsibility of educating the girls.

2 The Great Lake and Giant Slippery slide

The prisoners dammed the river upstream and raised the water level into two lakes. The smallest lake, closest to the prison, they called the Great Lake. This was the location of many activities. Swimming and boating were popular here, along with the more mundane job of washing. On the right bank of the Great Lake they constructed a giant slippery slide. The slide was an ingenious contraption. A carriage-like seat slid down a set of makeshift rails until it hit the water, catapulting the rider into the lake. They made the rails from saplings and held it up by a supporting frame. It was very popular with both the prisoners and locals. Usually, the prisoners were happy to share their slide, but the Christmas they were all confined to barracks because two captains ran away, the sounds of the locals playing on their slide added to the resentment they felt over their unjust punishment. It is to the credit of the Australian Army that when the prisoners sent a letter of complaint, the authorities (without bias) carefully investigated the charges and the commandant ruled in favour of the prisoners.

3 Schöne Aussicht Villa (The Emden Hut)

Building huts from bush materials was a popular pastime for the POWs. Individuals built small huts for private use, while groups of men banded together to build larger huts, which they used as club rooms. One such building was Schöne Aussicht Villa, otherwise known as the Emden Hut. It was built by seven crew members of the SMS Emden who were interned at Berrima. Unlike most of the prisoners who were merchant sailors, the Emden men had seen battle until their ship was destroyed by the HMS Sydney. The Emden hut was a handsome building made of brush and saplings. To add to its charm, it boasted a veranda and a small turret sat on its roof. Old photos show it surrounded by landscaped lawns, rock walls, and picturesque steps leading down to the river. Originally, it was located beyond the Hansa bridge, but when vandals from Sydney began causing problems, the authorities erected a protecting compound. On May 15th 1918, the POWs were ordered to move the huts located up river of the bridge, within the protecting fence. An old photo shows the prisoners carrying the Emden Hut to its new site. Initially, the POWs were afraid they would be confined to the compound and their long walks restricted, but this did not happen. Instead, the guards and prisoners worked together to patrol the surrounding fence against the threat of vandals and assault.

4 The Hansa Bridge

The left bank of the river was preferable to the right bank, but getting there was arduous. To overcome this problem, the prisoners built a bridge almost a hundred metres long. The men who built it were from the Hansa shipping line. Not surprisingly, they called it the Hansa bridge. The mariners put much thought into the construction of the bridge. A few weeks before their arrival, the river had flooded. By assessing the height of debris caught in trees and shrubs, they built the bridge five feet above the waterline. They used timber they cut from the bush, and work began with a platform suspended from a flying fox cable stretched across the river. Their calculations proved accurate when a flood in October 1918, came right up to the bridge but did not pass over it. It took three months to build the bridge, and at its completion the prisoners, guards and villagers celebrated its opening with a gala. The Hansa bridge gave quick and easy access to the internee's sport's fields, and was popular with the locals.

W.E. Hamilton

5 Frieda

Usually, the prisoners built their huts close to the river, for almost everyone made a boat. Karl Wirthgen, however, built his hut, Frieda, high up the bank, just below the sports field. And that was not the only peculiarity. While the others used material from the bush, Karl constructed Freida from ten thousand one hundred discarded jam and milk tins packed with clay. A keen musician, Karl and three other zither players practiced their music there, enjoying the reverberation of Frieda's metal walls.

6 White City

White city was perhaps the biggest villa. It sat by the water surrounded by elaborate veranda rails. A mast, eighteen to twenty metres high, towered above the surrounding trees. The mast was an antenna, the work of Eric Brauns and other wireless operators. In plain view, the guards overlooked the antenna because almost every hut had a flagpole. With plenty of time on their hands, it was a simple matter for the wireless operators among the internees to build an efficient receiver. Once this was done, they spent hours every day listening to morse code transmissions, much to the mystification of the guards who couldn't understand how they knew about world events before they hit the newspapers.

7 Sentry box and sunbathing enclosure

A sunny area on flat rocks was a popular area for sunbathing. In time, the POWs made the spot private by enclosing it with a fence of brush for the purpose of nude sunbathing. In addition, they constructed a sentry box.

8 Villa Marcella

Villa Marcella was built by a Hungarian called Julius Poszisch, captain of the steamer Turul. Julius was a flamboyant character with an unstable temperament. He was prone to fits of rage and jealousy over his Budapest girlfriend, Marcella. He built his villa and named it after her as a token of his love. It was approached via a bridge. At the entrance of the bridge, Julius constructed arches called Transylvanian lucky gates. Alas, the villa's luck ran out when Marcella broke up with him. As soon as Julius received her letter, he burnt Villa Marcella down in a fit of rage.

9 Alsterburg

Perhaps homesick men were thinking of Black Forest hunting lodges when they designed the Alsterburg. Set high and well back from the river, the Alsterburg was a communal cabin and a social hub. As one of the more substantial buildings, it took a team of men six months to build. The rock foundation, alone, took weeks to haul up from the river. Constructed from small upright logs, the villa boasted two spacious rooms with a storage loft overhanging the veranda. Over a hundred years later, you can still see the foundation and steps.

W.E. Hamilton

10   Alstertal

The Alstertal was the communal cabin of the men from the steamer the Cannstatt. Frau Hurtzig thought it was the prettiest villa, and sewed a pennant for its flagpole. In addition, the Cannstatt sailors built an outhouse and a laundry.

Captain Madsen was keen on music. He owned a gramophone and often rehearsed with small groups of musicians at the Alstertal.

11   Amphitheatre

The sloping ground rising behind the left bank by the first bend in the river, formed a natural amphitheatre. Here they built a simple wooden platform, and the prisoners gathered to enjoy open-air concerts and social events. Nearby was Heinrich Bartel's bakehouse. Heinrich did a roaring trade in authentic German cakes and pastries, especially when the band or choir was in full swing on Sunday afternoons.

12   Crow's Nest Lookout

The guards forbade alcohol, but that did not stop the POWs from getting it. Some smuggled it in, while others made moonshine from hidden stills in the bush. While obtaining alcohol was complex, drinking it posed another set of difficulties.

To overcome this, Engineer Heinrich Eckerlein built a tree hut at the top of Nobbys Hill, close to an overhanging rock where clandestine drinking parties took place. From his Crow's Nest Lookout, he warned revellers of approaching danger, resulting in the glasses and bottles hidden or buried long before the guards got up the hill.

13 Log cabin

At least four men each built a log cabin. A photograph of Paul Pann's cabin reveals a small chunky structure with cute little windows. Made of horizontal longs, the wonderful little building is more reminiscent of a child's playhouse than an American frontier dwelling. After armistice, the POWs were no longer locked in at night, so men with rented cottages or substantial huts like Pann's log cabin shifted into them for the rest of their time in Berrima.

14 Bark hut

Carl Euringer's bark hut was the most usual type of large hut. Neatly constructed, the steep gable roof sat over a front door and window (compete with curtains.) Generally, bark huts sat further back from the water than the flimsier summer houses made of brush. Their higher location made them less prone to flooding, while the bark walls kept them warmer so they could be used all year around.

15 Lloyd Halle I and II

Lloyd Halle I and II were built and used by the younger men of the NGL line. The second building was roomy and capable of housing several men at one time.

W.E. Hamilton

16 Lake Titicaca

Lake Titicaca was the name the POWs gave to the biggest of the two lakes that resulted from damming the river. Here is where they held their water carnivals, sports festivals, and aquatic spectaculars. The first gala in honour of the opening of the Hansa bridge, was a modest affair with little more than two boats. But increasingly, as dugout canoes and homemade boats proliferated, ingenious and elaborately decorated boats festooned Lake Titicaca.

17 Scheisshöh Vegetable Garden and Dam Site

Gardening started in a small way shortly after the prisoners arrived at Berrima, but when interned agriculturalist, Friedrich Machotka, arrived, production increased enormously. Gardening went from a hobby to a full commercial production. The prisoners had several large gardens that provided all the vegetables for the prison, with the excess going to the villagers. The produce made a big difference in the hungry local's lives, and was perhaps the biggest contributor to breaking down barriers between the Germans and Australians. Scheisshöh garden was one of the furthest gardens as it was located near the dam.

The Spot The War Forgot

Internees Berrima World War I[1]

The original records can be found at https://recordsearch.naa.gov.au/
Place in Keywords : Investigation Branch New South Wales, Register of World War I Internees in NSW

Ship Captains
H. Bahl
W. Brahms
L. Burmeister
P. Dahm
K. Dehnicke
W. Faas
E. Gattermann
M. Giesche
F. Gordes
T. Hanning
C. Haug
A. Hauth
C. Hermann
K. Heyenga
A. Hurtzig
A. Hurwitz
J. Kohler
D. Kuhlken
W. Kuhlken
G. Lorenzin
C. Madsen
H. Madsen
H. Meier
A. Meyer
E. Pahren
J. Paulsen
R. Paulsen
K. Poszpisch
J. Preiss
E von. Reeken

D. Reimers
J. Reinhold
K. Richter
P. Richter
A. Sandvei
N. Siemen
O. Stolberg
H . Strycker
E. Tonne
B. Voss
C. Wellhofer
J. Wenzel

Ship Officers
H. Albert
H. Bartels
M. Becker
E. Beckstadt
H. Behrens
H. Biet
O. Bock
R. Bose
E. Borgwardt
H. Brodersen
F. Bruschader
F. Bruse
M. Buschmann
A. Busing
R. Carstens
T. Christiansen
H. Cords

E. Dannemann
W. Denzin
H. Deslonder
A. Engfer
C. Euringer
G. Falkenberg
H. Fokken
V. Fulfs
R. Gerdan
M. Gohla
B. Gowers
H. Grabe
W. Greffrath
A. Grethe
C. Hanel
C. Hartwigsen
T. Hinisch
R. Hoffmann
W. Horstmann
H. Jacobs
L. Jensen
A. Johnsen
H. Josenhans
V. Josevekowski
G. Juricic
K. Kaufmann
J. Keitel
J. Kiesow
J. Korff
W. Koster

K. Kralapp
G. Kriegsmann
Krone
E. Krubbe
W. Kruger
G. Laas
G. Lachmann
D. Lange
C. Lerch
S. Mahler
G. Marcussen
C. Meyer
W. Mieendorf
C. Muller
H. Muller
H. Nagel
W. Niemann
H. Nusse
H. Ocke
H. Olhenberg
P. Paulsen
H. Peters
H. Peytsch
O. Pfingst
R. Preiss
J. Rasmussen
F. Reil
W. Reinhardt
C. Reinhold
C. Remmy
E. Richter

W.E. Hamilton

V. Schade
J. Schelein
F. Schellen-
berger
J. Schlesinger
J. Schliemann
M. Schmitt
M. Schmitt
E. Schnoor
B. Schulte
J. Schulz
A. Seidenzahl
J. Stang
J. Steinig
H. Steuer
P. Stoll
R. Stuparich
H. Timmermann
E. Trube
B. Usee
G. Voges
C. Voigt j
C. Vollmer
P. Voss
W. Wahlers
L. Wallner
W. Weltner
V. Wenk
E. Wessels
W. Wienecke
L. Willert
K. Wirthgen
H. Zeyen

Marine
Engineer
M. Adam
F. Behrend
F. Belle

K. Beth
H. Bohm
J. Boldibruch
J. Bruns
R. Buhler
E. Buhmann
G. Clausens
W. Collier
F. Cordes
A. Cortrie
W. Definer
J. Detlefsen
C. Doss
H. Eckerlein
B. Ewert
J. Fasshauer
C. Fischer
F. Fischer
O. Friede
B. Garves
E. Griefahn
K. Hahn
H. Hamann
W. Hammye
W. Hanke
A. Hansen
B. Hansen
G. Hansen
R. Heidermann
O. Henning
A. Hensen
F. Hesberg
C. Hess
F. Hinricke
G. Hoppe
R. Hoge
C. Japsen
A. Jensen
H. Juknath

W. Kamenz
H. Karkes
B. Karutz
J. Kinsele
W. Kiss
R. Kusner
W. Klein
J. Klesten
F. Knaack
P. Knoop
K. Kohler
O. Kohner
C. Konig
H. Kraus
H. Krieklow
O. Kretschmann
J. Kretschmer
G. Krock
G. Kruger
W. Landau
D. Lange
F. Lederhans
O. Lefie
J. Lohmar
H. Lojewski
N. Lubecke
A. Ludekin
W. Luttmann
H. Maass
W. Mahler
D. Malirnich
K. Mehne
R. Mieier
H. Menke
E. Meyer
G. Milossoov-
itch
E. Molnar
H. Muller

L. Mullmann
R. Nahke
J. Nommemsen
H. Oltmann
E. Paaschburg
P. Pann
G. Paradis
H. Peine
W. Petersen
R. Pfennig
C. Rabe
A. Rademacher
F. Rittig
K. Rode
W. Rohrs
K. Rupert!
H. Schilling
H. Schmidt
H. Schmidt
E. Schonfuss
F. Schopper
C. Schroder
H. Schroder
J. Schuller
W. Sievert
C. Sohrmann
M. Sontag
F. Steding
A. Steuernagel
A. Stover
G. Strietzel
O. Sulwald
J. Theil
H. Thiemer
F. Thiessen
A. Tiemann
A. Urra
H. Voges
E. Wagner

The Spot The War Forgot

J. Wagner
H. Warnke
E. Weinreich
R. Wendig
B. Wiedemann
J. Wilckens

Master Mariner
C. Jepsen
F. Jertrum
P. Schmidt
P. Schmidt

Harbour Master
J. Behur

Warrant Officer
W. Bergien
O. Fischer
G. Freund
O. Monkedieck
K. Muller
K. Velten

Wireless Engineer
E. Brauns

Wireless operator
C. Wittig

Army Reserve Officer
R von. Blumenthal
C von. Klewitz
F. Machotka
G. Mayer

Lieutenant
G. Meyer

M. Meyer
Manager
H. Reinecke

Supervisor
O. Pahnke

Assistant Supervisor
H. Wahlers

Inspector
P. Heunelein
R. Martens

Barber
J. Muller

Butcher
M. Schmid

Cabinetmaker
A. Gallwitze

Carpenter
H. Leyffer

Clerk
W. Maiwald

Cook
H. Becker
F. Fischer
F. Sellin

Labourer
M. Hildenhagen

Missionary

L. Aukenbrandt

Pilot
J. Buhrmann

Purser
F. Schmidt

Sailor
R. Mahn
F. Veile
S. Voss

Seaman
K. Burgdorf

Steward
F. Glinz

Tailor
P. Gohlich

Unknown Rank
O. Heidmann
P. Kulper

W.E. Hamilton

Berrima Guards WWI[2]

Major
W. Baxter
W. Evans

Captain
H. Foulkes
R. Stoddart

Lieutenant
W. Adams
C. Rouse
E. Samuels
K. Street
E. Williams

Sergeant Major
L. Hagon

Sergeant
H. Burton
Croll
Hill
J. Judd
J. Mcewen
Sawyer

Corporal
R. Adamson
R. Booth
E. Duff

Ellis
T. Green
B. Hardy
Heaney
J. Kelly
R. Latham
R. Long
N. Masters
F. Mcgovern
G. Murphy
O'Connell
C. Perry
R. Pilkington
E. Reid
Smith
J Williams

Buglers
Boswarva
Cochrane
Gregory
Yapping

Private
J. Birkhead
S. Bishop
A. Bisiker
S. Bridges
C. Burgin
T. Byrne

W. Castleman
R. Cheadle
Churton
P. Clements
Cusack
Deery
W. Denning
E. Downie
S. Elphick
S. Farmilio
W. Field
E. Fitzpatrick
W. Graham
W. Griffiths
Halle
L. Hall
A. Hanson
G. Harne
Heden
Hinge
P. Hughes
S. Hughes
Hooper
J. Innes
E. Jameson.
E. Jones
W. Kennedy
Knowles
Lamb
Martin

F. Mathieson
A. Mauley
W. Mcintyre
J. Molloy
H. Morris
Murray
Newe
Newling
Noakes
H. Noonan
Perkins
F. Rayner
W. Ross
C. Rouse
R. Russell
M. Shepherd
S. Short
Sim
J. Sproule
Standeva
G. Stokes
F. Sweetmam
Taylor
H. Thorpe
Wales
J. Wilson
Woodlands
Woods

1   https://recordsearch.naa.gov.au
2   Modified list from Simons, J "Prisoners in Arcady" Ausdoc on Demand, 1999, Pg 241 -243.

References

- SMS Emden Wikipedia.
- Diary of Berrima Internment Camp by Lieutenant Edmond Samuels
- Frau Hurtzig's diary
- Edna Machotka's diary
- Carmen Machotka's diary
- Prisoners in Arcady by John Simons
- Highlands History World War One German internees in Berrima Southern Highlands News Bowral NSW
- Historic Berrima by Jim Revitt
- Bibliography Australian Prisons project 2009
- Wikipedia based on Berrima internment camp group entry number 01848 New South Wales State Heritage register.

W.E. Hamilton

Glossary

- *Ach komm schon* Oh come on.
- *Auf wiedersehn* Goodbye.
- *Bratwurst* German sausage typically made with pork and veal.
- *Danka* Thank you.
- *Danke schoen* Than you very much.
- *Dekko* Australian slang for 'look.'
- *Eins zwei drei* one two three
- *Fraulein* Miss
- *Guten morgen* Good morning.
- *Guten tag* Good day
- *Ja* Yes.
- *Jawohl* Yes sir.
- *Komm herein* Come in.
- *Liebe Kinder* Dear Children
- *Liebling* Darling.
- *Nein* No.
- *Platzchen biscuits* Christmas shortbread
- *Schnell* Quickly.
- *Tochterschule* Girl's school
- *Wunderbar* Wonderful

The Spot The War Forgot

About the Author

Wendy Hamilton is a New Zealander who moved to Australia in 2014. For seven years she lived near Berrima and often wandered around the quaint village and along the riverbank where the German internees spent much of their time.

Nowadays, Wendy and her husband, Ian, live close to the Snowy Mountains. She spends her days writing and illustrating. Wendy is a diverse writer. This is one of her historical book. Her other works include books on home-schooling, parenting, life in New Zealand, children's novels, and picture books.

W.E. Hamilton

If you enjoyed "The Spot the War Forgot " you may be interested in Wendy's other books

Shipwrecks and Bush Felling.

The true story of George Meredith who in 1845 goes to sea at eleven, is shipwrecked twice, rescues a princess, and runs away to the gold rush in Melbourne. In New Zealand he meets a girl at the Lyttleton docks, marries her the next day, and carves out a life for himself and his family in the New Zealand bush.

It can be found at Amazon at
https://mybook.to/WEH_SABF
or at www.zealauspublishing.com

www.ingramcontent.com/pod-product-compliance
Lightning Source LLC
Chambersburg PA
CBHW071258110526
44591CB00010B/704